Moral Education
for Social Justice

"I'm talking, but I can't shut up!"

Moral Education for Social Justice

Larry Nucci
Robyn Ilten-Gee
Foreword by Carol D. Lee

TEACHERS COLLEGE PRESS
TEACHERS COLLEGE | COLUMBIA UNIVERSITY
NEW YORK AND LONDON

Published by Teachers College Press,® 1234 Amsterdam Avenue, New York, NY 10027

Copyright © 2021 by Teachers College, Columbia University

Cover design by Pete Donahue.

All rights reserved. No part of this publication may be reproduced or transmitted in any form or by any means, electronic or mechanical, including photocopy, or any information storage and retrieval system, without permission from the publisher. For reprint permission and other subsidiary rights requests, please contact Teachers College Press, Rights Dept.: tcpressrights@tc.columbia.edu

Library of Congress Cataloging-in-Publication Data

Names: Nucci, Larry P., author. | Ilten-Gee, Robyn, author.
Title: Moral education for social justice / Larry Nucci, Robyn Ilten-Gee ; foreword by Carol D. Lee.
Description: New York, NY : Teachers College Press, 2021. | Includes bibliographical references and index.
Identifiers: LCCN 2021012551 (print) | LCCN 2021012552 (ebook) | ISBN 9780807765630 (hardcover) | ISBN 9780807765623 (paperback) | ISBN 9780807779712 (ebook)
Subjects: LCSH: Moral education. | Social justice and education.
Classification: LCC LC268 .N838 2021 (print) | LCC LC268 (ebook) | DDC 370.11/4—dc23
LC record available at https://lccn.loc.gov/2021012551
LC ebook record available at https://lccn.loc.gov/2021012552

ISBN 978-0-8077-6562-3 (paper)
ISBN 978-0-8077-6563-0 (hardcover)
ISBN 978-0-8077-7971-2 (ebook)

Printed on acid-free paper
Manufactured in the United States of America

Contents

Foreword *Carol D. Lee*		ix
1.	**Situating Students' Moral Development Within the Context of Social Justice Education**	1

PART I: MORAL DEVELOPMENT AND CHARACTER FORMATION

2.	**Defining the Moral Domain**	9
	Morality and Social Convention	9
	Morality and Religious Rules	11
	The Personal Domain	17
	The Social Experiential Origins of Children's Morality	19
	Social Interactions and the Personal Domain	21
	Moral Complexity	24
	Informational Assumptions	27
3.	**Issues of Development**	29
	Age-Related Changes in the Personal Domain	30
	Developmental Dynamics Between the Personal and Conventional Domains	34
	The Development of Concepts of Social Convention	35
	The Development of Concepts of Morality in Childhood and Adolescence	45
	Development and Cross-Domain Interactions	56

4.	**Character as a Developmental System**	58
	The Limits of Traditional Views of Character	59
	The Components of Character	61
	Linking the Character System to Identity and the Self	66
	Conclusion	66

PART II: SOCIAL LIFE IN SCHOOLS AND CLASSROOMS: CREATING ENVIRONMENTS THAT PROMOTE MORAL DEVELOPMENT AND SOCIAL JUSTICE

5.	**Schools and Classrooms as Moral Institutions: Rules, Norms, and Procedures**	71
	Children's Concepts About School Rules	72
	When Worlds Collide: School Rules and Social Justice	77
6.	**Promoting Moral Wellness and Social Justice Through Classroom Management, Climate, and Disciplinary Policies and Practices**	82
	The Big 5: Basic Elements of a Moral Classroom Climate	83
	Facilitating Moral and Social Development Through Classroom Management: The Elementary Grades	89
	Restorative Justice	98

PART III: MORAL EDUCATION AND CRITICAL PEDAGOGY ENACTED: THE CURRICULUM, DIGITAL MEDIA, AND PRAXIS

7.	**Critical Pedagogy and Domain-Based Moral Education: Complementary Frameworks for Comprehensive Social Justice Education**	105
	Overview of Critical Pedagogy	106
	Alignment in Constructivist, Cognitive Foundations	107
	Alignment in Fostering Reasoning Transformations	109
	Alignment in Targeting Informational Assumptions	111
	Alignment in Classroom Strategies	112
	Critical Consciousness and Critical Moral Education: Even for Young Children!	114

Contents   vii

8. **Using the Academic Curriculum for Moral Development with a Social Justice Orientation: The Basics**   **117**
   Goals   119
   Basic Principles of Lesson Planning   122
   Putting This into Practice   123
   From Peer Discourse to Critical Moral Perspectives: Creating Discussion for Engaged Reasoning   126

9. **Lesson Plans for Moral Development and Social Justice: Some Examples**   **138**
   Morality   139
   Social Convention   145
   The Personal Domain   152
   Complex Multidomain Issues   155

10. **Critical Digital Pedagogy as a Component of Moral Education for Social Justice**   **163**
    What Is Critical Digital Pedagogy?   164
    Examples of Critical Digital Literacy   174

11. **Integrating Moral Education Within the Cycle of Praxis with Dr. Johari Harris, University of Virginia**   **177**
    Extending Curriculum-Based Moral Lessons to Include an Action Project   178
    Integrating Moral Development Within an Action Project   187
    Pivoting and Responding to an Emergent Issue   191
    Issues of Grading and Assessment   192

12. **Closing Thoughts**   **195**
    Addressing Student Emotions and Potential Resistance   196
    Walking the Walk: Steps for Educators   199
    Conclusion   201

References   203

Index   213

About the Authors   223

Foreword

When Larry Nucci first approached me about writing the foreword to this book, I immediately thought about the project I was chairing for the National Academy of Education: *Educating for Civic Reasoning and Discourse* (Lee, White, & Dong, 2021). In that report, we discuss the moral underpinnings of civic reasoning and discourse and the fact that children from a very young age are engaged in moral reasoning. We initially conceptualized the need for this report directly after the 2016 presidential election, dismayed by the deep divisions in the public domain. We did not imagine at that time how such divisions would proliferate, nor how these divisions would be intensified by the nation experiencing a health pandemic, an economic crisis, and racial divisions and challenges of climate change. The question we raised is what is the role of schooling, specifically public schooling in the K–12 sector, in preparing young people to engage in informative and thoughtful ways with the profound dilemmas in the public domain. I find this important volume contributes in multiple ways to these dilemmas in the United States (and certainly across other parts of the world), particularly around what schools as institutions and educators need to know and do to support the moral development of young people, precisely because moral moorings undergird our civic decision making.

A foundational question in this American democratic experiment to sustain the Union is, "How do we learn how to navigate difference?" The underlying structure of the government articulated in the U.S. Constitution is designed to create pathways for navigating difference. And the warrants articulated in both the Declaration of Independence and the U.S. Constitution assert moral claims about the inherent rights of people: "We hold these truths to be self-evident, that all men are created equal, that they are endowed by their Creator with certain unalienable Rights, that among these are Life, Liberty and the pursuit of Happiness.—That to secure these rights, Governments are instituted among Men, deriving their just powers from the consent of the governed. . . ."

Some argue that knowledge of how government is structured is sufficient to prepare young people to navigate the complex tensions that have always been present in this country about how these propositions actually unfold in civic life, including the moral dimensions of such negotiations.

However, in the *Educating for Civic Reasoning and Discourse* report and in this book, we argue that there are developmental dimensions that must be understood to prepare young people for these challenges, and that there is a research base to inform how we understand these developmental dimensions.

The first few chapters do a masterful job of discussing how moral development unfolds within complex ecologies, that it is not simply derived from stable internal traits of the individual. They discuss this unfolding as a complex system essential to human development (Nasir, Lee, Pea, & McKinney, 2020). In this argument, moral values are a lens through which we regulate our interactions with other humans (and while they don't discuss this, also nonhumans) while navigating our perceptions of our ego-focused needs. These interactions take place in social contexts that value particular social conventions. It is not unusual for the social conventions of these spaces to be in tension or even contradiction with basic understandings against doing harm to others and include conventions that reify unfairness. The authors document in detail how schools as institutions and classrooms as site of practice can reify and enforce social conventions that create moral conundrums with negative impacts for children, in particular for children who face societal stigmas with regard to race/ethnicity, gender, sexual orientation, and conceptions of ability. They offer very practical illustrations of how these tensions arise and examples from real classrooms and schools that seek to undo the negative impacts.

Rooted in a relational developmental systems framing (Overton & Learner, 2014), the authors carefully deconstruct how moral well-being develops from early childhood through adolescence. What I find most inspiring are the examples of how parents and extended caregivers—who may not be technically trained as we expect teachers to be—inherently understand these developmental dimensions. For example, how parents of children at different ages and different life course transition points understand how to respond to developmental differences in children's efforts to exert personal autonomy in ways that socialize basic moral groundings. These examples raise hopes for how teachers as professionals can, in many cases, learn to employ strategies they use with their own children with the children they teach. This can be complicated when the children being taught are very different from their own children. These differences can also be reflected in social conventions that may be valued in one community but not within a formal school context. These disconnects around social conventions can be most pronounced in late childhood and adolescence, in part because of developmental differences in how children and adolescence understand the role of social conventions, developmental differences in the need for autonomy, and moral moorings from which they view such social conventions. As the authors argue, these disconnects contribute to the disproportionate punitive disciplinary actions in schools against students of color.

The underlying propositions put forth around the centrality of moral development to the holistic development of young people and the role of schooling in such development intersect with traditions in schooling around character education and current attention to what is called SEL (Social Emotional Learning). However, the authors do a thoughtful job of examining the traditional ways schools have conceptualized character development and the current efforts to silo SEL. It is rare to find a book that combines a clear explication of complex scientific findings, in this case around moral development, with actionable practices that teachers and schools as organization can take up.

Even more unusual are publications that take up these scientific empirical findings as warrants for addressing persistent challenges of social justice in our society and our schools. Nucci and Ilten-Gee connect these scientific findings around children's development of what they call moral wellness with more recent research in education that include critical pedagogy, culturally sustaining pedagogy, restorative justice, and critical media studies. In each of these social justice–focused educational frameworks, they provide actual practices that teachers in real-world settings have employed with impact. Making these connections is very rare and indeed most welcome.

In conclusion, I applaud Nucci and Ilten-Gee for bringing to a wide audience a compelling arguments and challenges rooted in science, practice, and moral foundation around the urgency of preparing our young people to interrogate and resist social conventions that sustain inequalities. In our system of governance, where the outstanding question is how elastic can the system be to accommodate differences in point of view while sustaining and building on democratic value moorings, education plays a pivotal role in preparing young people to navigate such complexities. Nucci and Ilten-Gee offer a hopeful lens, showing us from empirical research across cultural communities and across ages and grades that children and adolescents, despite differences in cultural experiences and social conventions, display a tendency to value fairness. Perhaps our biggest conundrum is understanding how our schooling and broader societal conventions teach them to look down on the other.

Carol D. Lee
professor emeritus
School of Education and Social Policy,
and African American Studies
Northwestern University

REFERENCES

Lee, C. D., White, G., & Dong, D. (Eds.). (2021). *Educating for civic reasoning and discourse*. National Academy of Education.

Nasir, N., Lee, C. D., Pea, R., & McKinney de Royston, M. (2020). *Handbook of the cultural foundations of learning*. Routledge.

Overton, W. F., & Lerner, R. M. (2014). Fundamental concepts and methods in developmental science: A relational perspective. *Research in Human Development*, *11*(1), 63–73.

CHAPTER 1

Situating Students' Moral Development Within the Context of Social Justice Education

This is a book about moral development and moral education with a point of view. In it we situate educational practices intentionally designed to promote moral growth within the broader framework of social justice education. Moral development in itself has no social, political, or educational agenda. As will be made clear in these pages, moral development is a universal aspect of human functioning common to people across societies and cultural groups. <u>Moral education, however, is *an intentional process directed at achieving particular social goals*. These goals involve cultivating the ability not only to reason and act morally in everyday interactions, but also to recognize and perceive moral harm or injustice in one's immediate surroundings and act to address it.</u>

For many students in the United States today, schools themselves perpetuate this moral harm and injustice. One example of this systemic school-based injustice is that Black students and students with disabilities are disproportionately suspended from school, leading to a higher chance of dropping out and being incarcerated as a juvenile and as an adult, a trajectory known as the school-to-prison pipeline (Wald & Losen, 2003). In Flint, Michigan, 7-year-old Cameron McCadden, an African American boy with diagnosed attention deficit hyperactivity disorder, got an early jump on this progression when he allegedly ran across bleachers and kicked a supply cart. Rather than follow his Individualized Educational Plan (IEP), the after-school staff summoned a police officer, who placed the 7-year-old in handcuffs. The staff did not summon his mother, who discovered her boy in police custody when she arrived at her usual pickup time (Fancher, 2018). Turning to law enforcement is not something unique to this school in Michigan. The ACLU reported that Indigenous students in Montana were arrested six times more than their White peers in 2015–2016. Racial disparities in lost instruction time due to out-of-school suspensions persist in states like California, with Black and Latino students being suspended and asked to leave school at higher rates than their White peers. According to the Office of Civil Rights, students with disabilities are disproportionately restrained and secluded in involuntary confinement (U.S. Department of Education Office for Civil Rights, 2014).

Moral education must take into account students' own experiences of unfairness and harm, even if that means turning a critical eye toward the school and classroom itself. This framework for moral education is interested in moving students' understandings of moral harm and unfairness associated with social class, ethnicity, race, gender, and disability toward an understanding of those injustices in the context of larger social systems. Similarly, social justice educators help students make sense of everyday hurts in the context of structural, historical oppression. This involves enlisting the academic curriculum in literature, social studies, and the natural sciences as contexts in which to expand on students' direct experiences and promote their moral growth. In addressing issues of equity, schools also promote academic excellence. In this book, we listen to the call of social justice educators to embrace issues of power, systemic injustice, and sociopolitical inequities within moral pedagogy, because students are already encountering these forces every day.

Our stance on moral education draws from the work of the educational philosopher Winston Thompson (Erickson & Thompson, 2019), who argues that moral education *must* attend to social justice or suffer from incoherence. This attention to social justice by engaging students in open consideration of contentious social issues does *not* constitute a form of political indoctrination. On the contrary, it is the essence of civic engagement in a political democracy. The approach that we take makes great use of what we have learned about morality from developmental psychology. As we will describe in the following chapters, that research allows us to take a progressive approach to moral education that prioritizes attention to issues of justice and human welfare. In this book we will appeal to universals of human development to undergird our approach toward the goals and practices of moral education. At the same time, we will be directing our attention to the specific concern of social justice educators that education in North America is not meeting the needs of marginalized students.

Social justice education has been described as a process that encourages people to challenge oppression, distribute resources in an equitable fashion, and take charge of and participate in one's education (Hytten & Bettez, 2011). This means attending directly to the impact of factors of social inequality, power imbalances, and oppression on the lives of students as moral agents. Social justice education is rooted in several disciplines including democratic education, critical pedagogy, multiculturalism, poststructuralism, feminism, queer theory, anti-oppressive education, cultural studies, postcolonialism, globalization, and critical race theory (Hytten & Bettez, 2011). As these authors point out, social justice scholarship comes in various types and categories, such as philosophical, practical, or theoretically specific. In this book, we build specifically on the pioneering work of the Brazilian educator Paulo Freire (1973, 2005), who advocated for a problem-posing form of education that contradicted the traditional "banking" model in which teachers lecture on predetermined content and students receive and absorb this content. Instead, he developed strategies of discourse and critical literacy that promoted an awareness of oneself and one's own conditions in relation to societal and historical forces, power imbalances, and conflicts. Such a stance has inherent moral meaning and would appear to be the natural subject of attendant moral education. For the most part, however, the connections between social justice education and moral development have not been made.

Some social justice educators view moral education as either falling within the framework of virtue-based character education or connected to a religious framework. We will address the issues surrounding religion and morality in the next chapter. Writing in a *curriculum for equity* blog, Walsh (2017) speaks for many social justice educators by arguing that character education, as popularized by the Jubilee Center in Great Britain with its focus on the cultivation of virtue for personal "flourishing," overlooks or downplays the role of social forces that limit such "flourishing." Walsh objects to the position taken by James Arthur and colleagues (2017) in their recent book on character education, in which they conclude that it is far more practical to change individuals than to attempt to change societies. This individualist approach engages in what social psychologists refer to as the *fundamental attribution error* of assuming that human behavior is a function of individual internal characteristics (virtues) rather than contextual factors such as poverty or racism (Thrift & Sugarman, 2019). (We will raise additional challenges for virtue theory in subsequent chapters.)

Similar criticisms of an individualist emphasis can be leveled at moral education based on presumed universal developmental stages, when the educational goal is defined entirely in terms of stage change within students. We have contributed to educational research that has examined effective practices for stimulating students' socio-moral growth (Nucci et al., 2015). We would argue that such individual development of concepts of societal convention, social systems, and moral reasoning is essential for the formation of a critical moral orientation that would undergird any serious effort at social change. Thus, we would take issue with the position that attention to social-cognitive and moral development is not compatible with social justice education.

In our view, moral education that employs what we are learning about human development should be a factor in empowering all students to live as complete moral agents and to contribute toward a more just and moral society. The application of morality to society is an aspect of justice-oriented citizenship (Westheimer & Kahne, 2004) critical to a progressive democracy.

Moral education for social justice is not limited to any particular bracket of students, but to all students who are the potential contributors toward a more moral and just society. We include within our educational framework the moral development of students whose life circumstances have placed them at the apex of social privilege and economic potential. Moral education for social justice engages those students in becoming aware of, and critically examining, their privilege, and empowers them to contribute toward social progress out of a sense of proactive moral principle rather than from perspectives of guilt or noblesse oblige. As we will make clear in Chapter 7, we advocate for moral development lessons that fully integrate the lived experience components of social justice education alongside a *cycle of praxis*, engaging classmates in collectively searching for and enacting positive social change. We do this with attention to the developmental processes and age-appropriateness of these educational activities.

As we will explain more fully in Chapter 4, we do not view the development of social and moral cognition as taking place in isolation. Instead, our approach falls within the relational developmental systems framework (Overton & Lerner, 2014) for understanding developmental processes. A relational developmental systems perspective views each component of human development as interacting with each other as well as with the surrounding environment. The development of moral reasoning is a core component of *character*, which we conceptualize as a developmental system. Character is embedded within the self-system that includes other aspects of personal identity such as gender. The components of the character system include moral emotion, and the self-regarding skills of executive function and self-control. In addition, moral reasoning depends on the information provided through other-regarding skills of empathy and perspective taking. Each of these component processes is addressed through a comprehensive approach to moral education that makes use of the best techniques for addressing social and emotional learning (SEL), along with the dialogic processes that are central to the stimulation of moral cognition. This is concordant with what is referred to as *transformative SEL* (Jagers et al., 2019) with its attention to the reduction of social and educational inequity and the promotion of justice-oriented citizenship. The engagement in collective dialogue is viewed in our approach as essential to the linkage between moral development and attention to issues of social justice.

In this book, then, we take up the basic task that was set out in an earlier volume on moral education called *Nice Is Not Enough* (Nucci, 2009), in which the key challenge for moral education is to go beyond the creation of "nice people" who follow the norms and conventions of society and live their lives in ways that do not purposefully harm or exploit others. The limitation of "nice people" is that they too readily accept the structural inequalities and injustices that are built into the social systems they inherit. That is, while acting in ways that on the surface appear to be moral, such people are in effect enacting passive forms of oppression of others. Standard approaches to moral or character education that focus only on the cultivation of personal virtue or adherence to the norms and values of society are seen from our vantage point as forms of immoral education. In this sense, we are in accord with the critique of character education offered by Walsh (2017). We would extend this critique to schools and districts that rely entirely on conventional SEL programs to produce students of moral character (see Jagers et al., 2019 for an analysis of concerns and opportunities regarding social–emotional learning from an equity perspective).

Moral Education for Social Justice is structured in three major sections to address what educators would need to know in order to engage in this approach to moral education. The first section defines morality and differentiates it from societal convention and religious prescription. This section outlines the course of moral and social development and character formation, and provides the primary theory and research base for the sections that follow. The second section addresses issues of classroom structure and climate, school and classroom rules, and forms of discipline concordant with social justice and students' moral development and character formation. The third section begins with an exposition of critical pedagogy and how it relates to the pedagogical principles of domain-based moral education to form a comprehensive approach to moral education for social justice. This section then provides the principles for lesson construction, with specific examples for integration within the regular academic curriculum, the use of media, promoting a cycle of praxis, and how teachers can help students cope with the emotional feelings that may be unearthed through genuine engagement in the ethical dilemmas associated with social justice.

Part I

MORAL DEVELOPMENT AND CHARACTER FORMATION

CHAPTER 2

Defining the Moral Domain

If we are to engage in moral education, we need to agree on what we mean by morality. For the purposes of social justice education, we need to be able to link what we mean by morality to the goals of unraveling social inequity. Over the past half-century, we have learned a great deal about moral development and how morality differs from and interacts with other norms and rules. This research allows us to define a moral core while also accounting for cultural diversity in social values. As we will see, the universal core identified through research allows us to address students' moral development and to move them steadily toward consolidating and expanding their fair and compassionate treatment of others. Accounting for cultural variability in social norms while simultaneously focusing on a moral core—identified through what we have learned from research in developmental psychology—is critical to our ability to engage in moral education within the public schools of a culturally and religiously diverse society. It also provides the basis from which to enlist students in a moral critique of existing social norms and, in a developmentally appropriate and relevant fashion, engaging students in the examination of the historical and cultural antecedents of structural inequities.

MORALITY AND SOCIAL CONVENTION

Traditionally, morality has been defined in terms of the norms of society. Let's consider, however, what a 4-year-old girl in the U.S. Virgin Islands has to say about two of the rules of her preschool as she comments about social transgressions that she was witnessing taking place in her classroom (from Nucci et. al., 1983).

> ISSUE 1:
> *Interviewer (I):* Did you see what happened?
> *Child (C):* Yes. They were playing and John hit him too hard.
> *I:* Is that something you are supposed to do or not supposed to do?
> *C:* Not so hard to hurt.

I: Is there a rule about that?
C: Yes.
I: What is the rule?
C: You're not to hit hard.
I: What if there were no rule about hitting hard, would it be all right to do then?
C: No.
I: Why not?
C: Because he could get hurt and start to cry.

ISSUE 2:
I: Did you see what just happened?
C: Yes. They were noisy.
I: Is that something you are supposed to or not supposed to do?
C: Not do.
I: Is there a rule about that?
C: Yes. We have to be quiet.
I: What if there were no rule, would it be all right to do then?
C: Yes.
I: Why?
C: Because there is no rule.

Let's begin by considering this child's responses to Issue 2. The act of being noisy in the classroom, according to this girl, is only wrong when there is a rule in place: "We have to be quiet." In the absence of this social norm, being noisy in class would be all right, "Because there is no rule." The school norm of being quiet in the classroom is an example of a social convention. Social conventions are rules and norms established through consensus or authority that hold force within a particular society, culture, or group setting. Although conventions are arbitrary and variable from one context to another, they are constituent elements of social systems and essential for coordination within social groups (e.g., establishing norms of greeting, time for lunch breaks, etc.; see Turiel, 2002). Because conventions are arbitrary, children have a difficult time understanding their importance. As we will see in the next chapter, it is not until adolescence that a majority of children understand the relationship between social conventions and societies as systems of norms and rules (Midgette et al., 2016; Turiel, 1983).

In contrast with her responses regarding being noisy in the classroom, our 4-year-old girl judged the act of unprovoked hitting in Issue 1 to be wrong whether there was a rule in place or not. The act of hitting was evaluated in terms of its effects on the other child: "He could get hurt, and start to cry." Unprovoked hitting is a classic example of an issue of *morality*. Moral issues are those actions that have an impact on the well-being of others. Our moral judgments are not centered around our understandings of social norms, but instead are structured by our conceptions of justice, welfare, and rights (Nucci et al., 2017; Turiel, 1983, 2002).

The distinction made by the 4-year-old in the above interview has been replicated with thousands of subjects across more than a hundred studies in regions and cultural settings all over the world. This basic distinction between morality and social convention is one of the most robust findings in psychological research. There is now evidence that the precursors for the basic core of morality are present in infancy (Hamlin & Van de Vondervoort, 2018). However, babies do not have morality, as is sometimes claimed. In a paper in the journal *Science*, Audun Dahl (2016) reported on research that infants engage in unprovoked harm toward others at higher rates than older children and adults. Babies do not have a conceptual basis for judging the act of hurting someone else as wrong. During toddlerhood, children construct their moral knowledge through interactions with peers and with parents who provide specific feedback tied to emotions and verbal expressions of the impact the actions have on others (Dahl & Tran, 2016). By contrast, responses to violations of conventions focus on the governing norms or social expectations. By the time children are old enough to be interviewed (age 2–3 years), they differentially respond to moral and conventional transgressions (Smetana et al., 2018). By age 4, as illustrated by the young Virgin Islander in our example, children consistently and clearly articulate the distinction between morality and convention across a range of criteria, including the rule-independence of morality and the obligatory nature of moral actions across settings and cultures. In the next chapter, we will take up the developmental arc of moral reasoning from childhood through adolescence.

Across cultures, children and adults view conventions as norms that could be altered through social agreement, and as applying only to people within their own society (Turiel, 2002). However, cross-cultural studies have also shown that members of Arab villages, rural northeastern Brazil, and rural Nigeria are less willing than members of postindustrial societies, such as urban residents of Japan or the United States, to agree that it would be acceptable to alter or remove existing social conventions. However, even within the most traditional cultures, children and adults differentiate between matters of morality and social convention (Turiel, 2002).

MORALITY AND RELIGIOUS RULES

The research that has identified a basic core to human morality opens the prospect for an approach to moral and social justice education that is rooted in fundamental features of children's social reasoning rather than the views of a particular interest group. Along these lines, a central concern to many teachers in public schools is whether morality can be addressed without either promoting or undercutting the religious faith of their students. This is a legitimate worry given that many religious groups promote their values as equivalent to morality. Proponents of what is referred to as a "social foundations theory" (Haidt, 2012) have tried to make the case that aspects of religious faith comprise a separate moral strand. We will contest that position, but want to acknowledge it here. There is now empirical evidence that will help answer at least some of the questions and concerns regarding the role of religion in children's morality. This evidence comes from studies conducted with Christian along with Conservative and Orthodox Jewish children summarized in Nucci (2001), and from more recent work conducted with devout adult Muslims in Turkey (Kuyel & Cesur, 2013), Muslim immigrant adults in the United States (Kuyel et al., 2019), and Muslim and Hindu children and adolescents in northwestern India (Srinivasan et al., 2019). The studies with Christian children included Catholics, conservative Mennonites (Amish), and Dutch Reform Calvinists.

In each of these studies, participants were asked to make a series of judgments about the rules maintained within their religious faiths. Some of these judgments were about moral issues, having to do with actions affecting the welfare of another person. Others were rules maintained within each faith that were nonmoral issues akin to secular social conventions. Moral issues used in the studies included such things as stealing, hitting, slandering, and damaging another's property. The nonmoral (conventional) issues used with Jews and Christians included work on the Sabbath, the day of worship, wearing of head coverings, women leading religious services, baptism, and interfaith marriage. Adolescents over the age of 14 were also asked about consensual sex between two adults prior to marriage. Jews but not Christians were asked additional questions about dietary laws. In the studies with Muslim and Hindu children and adolescents, the nonmoral rules focused on such things as dietary laws, burial customs, clothing norms, and rules for prayer (i.e., five times per day for Muslims).

Findings across the studies were very similar. In all of the studies, judgments about moral issues were viewed as independent of the existence of a religious rule or biblical commandment. These actions were judged to be wrong because of the impact that such actions, such as stealing or unprovoked harm, would have on another person. In the study exploring the reasoning of Muslim and Hindu children in India (Srinivasan et al., 2019), children and adolescents in both groups maintained that it would be wrong to engage in the moral transgressions (e.g., unprovoked harm) whether one was a Muslim or Hindu. This was because these actions adversely impact the welfare of another person. However, violating a nonmoral rule was only considered wrong for a member within the religion in which the rule applied. For example, the prohibition against eating beef was considered by Hindu children and adolescents as wrong for a Hindu but not wrong for a Muslim. Interestingly, across groups, children and adolescents maintained that members of a religion were obligated to follow the nonmoral rules of their own faith. In sum, the Hindu and Muslim children and adults demonstrated systematic differences in their views of moral and nonmoral transgressions of religious rules.

The findings regarding nonmoral rules, particularly among conservative Christians, Muslims, and Orthodox Jews, however, were complex. In the case of these Abrahamic "revealed truth" religions, devout children and adolescents do not believe that religious authorities have the power to override rules set forth in scripture that are believed to have come from God (Kuyel & Cesur, 2013; Nucci, 2001). For example, less than 20% of the conservative Mennonite and Orthodox Jewish children thought that the authorities of their religions could alter the day of worship or the rules prohibiting work on the Sabbath. In order to further understand the thinking of members of these religious faiths, the participants were asked the following question: "Suppose God (Jesus) had said nothing about (the action), there was nothing in the Bible (Koran, Torah) about X, would it then be wrong or all right for a Jew (Christian, Muslim) to engage in (the behavior)." When asked this question, less than 10% of the Jewish and Christian children and adolescents on average stated that it would be wrong for a person to engage in the nonmoral acts. For the devout Muslim adults, 13% thought engaging in these nonmoral actions would continue to be wrong. In fact, for the majority of issues across faiths (work on the Sabbath, not wearing head coverings, and women leading religious services), *none* of the participants thought the actions would now be wrong. This finding is consistent with our definition of these actions as nonmoral. However, the finding is also consistent with the assumption that God's word determines right and wrong for these devout Christian and Jewish children and Muslim adults.

That latter interpretation does not, however, explain the findings obtained with moral issues. In contrast with their responses regarding nonmoral issues, the vast majority of Christian (87%) and Jewish (95%) children and 100% of Muslim adults (Kuyel & Cesur, 2013) judged that it would *still be wrong* to engage in actions entailing moral transgressions (hitting, stealing, slander, damaging property) even if there was nothing in scripture (God had said nothing) about the acts. These acts continued to be wrong according to these children and adults because of the effects they would have on other people.

The distinction that religious children and adults made between nonmoral religious rules and matters of morality is nicely illustrated in the following excerpt from an interview with a 9-year-old conservative Jewish girl given the pseudonym Marsha. In the excerpt, Marsha talks about stealing and the Jewish norm that requires boys to wear head coverings (Kippah) (Nucci, 2001, pp. 36–38). The interested reader can find other extended excerpts from these interviews with Christian and Jewish children in Nucci (2001).

Religious Convention: Men Wearing Head Coverings

> *I:* Was Jonathan right or wrong not to wear his kippah to the public school?
>
> *M:* It was wrong because he's not showing his, uh, his, like his religion. You should always show how good your religion is, and you should always keep the mitzvah. And also, he's probably disobeying his parents.
>
> *I:* Okay. Do you think it matters whether or not Jewish boys wear kippot?
>
> *M:* I think it matters. For one thing, you can never tell if it's a Jewish man or not a Jewish man and you could say, "Can I, uh, can I have, can you give charity to the people, to the poor people?" And they would say, "No, I'm not Jewish." How would I know? Like you'd get really embarrassed, because you don't really know, and also like, when you are trying to do something really good and you find out he's not wearing a kippah and also it shows that he doesn't like, go in the laws of HaShem (God).
>
> *I:* But why do Jewish boys dress differently? Why do they wear kippot?
>
> *M:* Because it's a law of HaShem, and they're just supposed to.
>
> *I:* Suppose that the rabbis got together and removed the rule about wearing kippot. Would that be all right?
>
> *M:* No.
>
> *I:* Why not?
>
> *M:* Because it's been that way and that's a rule.
>
> *I:* Well, if they did agree and removed the rule, then would it be all right for Jewish boys not to wear kippot?
>
> *M:* No.
>
> *I:* Why not?
>
> *M:* Because the rule is there and it was meant to stay there.
>
> *I:* The Christians don't require boys to wear kippot, is that all right?
>
> *M:* Yeah.
>
> *I:* Why?
>
> *M:* Because, well, because that's not one of their rules. They don't respect God in the same way.
>
> *I:* Is it okay that they respect God in a different way?
>
> *M:* Yes. The religion is different. What they do is not our business, and if they want to do that they can.
>
> *I:* Suppose that it never said in the Talmud or anywhere else in scripture anything about wearing kippot, then would it be all right for Jewish boys to read the Torah or pray without wearing a kippah?
>
> *M:* Yeah. I mean why would anybody need to if it wasn't there? How would anybody know?

Defining the Moral Domain 15

Moral Issue: Stealing

I: Is it okay to steal?
M: No, because it's a law in the Torah, and it's also one of the Ten Commandments.
I: Does that rule have to be followed?
M: Yeah.
I: Why?
M: Because HaShem said so in the Torah, and, uh, you should follow all the mitzvahs of HaShem. The Torah has 613 mitzvahs.
I: Suppose all the rabbis got together and decided not to have a rule about stealing. Would that be okay?
M: No.
I: Why not?
M: Because like I said before in some of the other questions, it's a rule of HaShem. They can't like change it 'cause like once when Moishe was walking his sons wanted, there was a law and they wanted to change it, and they changed it and their punishment was to die.
I: Suppose that people of another religion do not have a rule about stealing. Is that all right?
M: Probably yes—but no. So, it's like half yes and half no.
I: Could you explain that to me?
M: Well, like if they don't have a rule they might think that it's okay to steal, and no because it still wouldn't be.
I: Why would it still be wrong?
M: Because you're taking something from another person. And the other person—let's say it was a real gold pen or something and you really love it, like it was a present or something from your bar mitzvah or something, or bat mitzvah, and it would be really wrong for the other people. Because it's like a treasure to them. Like on a Peanuts show, Linus can't live without his blanket. It's like a beautiful present to him and he really needs it. It's like a treasure. Without it he probably can't live. And another thing is because, say there's one person and he steals from another person who steals from the first person who stole things. Well, he would feel, both, like one that got stealed from would get real angry and the one that already stole with the first stealer also would get angry because his stuff was stolen. That he already stole, probably.
I: Suppose that there was never a law in the Torah. God never made it one of the Ten Commandments or one of the 613. He just didn't say anything about stealing. Would it be okay to steal then?

M: No. Still I don't think it's right because you're taking something from somebody else. But to some people probably yes, because they think it's fair because, well, they might say, "Finders keepers, losers weepers."
I: I see. Is it right to say that?
M: No, because they really took it and they didn't just find it, and the other people didn't lose it. It's not fair. And besides, it's also a lie. So there are two wrong things in that then.

What is clear from this excerpt, typical of the hundreds of interviews conducted in these studies, is that the child being interviewed acknowledges that the rule about head coverings is based on the word of authority (God), that it is relative to a particular interpretation or view of that authority's norms, and that it serves the concrete social function of distinguishing girls from boys and members of her particular religious community from others. In contrast with her views about head coverings, she treated stealing as universally wrong, and wrong even if God did not have a rule about it. The wrongness of stealing, according to this child, is that it leads to hurtful and unjust consequences.

Summary of Findings on Morality and Religion

Taken as a whole, the findings from studies with religious children and adults indicate that moral understandings are independent of specific religious rules. Morality for the devoutly religious person as well as for secular people focuses on the same set of fundamental interpersonal issues: those that deal with justice and compassion. For the public schools, this means that there can be moral education compatible with and yet independent from religious doctrine. Such moral education would focus on developing children's concepts of justice, fairness, and concern for the welfare of others.

As we noted at the beginning of this section, religious systems are complex. They not only deal with issues of morality, but also provide believers with explanations for many existential questions. For this reason, nonmoral religious rules can take on a force for believers that is beyond that of secular conventions. This becomes of particular relevance when the pronouncements by a religious authority carry the weight of presumed divine sources. If any religious pronouncement is given the status of morality, because of the presumed connection to divinity (Haidt, 2012), then it becomes impossible to challenge, on moral grounds, religious edicts that do such things as grant authority of men over women, ban homosexuality, or as seen recently, sanction the capture and rape by ISIS fighters of non-Muslim women. Within religious communities, objections to such positions have been voiced on moral grounds by deeply religious people such as Mahatma Gandhi, Martin Luther

King Jr., Secretary of Education Pete Buttigieg, and Widad Akrawi through appeals to principles of fairness that they view as the moral core of their respective faiths. For those of us who are educators, it is important to recognize that the moral core is the same for religious and nonreligious students.

THE PERSONAL DOMAIN

"personal space"

Up to this point we have been discussing two forms of interpersonal and social regulation. But let's step back for a moment and consider the following set of questions:

- Who should determine who your best friend is?
- Who should decide what color shirt you wear on your day off from school or work?
- Who should be allowed to read your diary or journal?
- Who should decide what photos you post to social media?

Most people when asked these questions respond that they and they alone should have control over these personal matters. Research over the past 50 years has confirmed that people across cultures stake claim to a *personal domain* of privacy and prerogative, and reason about personal issues in ways that are distinct from their judgments about morality and the conventions of society (Nucci, 2014). A sense of how young people stake their claim to personal issues is illustrated in the following statements from daily online journals in which these adolescents were describing conflicts they had experienced with their parent or guardian that day.

> I went shopping with my mom. She wanted me to try on a skirt because she thought it was pretty. But in my eyes, it's totally out of date, and I desperately didn't want to try it on. So my mom felt mad with me. She seldom can understand my feelings. How can she force me to accept the things she likes!

> My dad entered my room without my permission when I was writing my diary. I have discussed this issue with him, but he always forgets it. Now I have grown up and should have my own privacy and space.

> When I received message from my friends on QQ [social messaging app], my mom always asked who was that? Male or female? I really feel bad about this. It's my freedom to communicate with my friends. Even if I have a boyfriend, it's my own business!

> My mom forced me to have a haircut, but I think it's OK to leave my hair longer. I think it's good to have long hair.

These examples are not from adolescents in the United States or Europe; they are from teens in Guangzhou, a large industrial city in China (Chen-Gaddini et al., 2020). The dynamics expressed in these excerpts are similar to what has been reported for teens from all over the world, including Iraqi, Syrian, and Palestinian adolescents living in refugee camps (Smetana et al., 2015). Control over the personal domain emerges from the need to establish boundaries between the self and others, and is critical to the formation of personal autonomy and individual identity (Nucci, 2014). Research has also shown that most parents across cultures allow a certain amount of privacy and personal choice, even to children as young as 3 to 4 years of age (Smetana, 2011). Reasons that children and their parents provide for why behaviors and decisions should be treated as personal and within the child's jurisdiction focus on the role of such choices in developing the child's autonomy and personal identity, and the child or adolescent's moral right to have such discretion (Smetana, 2011). Moreover, the ability of children and adolescents to respect the rights of others is affected by the degree to which they have a sense of control over what is personal and private (Nucci, 2014).

The basic function of the personal is nicely illustrated in the following excerpt from an interview with a 16-year-old American boy. He is responding to a hypothetical scenario in which a boy belongs to a club in which the rules are that everyone in the club can read everyone else's mail and listen in on their phone conversations. The protagonist in the story has to decide whether or not to go along with the club rule.

> *Question:* Should Jonathan [the main character] follow the club rules and let them read his mail, or should he keep them to himself?
> *Answer:* Well, if that's the club rule, he might have to. But if I were him, I wouldn't do it.
> *Question:* Why not?
> *Answer:* Well, it's carrying a group, a club, beyond the limits it needs in order to stay a group. It's just a desire to overstep and go into personal things.
> *Question:* Is it important to maintain the letters and phone calls private?
> *Answer:* Yes. It's an invasion of you, you as a person. You are losing a component of yourself. It's tearing away at that.
> *Question:* Why would a person want to keep things private if they aren't embarrassing or incriminating?
> *Answer:* It has its own importance. It's even one step further than being able to grow your hair the way you want. I guess your thoughts are as close to being able to describe the self that is possible. And then your physical freedoms, how long you grow your hair, just sort of build up yourself. They help to contribute on the outside to the core of your thoughts and personal ideas.

Defining the Moral Domain

A comprehensive approach to moral education would include allowance for and attention to this aspect of social life. Indeed, as will become clear in this book, many of the disputes that occur between students and their parents and teachers are over decisions that young people make within this personal zone (Smetana, 2011). As we explore issues of social justice education as they play out in school discipline policies, it will become evident that many of the conflicts occur at the boundaries of personal expression, and the norms of dress or decorum established at the school level.

THE SOCIAL EXPERIENTIAL ORIGINS OF CHILDREN'S MORALITY

As we have seen so far in this chapter, morality is distinct from other forms of social regulation and is different from a zone of personal choice. There is also evidence that the basic distinction between morality and convention is maintained by children with autism (Leslie et al., 2006). These sorts of findings have led to speculation that morality is innate. As we noted earlier, there is evidence that the precursors for the basic core of morality are present in infancy (Hamlin & Van de Vondervoort, 2018). This research has shown that preverbal infants will display a preference for a puppet that appears to be helpful over one that appears not to be helpful. Such findings showing that preverbal infants respond to emotional distress in others are indicators that humans are prepared to attend to social information relevant to the construction of moral knowledge and moral judgments. They do not mean, however, that morality is itself inborn. As we noted above, observations of infants younger than 2 years of age indicated that they engage in unprovoked acts of aggression (hitting) at higher rates than older children (Dahl, 2016). These actions were not brought about through frustration, but rather as unprovoked efforts by the infants to achieve goals such as getting a toy from another child. From this research we can conclude that infants do not hold the view, maintained at preschool age, that unprovoked hitting is wrong. Other research beginning with classic observational studies conducted in the 1970s has provided evidence that young children's concepts of morality, social convention, and the personal domain emerge from their efforts to make sense of everyday social experiences. This research done in classrooms, playgrounds, and family homes has demonstrated that the pattern of social interactions associated with morality is different from social interactions having to do with conventions and personal issues. As we will see in later sections of this book, understanding these natural social interaction patterns can help teachers in thinking about how to respond to misbehavior as part of classroom management.

Children's Responses to Moral and Conventional Transgressions

To explore these interaction patterns, researchers have looked at how children and adults respond to children's moral and social conventional transgressions. These patterns are illustrated in the following events observed in a study of children in free-play settings (Nucci & Nucci, 1982a). In each case, the transgression is italicized. In our studies of middle- and working-class children in free-play settings, we rarely witnessed children objecting to the use of profanity. The use of profanity was most common in response to moral transgressions, as will be seen in the following excerpts.

Moral

> *Two boys (1 and 2) are throwing sand at a smaller boy (3).* Boy 3 says, "Dammit—you got it in my eyes. It hurts like hell. Next time I'm gonna kick your heads in." Boy (1) says to boy (2), "Hey, did you hear that? Next time he's gonna kick our heads in." They both laugh and throw more sand in the face of boy (3). Boy (3) then spits at boy (1) and runs away.

> *Two boys have forcibly taken a sled away from a younger boy and are playing with it.* A girl who was watching says to the boys, "Hey, give it back a-holes. That's really even odds, the two of you against one little kid." The girl then pulls the sled away from one of the older boys, pushes him to the ground, and hands the sled back to the younger boy. He takes the sled and the incident ends.

As can be seen in these examples, children experience moral events as victims as well as perpetrators or third-person observers. The transgression (such as hitting, stealing, or damaging property) is followed by peer reactions that focus on the intrinsic effects of the act. An intrinsic effect of hitting someone, for example, is that the victim will be hurt. This will be true regardless of the children's cultural setting. Moral transgressions tend to be followed by statements of injury or loss, and evaluations of the act as unjust or hurtful. Generally, these reactions have a high degree of emotion. With very young children, the reaction may consist solely of crying. In addition, children may avenge moral transgressions, or try to avoid additional victimization through attempts at retaliation or, in the case of young children, by involving adults.

Social Convention

> *A boy and a girl are sitting together on the grass, away from the other children,* tying their shoes. Another boy (2) sings out to them, "Bobby and Alison sittin' in a tree, K-I-S-S-I-N-G," etc.

A girl (1) *is sucking on a piece of grass.* Girl (2) says to girl (3), "That's what she does, she sucks on weeds and spits them out." Girl (3) says, "Gross!" Girl (2) says, "That's disgusting!" Girl (1) then places the piece of grass down and ceases placing grass in her mouth.

Peer interactions involving violations of convention tend to arouse relatively little emotion. The transgression (such as sitting alone with someone of the opposite sex, or a breach of social decorum) is followed by peer responses focusing on social norms and social expectations. Respondents state governing rules, evaluate the acts as odd or disruptive ("gross"), and attempt to achieve conformity through good-natured teasing (see conventional example 1 above). These latter efforts to achieve compliance with peer norms are quite different in tone and intention from acts of peer harassment and ridicule that are evaluated by children and adolescents as forms of moral harm.

Adult Responses to Moral and Social Conventional Transgressions

The pattern of adult responses to children's transgressions is also different by domain. Adult responses to moral transgressions complement those of children and often follow them in time (Dahl & Tran, 2016). Research with mothers of toddlers showed that they provide social messages focusing on the hurtful effects of moral transgressions, the use of vocal tone indicative of the mother's own heightened emotional reaction, and also attempt to persuade children to engage in prosocial behaviors and share or "be nice." As children grow older, these adult responses become more elaborated as children are provided more explicit social messages regarding the harmful impact of their actions and are asked by teachers and parents to consider the perspective of the other person ("Mary, how do you feel when people lie to you?"), and to reflect on their own motivations for acting as they did ("Why did you do that?").

Adult responses to convention also complement those of children. Research with mothers and teachers showed that they provide statements regarding the underlying social rules and social expectations ("Raise your hand before talking."). They also provide statements labeling the transgressions as unruly, disorderly ("It's getting too noisy in here."), or unmannerly ("Chew with your mouth closed. Where are your manners?"), inappropriate for the context ("Dan, those ripped jeans are okay for play, but not for school."), and generally inconsistent with conventional expectations ("That's not the way for a Hawthorne student to act." "Susan, act your age.") (Nucci & Nucci, 1982b).

SOCIAL INTERACTIONS AND THE PERSONAL DOMAIN

The personal represents a boundary drawn between what individuals consider to be within their area of discretion and what is legitimately regulated by societal convention and interpersonal moral considerations. Thus, the development of the child's ideas about the personal emerges from social interactions in which they stake claim and/or negotiate for behavioral freedom. Observational studies of mother–child interactions with preschool-aged children within the United States have illustrated that children's construction of the personal is not simply a matter of accepting the default zones of control permitted by parents. This research uncovered three basic interaction patterns around personal issues (Nucci & Weber, 1995). In the first and least common pattern, mothers explicitly label certain things as decisions that were up the child. When they do give such explicit statements, they look like the following discussion between a mother and her daughter over the girl's hairstyle.

> *Mother:* If you want, we can get your hair cut. *It's your choice.*
> *Child:* I only want it that long—down to here. [Child points to where she wants her hair cut.]

More typically, the social messages mothers directed to children about personal issues were in the indirect form of offered choices, such as is illustrated in the following exchange:

> *Mother:* You need to decide what you want to wear to school today.
> *Child:* [Open a drawer.] Pants. Pants. Pants.
> *Mother.* Have you decided what to wear today?
> *Child:* I wear these.
> *Mother.* Okay, that's a good choice.
> *Mother:* How would you like your hair today?
> *Child:* Down. [Child stands by the bed, and her mother carefully combs her hair.]

In the above interaction, the mother offered choices conveying the idea that dress and hairstyle are matters for the child to decide. The child might then infer that such behavior is personal. Through both the direct and indirect forms of communication, mothers show a willingness to provide children areas of personal discretion. The fact that mothers are more likely to tell children what to do in the context of moral and conventional behaviors than in the context of personal ones is in itself an indication that mothers view the former as issues in which the child needs to accommodate to specific external social demands and meanings, while the personal issues are for the child to interpret and control.

Finally, there are interactions that reflect child resistance and parental negotiation. These situations often emerged when the child attempted to exert choice around a behavior or activity that overlapped or intersected with a social convention as illustrated in the following mother–child interaction.

Defining the Moral Domain

> *Mother:* Evan, it's your last day of nursery school. Why don't you wear your nursery sweatshirt?
> *Child:* I don't want to wear that one.
> *Mother:* This is the last day of nursery school, that's why we wear it. You want to wear that one?
> *Child:* Another one.
> *Mother:* Are you going to get it, or should I?
> *Child:* I will. First I got to get a shirt.
> *Mother:* [Goes to the child's dresser and starts picking out shirts.] This one? This one? Do you know which one you have in mind? Here, this is a new one.
> *Child:* No, it's too big.
> *Mother:* Oh, Evan, just wear one, and when you get home, you can pick whatever you want, and I won't even help you. [Child puts on shirt.]

This case presents a conflict between a dress convention (wearing a particular shirt on the last day of school) and the child's view that dress is a personal choice. The mother acknowledges the child's resistance and attempts to negotiate, finally offering the child a free choice once school is over. This example illustrates several things. For one, the mother provided direct information to the child about the convention in question: "This is the last day of nursery school, that's why we wear it." At the same time, she displayed an interest in fostering the child's autonomy and decisionmaking around the issue. The child's resistance, which conveyed his personal interest, was not simply cut off but was guided by the mother, who linked it to his autonomy: "Are you going to get it, or should I?" . . . "you can pick whatever you want, and *I won't even help you.*" In the end, there is compromise. The child got to choose, but within a more general conventional demand (enforced by the mother) that he wear a shirt.

The verbal dance engaged in by the mother and child in the above example illustrates that the mothers acted in ways that indicated an understanding that children should have areas of discretion and personal control. The excerpt also illustrates ways in which children, through their resistance, provided mothers with information about *their own* desires and needs for personal choice. We sometimes misinterpret children's resistance as instances of disobedience or the tantrums of a "spoiled child." No doubt there are such situations. However, few of the interactions that we observed fit those negative patterns. Instead, most of the children we observed complied with their parents when it came to moral issues. Children asserted prerogative or choice in 98% of the cases involving a personal domain issue. In contrast, children made such statements in less than 10% of the moral situations.

In sum, children construct their notions of morality, the conventions of society, and their sense of the personal out of different aspects of their social experiences. It is the qualitatively different nature of moral and nonmoral social interactions that accounts for the fact that children think about morality, convention, and the personal in such different ways. The important point to take away from these observational studies is that children's morality is a product of their efforts to make sense of actions that affect their own well-being and that of others. Children in every culture have experiences of kindness and harm, of sharing and of injustice. It is these commonalities of social life and not an innate moral sense that accounts for the universal aspects of morality.

MORAL COMPLEXITY

The conceptual frameworks that are used to understand and make judgments about morality, social convention, and personal matters form the basic windows through which we understand and reason about events in the socio-moral world. Many issues fall readily into one or another of these three basic frameworks. However, much of what we encounter requires us to coordinate or balance one or more of these basic considerations against one another. For example, most people in the United States or Europe have stood in line to buy movie or concert tickets, or to enter a stadium to see a sporting event. This is clearly a social convention, and we are sure that many readers of this book have been to places where people do not line up to buy things or to enter a ticketed event. On the other hand, anyone who has lined up only to have someone cut in recognizes that the social convention of queuing, by establishing turn-taking, serves the moral function of distributive justice. This is an example of domain interaction where the convention is in harmony with morality. One can also imagine domain overlap in which conventional concerns for social organization are in conflict with moral considerations of fairness and human welfare. An example would be gender-based norms that provide opportunities to males, such as career choices and advancement, not offered to women. These examples of domain overlap and interaction reflect the complex relations that exist between moral considerations and social structure. Our reasoning or understanding of such social issues may draw from our concepts from one or both social–cognitive domains.

For example, a dispute between a teenager and their parents over how to dress for school would require both the parent and teen to coordinate the personal aspects of self-expression through dress with the social conventions of the school and local community. In a constructive encounter, these *cross-domain coordinations* would occur both within the thought processes of the parent and teen, and in their conversations around the issue. The process of *domain coordination* required for the parent and teen to arrive at a shared resolution, however, may in fact not occur. Instead, the parent may frame the issue predominantly in terms of convention, while the teen might view the entire situation as a personal matter central to their own identity and autonomy. To the extent that the parent or teen is able to acknowledge the domain of the position taken by the other, they may discount or disregard the personal or conventional elements of the issue (see Smetana, 2011, for a thorough analysis of these parent–teen dynamics).

Domain Coordination and Social Justice

These sorts of encounters in which parties within a social space view the social world differently are at the heart of what is at stake in social justice education. Societies can only function as systems through the shared conventions more or less adhered to by their members. Over time, however, conventions may arise that privilege some members of society at the expense of others. To some extent this is inevitable given that societies can only function with some degree of hierarchy. It would be impossible to have a successful symphony orchestra without a conductor, or a successful American-style football team without a head coach and a skilled quarterback, or to have a functional family in which the parents did not have authority over their children. These positions of conductor, coach, quarterback, and parent all come with power and authority not afforded other members of the social group.

Similarly, complex societies and social institutions such as universities and businesses have people in leadership positions within levels of hierarchy. Generally, these hierarchies are accepted as legitimate, and as reflecting some degree of competence or culturally sanctioned achieved status (e.g., respect for the elderly). Questions of social justice arise when conventions sustain systems of oppression or privilege that cannot be justified in terms of the necessary smooth functioning of societies or groups. In such cases, moral reasoning and judgment needs to be applied to evaluate the legitimacy of the prevailing conventions.

Interestingly, where one sits within a system of hierarchy impacts how one perceives these situations of domain overlap (Turiel, 2002), as in the case of the teenager and parent described above. In societies where men have more legal rights than women, for example, men enjoy freedom of movement and power over their lives not enjoyed by women. The interpretations offered by men and boys in these societies regarding their own actions with respect to family decisions, such as where to go on vacation or what car to purchase, focus on the personal choice and discretion of the male making the decision. The men and boys also view the acquiescence of the girls and women to these "family" decisions as a function of the conventions and norms of society. The girls and women in these traditional male-dominated societies frame these same issues in terms of convention, but also view them in moral terms of unfairness because of the constraints placed on them that do not apply to the men. In effect, the women see and feel the injustice of the social system, while the men and boys appear to be oblivious to the moral implications of these same privileges granted to them and not to women. When asked directly about these differences, men and boys will admit that they would rather be male than to have the lives of a female. Nonetheless, they are content to live within the conventions that define gender in ways that favor men (see Turiel, 2002, for a detailed account of these gender-based cultural effects). Women and girls in these male-dominated societies often engage in subversive activities to get around the power of men (Turiel, 2002).

As mentioned earlier in the chapter, "women leading religious services" was used as a "conventional" rule in studies with children. However, women and LGBTQ+ people in many faiths have fought with their religious organizational bodies and won the right to be ordained, lead religious services, and bestow spiritual and pastoral care. Though the children in these studies viewed this rule as one that was written in scripture and obeyed "just because," others within the same faith may have perceived moral harm inherent in this discrimination. In their description of culturally sustaining pedagogy, Paris and Alim (2014) argue that while education should actively help students sustain cultural practices, "our pedagogical stance should also help youth, teachers, and researchers expose those practices that must be revised in the project of cultural justice" (p. 94). These practices may often be constructed around views on women, people with disabilities, LGBTQ+ and gender-nonconforming people that are problematic.

In sum, people in positions of privilege because of race, ethnicity, gender, or family social position tend to be less aware of the moral implications of their status than are the people in the less privileged cultural position. The conventions that sustain these positions of privilege are so normalized throughout history as to become invisible to the people who benefit from them. This was the point made with such power by Peggy McIntosh in her 1988 essay "White Privilege: Unpacking the Invisible Knapsack." Moral education for social justice is not only about raising the consciousness of students from oppressed groups, but of impacting in a constructive manner the moral responsibilities of students whose background and gender have placed them in positions of privilege. Addressing these situations in which societal conventions overlap with moral considerations requires that educators deconstruct the domain elements involved and direct student discourse accordingly.

Domain Coordination and Pedagogy

To illustrate how as educators we can address more than one conceptual framework within a single event, imagine the situation of four children trying to decide how to divide up the 10 dollars they earned for running errands. On the one hand, this is a mathematical problem requiring an understanding of how to divide 10 into 4 parts. On the other hand, this is a moral problem drawing on an understanding of equity and fair distribution. No mathematics teacher would reduce his subject matter to ethics, nor would an ethicist confuse her subject matter with mathematics. Yet in this example, we see that the problem solution requires knowledge from both domains. Similar situations arise in the context of multifaceted social situations. For example, a comprehensive understanding of social norms that distribute social roles and tasks requires an appreciation of the function that conventions serve for social groups such as the family to run smoothly, and a moral understanding of how such norms impact the need of individuals to be treated fairly. To reduce the issue to either a simple matter of convention or morality is to misconstrue the situation.

There are two clear educational implications of this social complexity. The first is that a comprehensive approach to students' moral and social development needs to differentially address their concepts of morality and societal convention if students are to be aided in their ability to comprehend, evaluate, and respond to everyday social situations. The second is that any approach that reduces moral education to the social transmission of existing social norms is inherently engaged in the perpetuation of whatever immorality may be embedded within those norms. This is why moral education worthy of the name cannot follow the path of inculcation and socialization advocated by traditional character education (Arthur et al., 2016). We will return to this point in greater detail when we take up issues regarding classroom practices in section III.

INFORMATIONAL ASSUMPTIONS

Part of what goes into our reading of the moral implications of actions are the facts and informational assumptions we have about the action. If we view a fertilized human egg as a person, abortion is not simply a matter of personal choice and control, but the taking of a human life. What changes the moral evaluation of abortion from being a decision within the personal domain is not the structure of someone's morality, but rather the assumptions about the status of the fertilized egg, embryo, and fetus as a person. Decisions over late-term abortions are especially thorny as they generally entail very problematic judgments about the viability of the unborn fetus and the health and welfare of the person pregnant.

The effects of informational assumptions on moral judgment can also be seen in cultural studies of social values. In one such study, University of Chicago anthropologist Richard Shweder and his colleagues (Shweder et al., 1987) asked adult members of a Hindu temple town in Odisha, India, to rank order from most to least wrong 39 behaviors that violated social norms within their culture. The act rated *most wrong* was for the eldest son in a family to get a haircut and eat chicken the day after his father died. Rated 35th in seriousness was a man beating his disobedient wife black-and-blue. From a Western perspective, these Hindu villagers would certainly appear to have a different morality from the Judeo-Christian community. (We saw earlier in this chapter that Hindus treat moral and nonmoral religious rules similarly to way people in the West do [Srinivasan et al., 2019]. So, these findings need some explanation.)

As it turns out, however, the Hindu judgments of the eldest son, while morally neutral from a Western point of view, take on a different meaning within the context of Hindu beliefs about the impact of the son's actions on the father. In particular, the judgments of these people must be seen from within the context of their beliefs about the ways in which events in the natural world operate in relation to *unobserved entities,* such as souls and spirits of the deceased. In this case, the father's soul would be placed in great jeopardy by the son's actions. If we allow ourselves to role-take for a moment and imagine that we are in the son's position, we can see how the acts of getting a haircut and eating chicken become a serious matter of causing grave harm to another person. We don't need to assume a new set of *moral* understandings, but rather to apply our moral concepts of fairness and human welfare to this situation once the *facts* are understood.

Within the United States, changes in factual assumptions have fed into shifting moral evaluations of such things as climate change. Advances in biological sciences may alter the ways we view such things as reproduction, aging, and even death. How those changes may affect social morality is hard to anticipate. An educational implication of the role of factual assumptions on moral judgment is that moral education should include attention to critical thinking and academic research skills.

In sum, we have seen in this chapter that moral decisionmaking can often be complex, requiring students to weigh and balance competing moral and nonmoral considerations. In the next chapter, we will take up issues of development within each domain, as well as the impact of development on the capacity of students to manage moral complexity.

CHAPTER 3

Issues of Development

In this chapter, we will learn about development within the moral, conventional, and personal domains and what those typical developmental changes mean in terms of students' behavior, and our sequencing of moral education. Advocates of social justice education face the question of determining at what age to begin integrating these concerns for moral growth as they apply to issues of gender, race, and social class. Recent work has indicated that honest discussions of these issues can begin as early as preschool (Brown & Anderson, 2019; Kelly & Brooks, 2009). We will take up specific recommendations for how to do this in Chapters 8 and 9. Issues of social justice generally involve the intersection between morality and the existing conventions of society as they are applied to different groups of people. Moreover, the lived experiences of young people often also embody the dynamics and tensions that exist between social conventions of institutions such as schools and the family, and the ways in which youth choose to express their identity and freedom of action within the personal sphere. To address these complexities, we will also look at how development within individual domains impacts social reasoning and behavior in situations that involve the application of social knowledge from more than one domain.

We will begin by looking at the broad picture of development in the personal domain, and especially its dynamic connection to social convention during adolescence. We begin with the personal domain for two reasons. First, morality and convention can be seen as regulating aspects of individual behavior. There is a tension between what individual students view as personal and what is regulated by convention and moral obligation. Therefore, we need to understand how development impacts this dynamic if we are to appropriately navigate resistance to school rules and authority, and effectively engage in moral and social justice education.

Second, it is essential for students to have a secure sense of what is personal in order to engage in activities like moral discourse. You can only operate maturely in the interpersonal realm of convention and morality if you also have a reasonably secure sense of the personal domain (Nucci, 2014). We tend to overlook this in programs of moral education because of our focus on having children reason and act in ways that are socially appropriate and morally right. Much of the emphasis in this book will be on forms of classroom structure and curricular lessons that will build students' capacities for understanding and critiquing social norms and existing social institutions, along with reasoning and acting in ways that are increasingly fair and compassionate. An important aspect of this developmental approach entails paying attention to the ways in which classroom structure and curricula support and foster growth in the personal domain.

AGE-RELATED CHANGES IN THE PERSONAL DOMAIN

The development of students' concepts about personal issues reflects their understanding of what it means to be a person, and how one establishes individual identity and autonomy (Nucci, 2014). The ages and grade levels associated with each developmental period in the sections that follow are derived from research with American children. Individual children may enter developmental phases at earlier or later ages than what is seen in the typical pattern. This caveat will hold true for development in all three domains of social reasoning.

Early Elementary

Children in the early elementary grades (K–3) base their intuitions about personal control on a physical and behavioral sense of self. Although very young children intuitively know that other people also have an interior mental life of emotions and intentions, children form their ideas about the personal domain in terms of physical and behavioral aspects of the self that are the easiest to apprehend. Susan Gelman (2003) describes young children as having the idea that the self is made up of components that are essential aspects of what that person is in actuality. We will see below that these early forms of essentialism are echoed in the adolescent's concepts of a "true" inner self. Parents and teachers are quite familiar with children who insist on wearing the same shirt to school day after day, or who cling to a particular activity such as riding their bike or playing video games. For young children, these clothing choices and behaviors are a part of who they are. In Chapter 5 and especially Chapter 6, we discuss how classroom rules and classroom climate should function to foster students' autonomy as well as their respect for morality and convention.

    The thinking of young children about the personal and its connection to a sense of identity is illustrated in the following brief excerpt of an interview with a 7-year-old girl. (Interviews in this section were conducted in research over many years. The interviews occasionally reference social situations that may seem less relevant to today's readers, but the conceptual thinking behind the responses is relevant to our argument.)

John goes to the principal and says that he wants to wear his hair the way that he wants to. What do you think about that?

I agree with him.

How come?

Because I wouldn't want to have to look like all the other boys, and I would want my hair a little different.

What would be wrong with having your hair like the other kids?

Well, he would like to be his own self, like there's all these people, they wouldn't want to look alike, then who would be who? It would really be weird.

As we consider this notion of the essentialist aspect of self as experienced by young children, we can also begin to appreciate how children who perceive themselves as not aligning with conventional social categories can experience school as a hostile environment. It is with this possibility in mind that a group of researchers from the nation's top pediatric hospitals (Hidalgo et al., 2014) joined together to advise educators to approach children with a "gender affirmative" orientation in which the educators accept the gender self-definition adopted by the given child along with the child's form of gender expression through dress and gendered activity.

Middle Elementary

Children grades 3–5 continue with the concrete foundation of the personal in observable aspects of self, but place even more emphasis than younger peers on behaviors as the critical component that defines your personal makeup. Personality is a matter of how you do things, as one 10-year-old put it: "Well some people play volleyball, and that's their personality. . . . God throws his voice; He has personality." Children at this age understand that being able to have control over aspects of your personal activities is critical to maintaining this essential component of self. Children also for the first time begin to interpret themselves in terms of their relative competence within favored, personal modes of acting. Educators are familiar with how these comparative evaluations can backfire when children are led to focus exclusively on measures of academic performance (Ryan & Deci, 2017). Thus, it is crucial that children have opportunities to explore a range of activities for finding and defining themselves. The proponents of what is referred to as *developmental discipline* (Watson, 2018) include attention to children's needs for autonomy and competence as essential elements of effective classroom management with elementary school–aged children. In

Chapter 6, we take up aspects of this approach to elementary school classrooms as a central feature of effective moral education.

Middle School

In late childhood and early adolescence, the elements that students use to define the self shift from the physical realm to their inner mental life. Control over the personal now takes on a new emphasis that includes maintaining privacy as well as behavioral choice. Personal diaries and journals now become staples for many adolescents. However, the "interior" life of an early adolescent lacks depth, and the basis for being an autonomous individual is expressed reactively in terms of "being different from others." There is a fear of losing oneself by too closely following the crowd. This reactive notion of self is expressed in terms of the need for f.eedom of choice, and the ability to be different from others.

> I mean everybody's got to be free you know, and growing your hair different is a way of being you know free, making a decision. I hate to be like everybody else. Because you know, I just like to look like myself, not like what somebody wanted me to look like, or you know, what my friends look like. —13-year-old girl

Teachers who work with middle school students will recognize in these claims an almost Shakespearean tendency to "protest too much." The freedom expressed by the 13-year-old girl in the excerpt above hangs on a rather fragile notion of self easily threatened by moving too far away from what is acceptable to the peer group. Consider the following statement from the interview with the same 13-year-old girl cited above. In this excerpt, she is talking about why she should be able to select what clothes she should wear.

> I mean your mother forces you to wear certain clothes. It makes you feel dumb, right? Dumb skirts or whatever, and then you go to school; you feel dumb, everybody's looking at you, and you can't concentrate on your work—you kind of daydream and wish you were somewhere else.

For all of her emphasis on the need for freedom and choice, this young adolescent girl is very much aware of her need for belonging, and the role of peer conventions in tying her into group membership. The personal domain of an early adolescent is unstable and in flux. The surface level of her sense of self as an interior set of opinions, values, thoughts, and emotions rests on a reactive employment of discretion in her personal sphere, rather than a deeper sense of self as something other than its overt, public manifestations.

High School

For the typical high school–aged student, the connection between maintaining control over personal issues and a sense of self is thought of as a process of bringing together all parts of oneself around a core inner true self or essence. Consciousness has depth. There is a real "me" that is the core of who I am. The task is to discover that inner core, and to bring the "outside self" of activities and public appearance in line with that true inner core. It is entirely possible that two people could elect to wear the same clothes and not be "phony." Since their inner selves are an essence of each person, they are not subject to change through the coincidental alignment of interests between two free people.

Control over a personal sphere of privacy and of thoughts is essential to discovery and maintenance of that true self, as was illustrated in the quotation from the 16-year-old boy in the section on the personal domain in Chapter 2. External control over what is private and personal disrupts that process and risks damage to the construction of the true self. This notion is expressed in the following excerpt from a 17-year-old explaining why she thinks that a boy in a scenario should be able to determine the length of his hair.

> That's the way he thinks, and the way he acts, and the way he wants to be, and the way he wants others to see him, and the way he sees himself. It seems that you should be able to be a whole person and have your outside look like your inside looks, and people can't determine what your inside looks like, the only person who can decide is you. So it seems that those should go together and that would be why people should determine their own appearance.

In the above excerpt, you can see how she is linking the boy's decisions over his external appearance to the core interior of his self. In the following excerpt, this same 17-year-old girl illustrates the self-constructive function of maintaining privacy over her personal diary:

> If I write something like that, it is really from deep down inside of me, and I feel very vulnerable . . . and to have someone just sit there and take part of that—I'd feel like it was damaged in some way.
>
> *Well, why write these things down?*
>
> Just to get your intimate thoughts on paper helps you think things out. . . . Then you have it out where you can examine yourself so to speak; your most intimate self, and you come to know how you feel and you just know more about yourself. It makes you closer to your true self I think.

The effort to align the outward expression of self with a perceived true inner core can lead to conflicts between students and the cultural norms of the school setting. Leoandra Onnie Rogers and Niobe Way (2018) detail how African American adolescent boys handle the conflict they perceive between their inner selves and the public presentation of self expected from school culture. For some male students, this conflict takes the form of overt resistance toward schooling itself. For others, the crosscurrents of a heteronormative ideology of the "boy code" that requires boys to display themselves as the opposite of a female social presentation, coupled with the disconnect between a Black identity and school culture, leads to a "cool pose" in which school is seen as only a passing interest. Trying to be true to one's inner core self—a developmental necessity in adolescence—is made more problematic when the conventions of the school restrict or condemn expressions of ethnic, racial, or gender identities.

DEVELOPMENTAL DYNAMICS BETWEEN THE PERSONAL AND CONVENTIONAL DOMAINS

As we have just seen, the interplay between the personal and conventional domains that takes place within individual students has important implications for educational practice. Part of the process of becoming an autonomous self involves what psychologists refer to as individuation. Generally, this refers to the gradual separation of children from the guidance of their parents. As was mentioned in Chapter 2, we have learned that a central part of this process involves the extension by older children and adolescence of what they consider to be personal matters beyond the authority of their parents. This dynamic of establishing boundaries around what is personal also plays out within the school setting.

As children get older, and especially as they enter adolescence, they begin to push for control over a wider range of their own behaviors (Smetana, 2011). This trend holds for issues that combine elements of the personal with convention, as well as their own personal health and safety (prudence). Typical issues over which American adolescents seek control include choice of movies to watch, how late they can stay out at night, where they can go for recreation, and when or whether to clean up their bedroom. Adolescents rarely argue against the legitimacy of parental authority over their moral conduct, adherence to basic cultural conventions, or basic safety such as drug or substance abuse. For their part, parents are also gradually giving over to their adolescent children greater authority and autonomy over personal matters. However, the timing at which parents tend to view their children as ready to assume authority lags behind the timing assumed by their adolescent children. As a consequence, these "border" disputes over what Judith Smetana refers to as "ambiguously personal issues" account for nearly all instances of adolescent–parent conflict. This is the case not only in the United States, but has been reported for teens from all over the world (Smetana, 2011; Smetana et al., 2015). The peak ages for these disputes within American middle-class samples correspond to the period from middle school through sophomore year of high school.

How parents approach their children's needs for a personal domain has an impact on adolescents' mental health. In a cross-national study of adolescents in the United States and Japan, adolescents who reported having parents who attempted to control personal issues such as the children's friendship choices, music, hairstyle, and issues of privacy such as reading their diary were also more likely to report experiencing internalizing symptoms of depression, anxiety, and somatization (Hasebe et al., 2004). Essentially the same outcome was reported in a study of urban Chinese adolescents (Chen-Gaddini et al., 2020), and middle-class African American adolescents and parents (Smetana, 2011). The negative effects of parental control over the personal on African Americans occurred at slightly older ages than had been found for the middle-class White students. For African Americans, parental control in early adolescence was associated with positive outcomes, while continued control into middle adolescence (age 14 and older) was associated with negative psychological outcomes.

As one would expect, there is a similar age-related trend toward greater control over the personal within the school setting. As we will see in the next section on developmental changes in concepts of social convention, these normal developmental shifts may help to account for some of the behavioral issues teachers and schools contend with during this same early adolescent age period. Middle school and high school students are generally aware of the differences between the institutional setting of school and the more intimate setting of the family. Most students grant school authority over "ambiguously personal issues" such as "public displays of affection" between boyfriend and girlfriend that they would insist on as personal matters outside of the school context. School rules about hairstyle and dress based on White cultural standards can result in punishing students for expressing themselves in culturally relevant ways (reported by the *New York Times*: Jacobs & Levin, 2018; Vigdor, 2019). For the African American middle and high school students in these news articles, such school rules are in direct conflict with the students' claims to a personal domain, which are essential to their construction of a coherent and genuine expression of selfhood and identity. We take this up in greater detail in discussions about school rules and school culture.

THE DEVELOPMENT OF CONCEPTS OF SOCIAL CONVENTION

Children's understandings of convention progress through seven developmental levels that extend into young adulthood (Turiel, 1983). These seven levels follow a pattern that alternates between periods affirming the importance of convention and transitional phases in which children appear to doubt or negate the reasons that they had previously given for maintaining convention. This oscillation indicates the difficulty children have in accounting for the function of arbitrary social norms and illustrates the slow process of reflection and construction that precedes the older adolescent's understanding of convention as important to maintaining the social system. We will see a similar U-shaped pattern of seeming progress and regression in the section below when we look at the development of moral concepts regarding helping someone in need and actions that indirectly result in harm to others. Teachers are generally familiar with what psychologists refer to as U-shaped growth patterns. Students often seem to be less competent just as they are about to make a shift to a more complex academic skill. These U-shaped patterns occur across many developmental tasks and may actually be more common than the linear patterns of steady developmental progress usually described in child development textbooks (Stavy, 2012). Most teachers also understand that these "regressions" are not steps backward, but are part of the process of moving toward newer levels of competence and complexity. From an educational point of view, periods of transition are critical junctures where proper guidance can assist the developmental process. The levels of development for school-aged children have been verified through multiple studies conducted in the United States as well as Asia (Midgette et al., 2016).

Early Elementary (Level I Grades K–2). Convention as Reflecting Observed Social Regularities

Young children already understand that behaviors governed by social convention are only right or wrong if there is a social rule in place. For this reason, children need to make sense of conventions by focusing on the rules rather than the acts that rules regulate. Just as they do with rules of grammar, young children search for patterns in social rules. For children approximately 5 to 7 years of age (roughly kindergarten to 2nd grade), the patterns that they observe in how rules are applied, combined with the explicit information they are told by parent or teachers, leads them to establish a sensible but overly rigid idea about social expectations. For example, children may observe that women sometimes wear dresses. From this observed regularity, children construct a straightforward set of conclusions: Men don't wear dresses because men aren't women; therefore, only women and girls should wear dresses. For a man or a boy to wear a dress would be to violate this observed regularity of the social world. Teachers of young children will recognize this rigidity about convention as similar to what children do when they overgeneralize the rules for such things as past tense and pluralization, and put "ed" endings for irregular verbs such as "drinked" for "drank," and "s" as plurals for nouns such as "sheeps" rather than sheep and "gooses" for geese. Reasoning about convention typical of young children in early elementary grades is illustrated in the following excerpt from research by Elliot Turiel (1983) in which a 6-year-old girl is responding to a scenario depicting a boy who wants to grow up to become an infant nurse, something that was less common in the 1980s.

Should he become a nurse?

Well, no because he could easily be a doctor and he could take care of babies in the hospital.

Why shouldn't he be a nurse?

Well, because a nurse is a lady and the boys, the other men would just laugh at them.

Why shouldn't a man be a nurse?

Well, because it would be sort of silly because ladies wear those kind of dresses and those kind of shoes and hats.

Middle Elementary (Level II Grades 3-4). Negation of Convention as Empirical Regularity

Children at age 5 to 7 years are aware of counterexamples to the regularities that they use to base their notions of convention. For example, they may have a teacher who allows children to call him by his first name rather than by the title Mister and his last name. For the 5- to 7-year-old, such a counterexample is simply chalked up to error. The teacher is simply "wrong." As children get older, however, this instability in their assumptions about convention leads them to reconsider their position. Now such contradictions are viewed as evidence that conventions don't really matter. Children reason, if you can call one adult by his first name, why can't you call all teachers by their first names at school? As one would expect, observational studies of children's violations of classroom social convention report a rise in 3rd and 4th grade in the rate at which children break classroom rules about such things as raising your hand to speak, getting the teacher's permission to leave one's seat to sharpen a pencil, and lining up to enter the class or school (Nucci & Nucci, 1982b). Reasoning about convention at this point in development is illustrated in the following excerpt with an 8-year-old girl again from Turiel (1983).

Right, because it doesn't matter. There are men nurses in hospitals.

What if there were not any in Joe's time, do you think he should have done it?

Yes. It doesn't matter if it is a man or a woman it is just your job taking care of little children.

Middle Elementary (Level III Grades 5–6) Affirmation of Convention as Authority-Based Rules for Social Order. Early Concrete Conception of Social System

At approximately 5th grade (about age 10), children tend to replace the negation of the previous level with a concrete affirmation of the functional value of conventions as serving to maintain social order. Children recognize that conventions vary by context, and that exceptions exist within contexts. However, they also maintain that things work "better" when there is some organization established by rules. For example, rules are needed in order to keep everyone from running in the school hallways and creating chaos. Along with this concrete conception of social order is a concrete notion of social hierarchy. People in charge make the rules, which others are expected to follow. As one might expect, classroom observations of violations of school conventions show a decline in 5th grade relative to the levels observed in grades 3 and 4 (Nucci & Nucci, 1982b).

There is, however, no understanding of societies as systems, and thus, no way of justifying particular social norms beyond very obvious concrete givens. For example, children at this level do not understand the functional significance of titles (e.g., Mr., Mrs., Dr.) in forms of address as reflecting hierarchical social position. Children often state that one should use titles as a sign of respect for the person being addressed. When asked why the use of the title is more respectful than use of a first name, the children are unable to answer other than to say that the authorities who have organized things favor the rule.

The following excerpt is from the responses produced by an 11-year-old girl, and illustrates the reasoning of a child at this point in development. The child is responding to a scenario in which a student refers to his teacher by her first name. She has already judged that it was wrong to do so, and is now providing her justifications.

Why was Alec wrong to use his teachers' first names?

Because that is a sign by disrespect and the teacher asked him nicely to stop but he kept doing it.

Why is it more respectful to use titles rather than first names? What makes saying Mrs. Johnson more respectful than calling her Alicia?

Because some people like to sound older by calling them Mrs. Johnson but some people like to sound younger and calling them by their first name.

Middle School (Level IV Grades 6–8): Negation of Convention as Part of a Rule System; Conventions Simply the Dictates of Authority

As children enter early adolescence (age 12 to 14), they tend to reflect on the fact that the actions regulated by conventions are arbitrary. While they acknowledge that such norms tend to reduce chaos in some cases, such as running in the halls, many conventions, such as calling teachers by titles and surnames, seem superfluous and pointless. From the point of view of the typical middle school student or even many high school freshmen, conventions are nothing more than arbitrary rules imposed on them by authorities. At this point, young people still have no clear conception of societies as systems, and thus have no sense of conventions as helping to form social systems.

Students who tend to be well mannered and well behaved will often follow these norms out of respect for their teachers, and in order to not get into trouble. In some cases, such as in regards to norms about running in the halls, they will base their adherence on an evaluation of the behavior and go along with the rule because it seems sensible. Thus, students at this point in development will appear to selectively adhere to some conventions while disregarding others. Adding to the complexity for social reasoning at this age is the concurrent expansion of what young people consider to be personal matters. Accordingly, schools and teachers, especially in democratic societies, face resistance to conventions such as school dress codes that overlap with what young people view as personal matters. As can be readily imagined, observational studies have reported that the rate of violations of classroom and school conventions is higher in 7th-grade than in 5th-grade classrooms (Nucci & Nucci, 1982b).

In later sections of the book, we will take up the implications for classroom management and the curriculum that this transitional developmental period affords. The following excerpts provide a good illustration of how young people at this level reason about social conventions. The issue is the same one of teacher names as in the above excerpt with an 11-year-old.

What do you think? Was Alec right or wrong to call his teachers by their first names?

Alec was right to call his teachers by their first names because he should be allowed to say what he wants, that's a stupid rule because just calling your teacher by whatever you want to call them should be up to you not up to a school.

Why doesn't it matter if you use first names or titles?

Because a lot of people say it's a sign of respect, but just being nice is enough respect and just being kind would be respectful.

Why do you think the school would have a rule about calling teachers by titles?

For respect issues.

People sometimes respond by saying that it is more respectful to call a teacher by titles and last names rather than using first names. Do you agree with that?

No, I don't think it's more respectful to use titles because if you get a letter when you are five and its addressed to you as Miss, or Mr, you usually don't think of it much different as if they put your regular name.

This early adolescent rejection of convention is not confined to American children as evidenced in the following brief excerpt of an interview with a middle school boy in South Korea (Midgette et al., 2016). Confucianism, which emphasizes social hierarchy that extends into the family system, is an influential part of Korean society. What was found in this research was that Korean students display the same U-shaped developmental pattern when it comes to social convention as has been reported for students in Western societies. In this scenario, the child being interviewed is responding to a situation in which a boy, Youngsoo, has an uncle who is actually younger than him. Youngsoo calls his uncle by his first name, rather than using the title "uncle." The interview excerpt follows:

Youngsoo called his uncle Minwoo by his name. What do you think about this? Do you think it is alright or not alright to call him by his name and not call him as uncle?

I think it's ok.

Why?

Because he is younger, I don't think it matters.

High School—Grades 9-10 (Level V): Affirmation of Convention as Mediated by Social System; Conventions as Constituent Elements of Society

It is in middle adolescence that the dismissal of convention as simply the dictates of authority is replaced by an understanding that conventions have meaning within a larger social framework. Conventions are viewed as binding within a social system of fixed roles and hierarchical organization. At this point in development, violations of convention are viewed as potentially disruptive of the social system. Participants within a system are expected to abide by the norms and conventions of that system.

This more sophisticated understanding of convention is illustrated in the following two excerpts. The first presents a 15-year-old American student's response to the issue concerning teacher names. The second is an excerpt from an interview with a Korean high school student regarding how to address the uncle (from Midgette et al., 2016).

Level V (High School)

U.S. Student:

Why is it more respectful to use titles rather than first names? What makes saying Mrs. Johnson more respectful than calling her Alicia?

It's more respectful because it gives Mrs. Johnson authority, and allows her to rise above her students and not give her a strive for power, but more of a reassurance that she's "the boss," and that she teaches the students; the students don't teach her.

Korean Student:

Youngsoo called his uncle Minwoo by his name. What do you think about this?

You should not call your uncle by his name.

Why do you think so?

There is a family structure and accordingly to this, it is without doubt that you should call him as uncle.

What is the purpose of calling the uncle by his title?

Because in our country, there is the notion of filial duty (A duty to one's parents), and there is a significant hierarchy. This is the norm for our country and I think this is natural.

The 15-year-olds in the above excerpts affirm the convention of students calling teachers by titles and surnames (and children referring to their uncles by titles) on the basis of the differential role relationships, and their respective roles within the school and family as social institutions. The excerpts that follow even more clearly illustrate the differences in thinking between Middle School Negation and High School Affirmation. The responses address a series of questions based on an actual event from the period just following the American Revolutionary War with England. In this incident, King George of England sends a letter to George Washington, to open diplomatic relations. England, however, had not as yet recognized the United States as a country. King George addressed the letter to George Washington, rather than to President George Washington. George Washington did not open the letter, but instead returned it to King George unread. First are the responses of a Level IV female. These same questions were also posed to South Korean students who were well versed in American history (Midgette et al., 2016).

Level IV (Middle School)

USA student:

Why was Washington wrong to return the letter?

Even though he is the president, he is still Mr. Washington so it is okay to call him that.

Why shouldn't it matter how the king addressed the letter?

I don't think it mattered because like I said, that is still his name.

Why did it matter so much to him that the letter be addressed "President Washington"?

I think it mattered a lot to him because he wanted to be called the president because it made him feel good about himself and he wouldn't take anything else for an answer.

Does the way in which the letter is addressed have anything to do with having England recognize the United States as a country?

I have no idea.

Korean Student:

Why do you think he returned the letter?

He thought the letter would be addressed as President but it wasn't. So Washington was disappointed.

Why was he disappointed?

He was expecting some better titles.

Does the way in which the letter is addressed have anything to do with having England recognize the United States as a country?

I don't know.

The middle school students providing these Level IV responses had no real understanding of why Washington would have returned the letter. This extended to the Korean student despite the cultural emphasis on social hierarchy. Their best guesses were that Washington was expecting to be addressed with "better" titles that would make him "feel good about himself." They had no sense of the connection between the formal title and Washington's role within the United States as a social system. When asked about the connection to diplomatic recognition of the United States, both students answered honestly, "I have no idea." In contrast, the following responses from Level 5 high school students in each country illustrate an integration of concepts about the social function conventions of titles as indicative of social status with their larger function as organizing elements of a social system.

Level V (High School)

USA Student:

Why was Washington right to return the letter?

If the problem at that time was that England wasn't giving the United States recognition, then Washington's decision paralleled the reason they were upset.

Why does it matter how the king addressed the letter?

The whole point in their disputes was that he wasn't thinking of Washington as the leader of a real country. The king would have been pretty mad if Washington called him "Mr. George guy from that place in Europe" so I don't see why he didn't have to give Washington the same amount of respect as he expected from the rest of the world.

Why do you think Washington returned the letter?

Washington was offended with the way England constantly didn't believe the United States was a real country. If King George had referred to him as President then he would finally be saying that Washington was in charge of something real.

Korean Student:

So remember that the letter said "Mr. Washington" instead of "President Washington," and thus, he returned the letter without opening this? Do you think such an act was all right or not all right?

It was alright.

Why?

He is the president of a country. Clearly a country and citizens in that country exists. I think it is wrong for England to disregard someone like him and call him as if he was a regular person.

Why did it matter so much to him that the letter be addressed: President Washington?

Because Washington is the president of US and US is independent from England. I think it is right for the King to call Washington president.

Does the way in which the letter is addressed have anything to do with having England recognize the United States as a country?

Yes, there is a relationship. President is a representative of a country. If you accept someone who represents a country, it means you accept the independence of the country.

In sum, by the sophomore year of high school most adolescents have constructed a view of societies as systems of norms. This is a considerable achievement and for the first time positions students to talk coherently about social systems. We will suggest ways in which to make use of this developmental achievement in our approach to moral and social justice education. This initial conceptualization treats society as somewhat static, with norms and conventions that seemingly must be adhered to. This can translate into rigid social conformity, particularly with respect to peer culture. Stacey Horn (2003) has identified the 9th grade, in contrast with 11th grade, as a period during which high school students are most willing to exclude LGBTQ+ peers. In her analysis, Horn concludes that this acceptance of exclusion among 9th-graders is based on perceptions of gender atypicality as going against gender conventions. It is the perceived need for adherence to gender conventions rather than sexual orientation per se that is often the primary driving force supporting such peer exclusion.

High School—Upper Grades 11-12 (Level VI): Negation of Convention as Societal Standards

During the junior and senior years of high school, most adolescents reflect on their views of convention and conclude that although conventions reflect the standards set by the social system, there is no necessary connection between a given societal standard and the functions that they serve. In essence, these older adolescents replace the middle school argument that conventions are nothing but the dictates of authority with the idea that these standards are nothing more than the norms established by a particular society or social organization. This type of reasoning is exemplified in the following statement by a 17-year-old quoted in Turiel (1983, p. 111) responding to the scenario regarding calling teachers by titles rather than their first names.

> Just the fact that teachers in schools have to be called Mr. and Mrs. is no valid reason for that. And also, they simply refuse to acknowledge the fact that he's used to calling people by their first names. . . . There is no good reason for it, the reason is to give the teacher in the classroom respect and give him a feeling of power and authority over the kids in the class.

As was the case with the middle school students, this point of transition is an inflection point in which young people are open to being critical of the norms around them. Unlike the middle school students who have not as yet constructed a conception of societies as systems of norms, these older adolescents are now positioned to critique the social system itself. For social justice education, this period from late elementary through middle school and high school is an especially rich time in which to coordinate attention to the norms of the school culture with the information obtained through the academic curriculum to examine anew the societal assumptions that guide our views around gender, race, ethnicity, power, privilege, sexual orientation, and disability.

College Age (Level VII): Convention as Coordination of Social Interactions

Finally, in young adulthood, conventions are understood to be necessary for the coordination of social interactions among members of social groups. Shared knowledge of social conventions allows for members of groups to have predictability in their social interactions and for the social system to function. However, the overly rigid view of convention maintained during early high school is replaced by the notion of a voluntary participation within the conventions of society rather than unquestioned adherence to rules established by authority or social history.

THE DEVELOPMENT OF CONCEPTS OF MORALITY IN CHILDHOOD AND ADOLESCENCE

Moral development involves shifts in reasoning about fairness and situations involving helping or harm to others. Moral reasoning is more than social logic. It includes concerns for care and compassion (Noddings, 2002). Moral development also involves changes in the ability to integrate or coordinate competing elements of moral situations. For some moral situations, such as unprovoked harm, the moral consequences of actions are clear-cut, and children construct moral judgments about such actions at very early ages. There are no age-related developmental changes in moral reasoning around such clear-cut moral issues after early childhood. There are, however, developmental changes in early childhood associated with interpreting instances of psychological versus physical harm. Young children do not interpret situations of psychological harm as readily as they can interpret the welfare involved in acts of physical harm (Helwig et al., 2001; Jambon & Smetana, 2014). Concepts about fairness emerge later in early childhood than judgments about harm, with language around fairness becoming more common by age six (Turiel, 1983) than among preschool-aged children.

The early development of moral concepts, along with different patterns in applications in situational contexts, is also evident in evaluations and judgments about inclusion and exclusion within group activities. Some of those studies were conducted by presenting children with situations in which a child is excluded from a group activity because of gender or race. As examples, children were asked if it is all right for a group of girls playing with dolls to exclude a boy; or a group of boys playing with trucks to exclude a girl (Killen et al, 2001). In line with findings on harm, children of different ages, starting with preschoolers, judged it wrong and unfair to exclude a child solely on the basis of gender or race. Similarly, the large majority of children and adolescents judged it wrong to deny educational opportunities because of gender or race (Killen et al., 2002). In contrast with the judgments made about such straightforward situations, it has been found that exclusion was not judged to be wrong when due to reasons pertaining to the optimal functioning of a group in particular activities. For instance, even older children and adolescents judge exclusion as acceptable when it occurs because the child does not have as much ability as another for the activity. It has also been found that exclusion is judged differently in the contexts of friendships, peer groups, and the school as a social institution—with greater acceptance of exclusion in friendships and peer groups than in the school context. We will take up these complex issues of social exclusion in later chapters when we look at the application of attention to moral development in school contexts.

Therefore, when we speak about moral development, we need to consider the continuities in basic moral judgments around such clear-cut issues as unprovoked physical harm, along with the changes or discontinuities that occur with applications of moral reasoning around more complex or ambiguous situations. In our more recent work (Nucci et al., 2017), we have described how the child's increased capacity for attention to moral complexity leads to a period of moral ambiguity or uncertainty in early adolescence, relative to the morality of younger children and older adolescents. These changes result in a U-shaped pattern of development similar to the transitional phases we saw with social convention. We will continue our discussion of moral development by looking at changes in how children evaluate or decide on the fairest way to distribute or share things between two or more people. We will then look at the recent findings that have focused on the development of moral concepts of harm and welfare.

The Development of Distributive Justice/Fairness

Early Elementary (Grades K–2): Intuitive Morality

Up to about age 7, children's moral judgment is primarily regulated by concerns for maintaining welfare and avoiding harm and is limited to directly accessible acts. Young children's morality, however, is not yet structured by understandings of fairness as reciprocity. In settings where the child's own interests are not importantly at stake, young children can be touchingly generous and benevolent (Eisenberg, 2014). Preschool teachers often remark on the kindness exhibited by the children in their classrooms. At the same time, however, young children have difficulty balancing the needs of more than one person at a time. In the absence of some clear procedure for resolving competing moral needs, young children appear to use arbitrary standards for assigning value to persons (e.g., age, gender), and have particular difficulty in weighing the needs of others against their own desires (Damon, 1977). Thus, we witness the contradiction of the generosity and openness of young children, and an arbitrariness and selfishness characteristic of the age. Resolving these contradictions involves changes in a) the child's conceptions of persons, b) in their understandings of what is required to maintain interpersonal relations, and c) in their general intellectual capacity to comprehend the implications for how what you do might affect others. This is a tall order. And these issues are revisited throughout the course of moral development.

William Damon (1977) captured the moral reasoning of young children in a series of creative studies in which he asked children to decide what would be the best way to divide up candies between themselves and another child friend. In a typical situation, a 5-year-old child would be asked to tell an interviewer what her favorite color of M&Ms is. She would then be shown a group of M&Ms in which the majority was of the child's favorite color. When asked the best way to divide up the M&Ms between themself and their friend, the child would generally keep all of the M&Ms of their favorite color and give their friend the remainder. This is considered fair by the young child because they didn't keep everything to themselves, but shared some with the other child.

Middle Elementary (Grades 2–5): Morality as Strict Equality

The great accomplishment of early childhood moral development is the construction of notions of moral action tied to structures of "just" reciprocity (Damon, 1977). By approximately 6 to 8 years of age, children begin to construct a set of moral understandings that compellingly tie the actions of one person to the reactions or responses of the other. By age 10, these notions of reciprocity are generally consolidated into notions of moral "necessity" resulting from a moral logic that requires equal treatment of persons. In the case of distributing candies described above, the typical 3rd- to 5th-grade child would distribute all of the candies, including the ones of their favorite color, equally between themselves and their friend. Many parents have understood this child moral logic, and solve such distributive justice problems such as sharing a candy bar by having one child do the cutting and the other one getting to choose which "half" to keep.

This "strict" reading of equal treatment, however, may allow for a kind of tit-for-tat morality in which moral obligation extends only to those with whom one can expect something in return, and only to the extent that actions maintain a balanced "moral ledger." On the playground, this too often translates into the tit-for-tat of getting even with name-calling, or even one's fists.

Middle School (Grades 6–8): Morality of Equity and Equality

Beginning around 3rd grade, children show signs of an awareness that differences in the capacities and needs of individuals should be met with special considerations. These intuitions are coordinated between the ages of 10 and 14 years into a notion of fairness as requiring more than strict equality (Damon, 1977). Treating others fairly may mean treating people unequally in the sense that equity requires adjustments that bring people into more comparable statuses. This expansion of morality frees the child from considering what is fair solely in terms of direct reciprocal exchange, and allows for extensions of moral (fair) treatment to those from whom one has no expected repayment, and to those who have even been ungracious or unfair to the self. With respect to this latter point, it allows the child to go beyond a tit-for-tat morality of retribution to deal with transgressors without resorting to the same kinds of hurtful acts employed by the transgressor.

This depiction of the sequence of changes in moral judgments around distributive and retributive justice describes children's reasoning in typical everyday contexts. As we noted above, however, increasing the salience of the moral consequences can engage even very young children into making more sophisticated judgments than when the moral consequences are less salient. In particular, the ages at which children are capable of displaying judgments about fair distribution of goods have been found to be associated with whether the goods to be distributed are necessities. As just described, when asked to distribute goods that are nice to have (such as M&Ms) or fun to play with, children below the age of 10 tend to employ concepts of equality and not equity. However, when the goods are described as necessary (e.g., school supplies, medical equipment), children of the ages of 5 or 6 employ concepts of equity to insure that disadvantaged children have access to needed goods (Rizzo et al., 2016). This suggests that the underlying capacity to attend to issues of social justice is present in children's moral thinking from a very early age if the maldistribution of goods is made sufficiently salient. However, a fully stable and broadly applied notion of fairness as equity does not emerge until late in childhood. Nonetheless, the underlying capacity to attend to inequities in the distribution of necessary goods means that educators can appeal to children's sense of fairness around these aspects of inequality at very early ages.

The U-Shaped Development of Concepts of Harm and Welfare

While the picture of moral development just described is one of "progress," there is another side to the emerging capacity for moral complexity as children shift to the more abstract reasoning of adolescence. Although young adolescents have moved beyond the tit-for-tat direct reciprocity of middle childhood, their moral thinking remains in transition. This is most evident in situations where there is moral ambiguity in relation to the harm caused and the personal choice available to the actor to behave in their own self-interest.

A recent study (Nucci et al., 2017) explored the development of children's and adolescents' reasoning about situations in which they had to weigh their own self-interests against whether to help someone in need, or refrain from engaging in harm to the other person. The study investigated many variables beyond the scope of this book. However, the basic findings can be summarized in terms of the central developmental patterns. The helping situations describe a child who falls and is injured. The protagonist must decide whether to seek help for the injured child or continue on without helping in order to be on time for an activity that they want to do. The harm conditions are of two types. In one case, the harm involves directly hitting and hurting another person without provocation.* In the second, indirect harm situation, the protagonist in the scenario does not have enough money to participate in an activity with their friends. The protagonist had tried to earn the money to be able to participate, but came up $10 ($20 in adolescent

---

* The hitting scenario involves two other conditions with findings that are too complex to report in this chapter. In one, the protagonist has to decide whether it is right to hit in self-defense. In the second, the decision is whether to hit in order to protect a child who is being attacked. The basic U-shaped developmental patterns also hold for these situations.

scenarios) short. A few days before the day of the activity, the protagonist boards an empty bus. Soon afterward a second person boards the bus and drops a $10 bill while reaching for the money to pay the bus fare. Neither the driver nor the passenger is aware of the $10 bill on the floor. The protagonist has to decide whether to tell the passenger that they dropped the $10 bill or stay silent and keep the bill themself. In addition to varying the nature of the act, the scenarios also varied the characteristics of the other child depicted in the situation. The other child was described a) simply as a "girl" or "boy," b) as someone who had antagonized the child the previous day by teasing them the day before, or c) as a child who falls or drops money because of a physical disability. These changing characteristics were intended to impact the degree of empathy for the other child in the moral conflict situations.

In addition to children and adolescents being asked whether it would be wrong or all right to engage in the action, they were asked whether the protagonist would have the "right" to engage in the action if that was the protagonist's decision. In response to the unprovoked direct harm situations, virtually all respondents across ages indicated that the protagonist would be wrong to engage in hitting, and that the protagonist had no right to engage in the behavior. This is not surprising given that a typical 3-year-old would treat unprovoked hitting as wrong. The helping and indirect harm conditions, however, produced very different types of results. Most of the children and adolescents in the study viewed it as wrong to not offer help in situations that did not pose a conflict with the interests or needs of the protagonist. However, whether or not to help was viewed as more discretionary than to refrain from engaging in harm. The acceptance of a right-not-to-help in an unconflicted context was greater than for judgments of a right either to hit or to keep the money in unconflicted situations. There were also age-related effects on judgments about the right to not offer help, especially in conflict situations that pitted helping against the needs and desires of the protagonist. This curvilinear trend can be seen in Figure 3.1, which shows that the 8-year-olds and 16-year-olds were less likely to make the judgment of a right not to help than were the 11-year-olds and 14-year-olds.

Similar developmental trends appeared in the judgments children and adolescents made regarding decisions about whether or not to return money to a person who had unknowingly dropped it. Unlike the act of physically hitting someone, keeping the money does not result from an intentional act by the protagonist to steal from the other person. Instead, the situation presents itself entirely by chance. When the person dropping the money was described in generic terms, or as an antagonist, the responses varied by age. Young children and 17-year-old adolescents generally viewed keeping the money to be wrong. However, 10-year-olds, and especially 14-year-olds, were more likely to express ambivalence as to whether it might be all right to keep the money. These developmental trends become even more apparent when the children were asked to judge whether or not the protagonist would

Figure 3.1 Percentage of Participants by Age Judging That the Protagonist Would Have a Right to Keep the Money, to Not Help

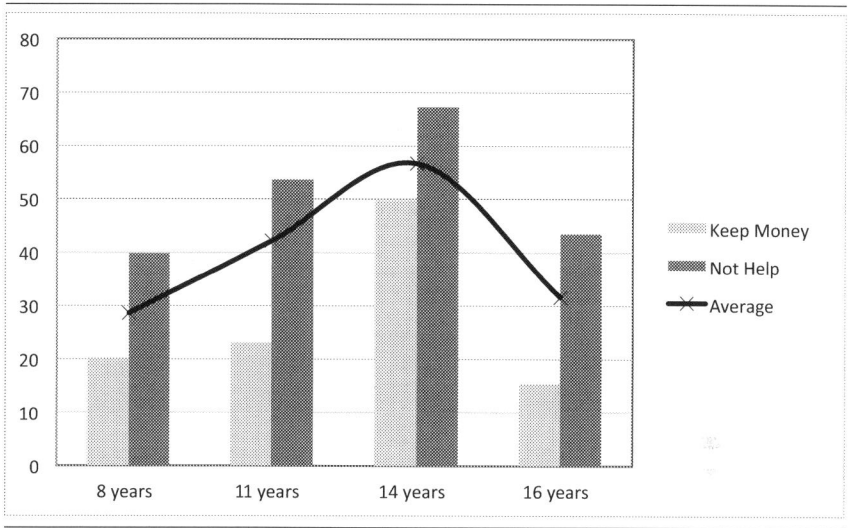

have a "right" to keep the money if that is what they wanted to do. Here the results look very much like the age-related trends observed with helping.

Figure 3.1 presents the proportions of participants at each age who argued that you would have a "right" to keep the money. As can be seen in Figure 3.1, young children generally maintained that the protagonist does NOT have a right to keep the money as this would be a simple case of theft. More than half of the 14-year-olds, however, were of the opinion that the protagonist has a "right" to keep the money. By age 16–17, the majority of respondents again took the position that the protagonist did not have a right to keep the money.

The reasoning used in support of the decisions regarding indirect stealing, helping, and hitting (in conflicted situations) fell into three types or *Levels* that represented age-related forms of coordination. What follows are descriptions of these levels with examples of reasoning about indirect stealing and helping (from Nucci et al., 2017).

Early–Middle Elementary (Grades 2–5) Level 1: Straightforward: One-Dimensional Decisions

The first level describes moral judgments in which evaluation of the right or wrong of an action is based on the most salient moral elements of harm or welfare presented in the situation and not other features. The decisions made using this pattern appear non-wavering and unambiguous. Individuals may recognize or mention other elements, or can recognize other elements if they are brought to the person's attention, but these are not integrated within the person's reasoning; they are merely noted.

Indirect Stealing:

8-year-old female

Would it be wrong or all right for (protagonist) to keep the money instead of giving it back to the other girl?

No, because it's someone else's $10 bill, she shouldn't keep it because it's not hers.

8-year-old male

Would it be wrong or all right for (protagonist) to keep the money instead of giving it back to the other boy?

He's stealing, and you don't want to, it's not good to steal.

Suppose he decides to keep the money. Does he have the right to keep the money if he wants to?

No, because it's someone else's $10 bill.

Middle School and Early High School (Grades 6-9) Level 2: Multidimensional Uncoordinated Decisions

The second level, referred to as multidimensional uncoordinated, is characterized by attention to different features of a situation, and a recognition of ambiguity, but without resolution or evidence of coordinating the moral and nonmoral concerns in a systematic way. This process is manifested by inconsistency and ambivalence that sometimes result in a reading of moral ambiguity as allowing for selection of an action that fits the needs and desires of the actor. At this level, judgments about whether an act is right or wrong are not coordinated with judgments about whether one would have a right to engage in a given action. Thus, it is frequently maintained that one would have a right to engage in an action even though the act could be considered wrong.

It is important to point out, however, that the reasoning of these early adolescents should not be characterized as uncaring, or operating solely from self-interest. The decisions to keep the money or to help someone in need were quite different when the other person in the situation was described as vulnerable. In the case of a person with a visible physical disability, the decision of nearly all participants was to help the person or to return the money.

Indirect Stealing:

13-year-old female

Would it be wrong or all right for (protagonist) to keep the money instead of giving it back to the other girl?

He's not doing anything wrong. He's not necessarily doing something wrong, but the right thing to do would be to give it back, but he's not necessarily, he doesn't necessarily have any wrongdoing.

13-year-old male

Suppose he decides to keep the money. Does he have the right to keep the money if he wants to?

He's got every right to keep the ten dollars, like I said, because it's in nowhere land. And it's his, he found it. It's not in the kid's house or anything. . . . However wrong it seems for him to keep the money, he has the right to. It is the same thing as finding $10 on the bus with nobody else around. Lost money is up for grabs. He has the right to keep it because that person dropped it and it's a free country.

Helping:

14-year-old male

Would it be all right or not all right for John to keep walking so he could get to the soccer tryout on time without helping the kid in this situation?

I guess it would still be all right, it would be nicer if he just helped the kid.

Would he have a right not to help in this situation so he can get to the tryout on time?

Ah, yeah, 'cause it's really, it's not his fault that the kid fell or anything.

So, would it be right or wrong for him to do it?

It wouldn't be a bad thing that he didn't do it, but it wouldn't be wrong that he didn't do it, I mean, it wouldn't be wrong that he didn't do it, but it wouldn't be a good thing that he didn't do it.

Can you explain that to me?

It's a good thing, if he did do it, it'd be a good thing 'cause like he helped out the kid, but if he just went to the soccer thing, it wouldn't be horrible, because like, I don't know, I guess.

So how should he decide what's the right thing to do here?

It's kind of a tough situation, just like.

How should he decide it, though?

I'm not sure.

Okay, well what things do you think he's going to have to balance out here?

Making the team and helping out the kid and what to do before.

And is there any way for him to decide what's the right thing to do here?

Not really, it's just, there's no really right way to do it.

Level 3: Multidimensional Coordinated Decisions

At the third level, labeled as multidimensional coordinated, there is evidence of consideration and weighing of multiple (moral and nonmoral) aspects or considerations with a resolution. Individuals who engage in a *coordinated* process demonstrate an awareness of moral ambiguity and the arguments that can be made for acting in self-interest in such situations. However, they engage in reasoning that leads to resolution of that moral ambiguity with the integration of nonmoral concerns in a consistent and systematic way.

Indirect Stealing:

17-year-old female

Would it be wrong or all right for (protagonist) to keep the money instead of giving it back to the other girl?

Well, in reality, would it be all right or not all right? You should always give the money back. But, I can understand the thought process for not giving the money back. Well in reality, if something, I don't know how to say that, if someone loses money, it's theirs and if you know that, she should give it back. But, if you just saw ten dollars on the street and you have no idea who it belongs to, keep it, but if you know who it belongs to, it's your duty to give it back. But I can understand the thought process.

Helping:

16-year-old male

Would it be all right or not all right for John to keep walking so that he can get to the soccer tryout on time?

I think it would be a good thing for him to stop and help the kid because you know, he has to get his priorities straight. And, it'll be a tough decision for him to make because one (decision) benefits him, and the other benefits someone else and it won't be natural to go for the benefit of someone else but he should stop and help the kid.

Would John have a right not to help in this situation so that he can get to his tryout on time?

He does have a right not to help him because he doesn't have to help him. It's morally the right thing to help someone else over helping yourself but it's definitely as a person a bonus and an extra quality to be moral like that and help someone else. But he definitely has the right to go and do what he wants to do and what will benefit him because you don't have a right or obligation to help anyone else because there's no reason that you have to. It's a very nice thing to do but you don't have to do it.

How should he decide what the right thing to do is in this situation?

He should probably think about what will happen in each case which will be he'll get cut versus the kid will be stranded and possibly having no help and he should weigh those options and say "You know, I could play soccer next year or sometime else but you know this kid really needs my help." So he should weigh the negative benefits. In this case, I would say that helping should take priority.

Summary of Findings on Moral Development

With age, children and adolescents move toward increasingly coherent conceptions of fairness. Development moves from an early childhood set of intuitions about unprovoked harm to notions of fairness as regulated by direct reciprocity. This morality of reciprocity shifts from direct equality toward conceptions of morality in which equality is coordinated with equity.

Along with this greater understanding of fairness, however, comes an expanded capacity for incorporating facets of moral situations that render the application of morality more ambiguous and divergent. Rather than presenting a straightforward picture of moral development as linear moral "progress" toward shared answers to moral situations, moral development includes periods of transition in which the expanded capacity to consider aspects of moral situations leads to variations in the application of moral criteria. In early adolescence in particular, the effort to establish the personal domain results in the overapplication of conceptions of *rights* in contexts that are morally ambiguous. With development, adolescents sort out notions of free choice, from conceptions of rights. They also become better able to coordinate multifaceted moral situations, and to weigh the moral and nonmoral (societal, personal, prudential) aspects of particular social contexts and events.

DEVELOPMENT AND CROSS-DOMAIN INTERACTIONS

Chapter 2 ended with a discussion of moral complexity and domain overlap. If we apply the lessons from that chapter to the patterns of development within domains, we can begin to anticipate how students at various grade levels are likely to reason about multifaceted social situations. By way of illustration, let's consider how a cross-domain analysis affords a window into the workings of the early adolescent in middle school and the freshman year of high school. A student at this point in development is expanding the list of personal behaviors that should be matters of personal discretion and privacy rather than subject to family or school conventions. This expansion of the personal is closely linked with the young person's efforts to establish personal autonomy and personal identity. These developmental changes in the personal are occurring at the same time as the normative development of a phase of negation of social convention as "simply the dictates of authority." Thus, even those conventions the adolescent acknowledges as legitimate have little regulatory force. Finally, the young adolescent's morality is characterized by a more mature integration of notions of equality and equity in reasoning about fairness. However, moral thinking is also defined at this developmental age by an increased tendency to see the "shades of gray" in moral situations, and to at times confuse personal expression of freedom of choice in such ambiguous situations with a right to act in ways that are understood to be morally wrong.

Given this developmental constellation, we should expect to be engaged with a young person who cares deeply about social justice, and about respect for personal rights and freedoms. We should also expect to interact with someone who questions existing social norms, and who defines authority in terms of interpersonal qualities rather than social position (e.g., as a teacher). Personal expression in the areas of music, dress, and language will come to the forefront and may lead to conflict with parental and school rules. Our young person will also be someone who finds new complexities and ambiguities in moral situations. At a behavioral level we would expect an increase in social experimentation, challenges to authority, and engagement in petty crimes that have little or no direct impact on individuals. Shoplifting, for example, tends to peak between the ages of 12 and 14.

This middle school period is often experienced by teachers as particularly challenging in terms of classroom management and adherence to school policies of dress and decorum. We will take up developmentally appropriate approaches to classroom management in upcoming chapters. However, this transition period is also an inflection point in which the students' challenges to convention along with their transitional moral thinking can be viewed as an opportunity for social justice educators to engage students in the beginnings of a critical analysis of society. A fully formed analysis would await the construction of deeper understandings of convention and morality that emerge during the high school years. The point that we are making here, however, is that periods of transition should be viewed as opportunities to engage students in critical social and moral thinking rather than times to simply manage and outlast. Engaging students in opportunities for translating social justice concerns into praxis, as we describe in Chapter 11, harnesses these developmental dynamics into positive engagement as citizens and critical moral people.

CHAPTER 4

Character as a Developmental System

When we engage in moral education, we are not simply addressing moral reasoning or values; we are impacting the child or adolescent as a person. Our moral judgments do not take place in isolation. They draw on the broader set of social and emotional capacities that allow us to function as social beings, and they reflect the competing goals and biases that make up the totality of our selves as individual people. Moral education will impact the very kinds of people our students will become as adults, participating as members of families, communities, and citizens of their countries.

Historically, viewing morality as an aspect of the person has been referred to as *character*. This is an old and enduring way of looking at the qualities that together comprise a "good" person. In Europe and North America, this focus on character has its roots in the philosophy of Aristotle. In Asian countries such as China and Korea, the focus on character is grounded in the writings and sayings of Confucius and his followers. Many teachers in North America are familiar with a traditional approach to what is referred to as character education. In the traditional approach, character education is about transmitting social values to children through direct teaching, role models, and systems of positive and negative consequences. The goal is to build up habits of conduct or virtues that automatically guide a student's behavior toward doing the right thing (Narvaez, 2008).

Historically, character education has been employed to socialize each new generation into the values and traditions of the dominant culture. Character has also been used as a notion by European settlers to create narratives of racial superiority over Indigenous peoples (Stanley, 2003). In a case study of White supremacy and imperialist narratives in Canadian textbooks, Stanley wrote:

> An imperialist ethic constructed around the notion of "character" transformed [British Columbia] classrooms into imperial outposts and allowed *students* personally to become part of, and share in the responsibility for, this imperial mission. Third, by explaining the Empire as the product of genetically based moral superiority, they presented subject peoples as morally deficient Others. (p. 148)

As we move on to discussing a model of character that is sensitive to the role of cultural heritage and traditional ways of being, it is important to note the ways in which character has been weaponized by colonial powers to justify dominance over Indigenous peoples and people who were captured, sold, and enslaved. "Good character" in these contexts divided people along racial lines and lines of social conformity to White, European values.

In the first chapter of this book, we mentioned that contemporary proponents of character education do not view attention to character formation as compatible with the goals of social justice education (Arthur et al., 2016). This is because of the mistaken notion that character is something that exists as a set of discrete qualities or virtues within the person that function apart from the context. From this view, character is a set of objectively positive qualities that individuals apply across social and cultural settings.

In this chapter, we will challenge this position and offer an alternative view of character as a developmental system. This developmental view of character is consistent with current research, and coherent with a commitment to the goals of social justice education. It recognizes that moral education impacts the very core identity of students. This developmental system view also understands that individual students are embedded within a cultural context that is mutually constitutive and impacted by the actions of its members. A person with mature moral character will participate in the collective process of either sustaining the status quo or moving the society and culture toward justice. We begin with a critique of the traditional view of character.

THE LIMITS OF TRADITIONAL VIEWS OF CHARACTER

Character as Virtues

As we noted above, character has traditionally been defined in terms of virtues that emerge from socialization practices fostering culturally valued qualities that guide behaviors. There are several fundamental problems with this traditional approach to character. The first is the lack of agreement across cultures and historical periods as to which qualities count as virtues. If there is no agreement, then the idea that these virtues hold some objective significance across time and place cannot be true. A systematic recent historical analysis by Robert McGrath (2016), for example, found that of the five primary virtues identified by Plato, two (courage, prudence) made it into the list of 16 primary virtues identified by Aristotle, and only one of the virtues maintained by Aristotle (justice) made it onto the list of seven core virtues identified by Catholicism.

In addition, defining character in terms of virtues that are to be upheld in all situations runs contrary to evidence beginning with Hartshorne and May (1928) that demonstrated that people are inconsistent in their application of virtues—basically, people behave differently as a function of context (Nucci et. al., 2017). Readers of this book can readily understand this by simply reflecting back on times when they may have copied or shared homework assignments, or cheated on a test, and other situations in which the reader resisted such behavior even though others were engaging in cheating. Readers can probably also recall instances in which they lied in order to protect themselves or a friend, and other times when they told the truth even though it may have gotten themselves in trouble. Anyone who lives an actual social life understands the complexity of real social situations and the impossibility of remaining "honest" or "virtuous" in this simplistic sense in every social context.

Contemporary virtue philosophers and like-minded psychologists (Narvaez, 2008) address these shortcomings of virtue theory by appealing to processes that guide the application of judgments in context through "practical expertise," referred to by Aristotelians as *phronesis* (Darnell et al., 2019). Such interpretations and adjustments in virtue theory, however, are acknowledgments that the core of moral action lies in the judgments made within context rather than static abstract qualities of the person.

Character and the Self-System

The best way to view character is as a system operating within the self as a whole. The self-system includes our overall sense of agency and unique personal identity. When we talk about character, we refer to those capacities and characteristics that motivate and enable the student to act as a moral agent. Moral agency (Pasupathi & Wainryb, 2010) refers to the student's understanding and experiences of themselves as the source of their own moral actions. How a student manages their own emotional states, desires, and moral decisions forms the basis of character. Being a moral agent includes a capacity for self-correction or improvement in response to wrongdoing (Midgette, 2018). Moral agency is a critical component of what we refer to as basic moral wellness. Moral agency emerges throughout childhood through reflections on positive actions, but also very powerfully as children account for their own harmful actions and the harmful actions of others (Recchia et al., 2015). Educators should note the fact that experiences of trauma and engagement in acts of violence can impact and disrupt the formation and status of constructive moral agency (Wainryb, 2011).

A second thing to keep in mind is that teachers can take snapshot views of students within a given moment that may illuminate features of moral development and character, as long as we understand that these are moments in the course of development. They are not frozen entities (virtues, traits). For this reason, what we should be looking for in terms of character within our students is not consistency across contexts, but coherence. Character is not a matter of acting in the same (consistent) way (e.g., "honest") irrespective of the situation, but in a manner that is morally sensible (coherent) across situations. For example, whether to participate in excluding an unpopular peer from a group activity would involve weighing the harm caused to the peer, the norms of the peer group, and the child's own self-interest and personal preferences (Killen, et. al., 2002). That decision will be one that feels sensible to that particular student in that particular context. Decisions over time generated by the character system alter how that person will respond to similar moral situations in the future, but will not determine future contextualized moral decisions. When we view our students, we are not just seeing spontaneous actions. We are viewing an outcome of the trajectory of their prior action decisions along with the dynamics of development. Teachers who know their students well can predict with some accuracy how a given student is likely to behave. As any experienced teacher knows, however, students will always surprise us with actions that seem "out of character." This is because coherence at any point in time is subjective to the person making the action choice. In this same way, our knowledge of a student's history does not allow us to infer conclusively how that same student will act in the future. We need to keep this in mind when we think about our approaches to student discipline.

Finally, the notion of a dynamic relationship between person and context means that over time we will see evidence not only of the impact of the context on the person, but the impact of the person on the context. A comprehensive understanding of character involves the systematic analysis of our role in transforming others with whom we come into contact, along with the larger society. Therefore, peer relations are an important consideration for effective teachers.

THE COMPONENTS OF CHARACTER

Let's now turn to the basic components that collectively contribute to and comprise "character." There are four basic components. Development of the first three aspects of character results in what we refer to as basic *moral wellness*. The reader may be familiar with how the term wellness is used in talking about our physical well-being. Wellness connotes normative basic health, but also includes the daily practices of good nutrition and exercise that keep us healthy. Similarly, establishing moral well-being is an ongoing process requiring active attention and nurturing. This has important implications for teachers. Teachers, like good health care providers, make sure that their students are exposed to sound classroom environments and educational practices that foster moral growth and help the student maintain moral wellness.

The three components of moral wellness are: 1) basic moral cognition, 2) other-regarding social–emotional capacities and skills such as empathy and perspective taking, and 3) self-regarding capacities for executive control and self-regulation of emotions and desires. This third component is employed both in the enactment of moral actions and in the completion of nonmoral tasks that require steadfast commitment and engagement.

In other places, the steadfast commitment to the completion of nonmoral tasks has been referred to as "performance character." Examples of performance character in educational settings include such things as getting assignments done on time and doing one's best work. At times it may seem that the only aspects of character that are of interest to the educational establishment is performance character as applied to academic achievement. It is an open question, however, as to whether self-regarding capacities such as industriousness, grit, or courage function in the same way in nonmoral contexts as within moral contexts. What is important for our discussion about education is that it is very problematic to apply the notion of character to particular skills or propensities in the absence of their connection to morality. For example, the Nazis were certainly industrious when it came to their enactment of their "final solution" toward the Jewish people. Similarly, it can be argued that the individuals engaging in school shootings have shown grit and perhaps even courage. We would be hard-pressed to argue that these displays of self-regarding capacities constitute character in the absence of an evaluation of their moral impact. Finally, a student displaying morally neutral capacities of industriousness in the classroom, or grit and courage on the playing field, would not be judged to have "good" character if that same student was abusive toward classmates or to their friends. This is because the evaluative meaning of character is inexorably tied into the expression of morality as an aspect of the self-system.

Our view of character includes a fourth component, which is the discourse and communication skills, and critical orientation for principled moral change at the social level. This fourth component is not generally included within discussions of moral character. However, the standard depiction of character does not account for the potential impact of a person on the social context. Inclusion of this aspect of character is consistent with comprehensive views of development that attend to socio-genetic processes along with individual aspects of development. This attention to the sociocultural connects character with social justice. It envisions a person of character as more than a product of society, but as a potential moral agent of social change. Figure 4.1 represents the relationship between this character system and the self-system as a whole. In the following sections, we elaborate on each component of the character system.

Morality and Moral Cognition

Character is, at its core, about engagement in moral choices. As we have described in detail in the previous chapters, moral judgments center on issues of fairness, welfare, and rights, and are distinct from judgments about

Figure 4.1. Character Within the Self-System

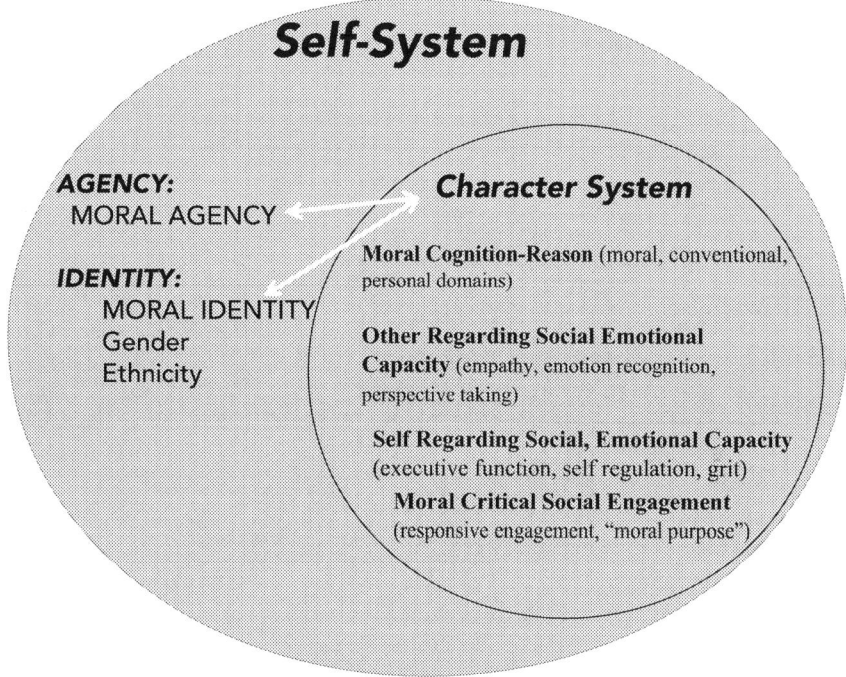

consensually determined conventions, and matters of personal choice and privacy. Developmental analyses have identified continuities in moral judgments within prototypical situations, such as unprovoked harm, as well as age-typical, cross-domain coordination (Nucci et al., 2017). These structural aspects of moral cognition contribute to observed consistencies in moral judgments and action. For example, individuals across age rarely endorse unprovoked harm. As we saw in the preceding chapters, the trajectory of development within the moral and conventional domains, however, is not linear, but follows curvilinear oscillating patterns. These developmental findings are strong evidence against accounts of character formation in terms of habits or chronic, easily accessed cognitive schemes (Narvaez, 2008), since one would need to explain how and why moral virtue (expertise) disappears (and reappears) once it has been formed.

As we have also described, social contexts may also be multifaceted, requiring the coordination of concepts from more than one domain. Older adolescents are better able to coordinate competing elements in ambiguous moral situations than are younger adolescents. Character formation is impacted by development within domains as well as the capacity to coordinate competing considerations across domains. The contextual multidomain nature of the application of morality to lived situations is why any definition of character must be framed in terms of coherence in moral judgments rather than context-independent consistency. Those moral decisions are the outcome of the character system engaging with particular contexts. Each decision impacts the ways in which students approach future moral choices, and in this way forms the moral character of the person that the student is becoming. We will say more about this below when we discuss the connections to moral identity.

Other-Regarding Social–Emotional Capacities

The second component of character is comprised of the social–emotional capacities for engaging the motives and needs of others. This includes the capacity for empathy, the ability to accurately read the emotions of others, and perspective taking. These components provide the inputs for the universal capacity of human beings to generate moral judgments about harm and human welfare.

Some forms of pathology exhibited by psychopaths and sociopaths are not the result of flaws or lacks in the development of basic moral cognition or social intelligence. Adolescents who score high on psychopathy do not show impairments in making the distinction between morality and convention, and do not appear markedly different in their capacity for perspective taking (Dolan & Fullam, 2010). In fact, it is their capacity for understanding the motives and needs of others that allows psychopaths and sociopaths to be so effective in exploiting or causing harm. There is research indicating that psychopaths display deficits when it comes to affective empathy, with corresponding differences in responses within brain regions associated with empathic arousal (Blair et al., 2005). Traumatic or extremely negative experiences can impact the development of empathy and related emotional competencies. As Wainryb's (2011) work has shown, for example, one's moral agency can be impacted by direct exposure to violence.

Self-Regarding Social–Emotional Capacities

Character is more than the capacity for judging the right thing to do; it is the propensity to act on that judgment. This has often been mischaracterized as a problem of moral motivation. Morality, however, is intrinsically motivating. Children 23 months of age, for example, display greater happiness when giving away treats to a puppet than when receiving treats themselves, and display greatest happiness when voluntarily giving something of their own (Aknin et al., 2012). Adult readers of this book would hopefully not expect an external reward for going through a typical day without engaging in unprovoked harm to colleagues, or stealing from strangers. Nonetheless, engaging in moral action sometimes requires supportive personal traits and social–emotional skills. The third component of character is the capacity for self-regulation and follow-through. This is the subject of research on emotion regulation and executive function. Emotion regulation allows for the person to act on the basis of rational choice, rather than the heat of the moment. Executive function serves to enable the coordination of cross-domain considerations and enhance impulse control.

Nice Is Not Enough: Discourse Skills for Responsive Engagement and a Critical Orientation for Principled Moral Change

The components listed thus far account for conventional notions of character and morality. They describe the development of the person who will operate morally in everyday life. Achieving this level of moral wellness should be the baseline expectation of our educational systems. However, the limitation of basic moral wellness is that it allows for the person who will live quite happily within a culture or society with structural inequalities or structural practices that are themselves immoral. There is ample evidence from history and contemporary research that resistance to unfair practices is common and especially prevalent among individuals in positions of lesser power or privilege (Turiel, 2002). However, translating personal moral opposition into a principled moral perspective is something that may not be possible at an individual level. This is the argument made by philosophers (Rawls, 2001) who maintain that abstract moral principles cannot be translated into genuine moral positions in the absence of dialogue with those for whom those principles are meant to apply. For example, an abstract principle of justice as fairness cannot in itself lead a person of privilege to recognize injustice within social arrangements that are longstanding and taken as working well. As we noted earlier, Peggy McIntosh (2018) pointed this out in her highly influential essay "White Privilege: Unpacking the Invisible Knapsack" describing how as a White person one can be unaware of the many ways that simply being White affords access to goods and services not as available to a person of color. For moral education to address the concerns of social justice, it must embrace practices that resolve the limitations of individual moral development.

Our approach to the development of moral character addresses this challenge by drawing from what the political philosopher Anthony Laden (2012) refers to as "responsive engagement." This is a form of conversation that has as its goal, finding a conceptual space that all can share and accept as their own. This is in contrast with debates or other forms of discourse that either ignore the positions of others or merely seek to defeat or convert competing viewpoints. The educational practices we describe in the following chapters include a process for developing a discourse orientation and skill set in students that would increase the likelihood of their engagement in principled moral change in the social system.

LINKING THE CHARACTER SYSTEM TO IDENTITY AND THE SELF

Character is not a set of static virtues but the cumulative result of moral choices that alter who we are and that establish the framework for our contextualized future moral decisions. It is a developmental subsystem that is impacted by emerging social and emotional skills and knowledge structures that undergird our moral decisions. This developmental subsystem is linked to our construction of identity and sense of self. With the exception of psychopaths and sociopaths, all people care about morality and view being moral as a core aspect of their identity. In a recent comprehensive review of the research on moral identity, Lapsley (2016) reports that moral categories are more readily accessible than competence traits and dominate our impression formation. In a fascinating recent study, Lefebvre and Krettenauer (2020) found that beginning with preschool age and continuing through adolescence and adulthood, people judged that if a person altered their stance toward a moral value (e.g., okay to steal or hurt others), they would no longer be the "same person" as before. If the same person had instead changed their view about social conventions (forms of greeting, punctuality) or personal preferences (music choices), they would still be the same person. In other words, one's moral positions and decisions are understood even by children to be core aspects of the self.

As we learned in Chapter 3, there are age-related shifts in how children and adolescents conceptualize the self. For children, the self is understood literally to be one's physical makeup and characteristic actions. A morally "good" person is defined by corresponding tendencies to act in harmony with what is morally right. In early adolescence, this sense of self is tied to core ideas and values that in middle adolescence become the defining essence of a core inner true self. For the adolescent, the task of building the self entails bringing all aspects of one's actions and public expression into line with this core "true" self. In later adolescence, the notion of essence is replaced with the understanding that self is the evolving product of one's daily decisions and actions.

CONCLUSION

Character is a developmental system that enables the person to engage with the social world as a moral agent. As a self-generating and self-sustaining system, character provides coherence to moral action, but not complete consistency. The lack of consistency is not a sign of moral failing or weakness of character, but the normative and expected adjustments to the social context by a functioning moral agent. As teachers, we should attend to the trajectory of our students' action choices and view them as pieces of a whole, rather than interpreting particular actions as indicative of character. The core of character is morality, defined in terms of fairness and human welfare. Thus, it would be a disservice to our students to place complete emphasis on SEL skills without attention to the development of moral reasoning. It is equally mistaken to elevate attention toward any particular expression of morality, such as gratitude or compassionate love, as having particular relevance outside of its role or position within the character system. In the remainder of this book, we will discuss the specific practices that teachers may engage in to foster morally healthy and critical students prepared to contribute to social justice.

Part II

SOCIAL LIFE IN SCHOOLS AND CLASSROOMS

Creating Environments That Promote Moral Development and Social Justice

CHAPTER 5

Schools and Classrooms as Moral Institutions
Rules, Norms, and Procedures

> I think there would have to be a lot of rules about hitting at school because it would hurt somebody!
>
> —Marisha, 5 years old

Children's moral development originates in their attempts to make meaning out of social experience. The social life of school is not experienced as an abstraction, but confronts children in their everyday efforts to negotiate their desires and needs in relation to those of others, the social rules and norms that structure social interactions, and the feelings that come along with those social experiences. How we structure educational environments and respond to student behavior forms part of what has been referred to as the moral life of schools and classrooms (Kumashiro, 2000). There are three basic aspects to schools and classrooms as social environments. These are 1) the rules, norms, and procedures, 2) the emotional or affective climate, and 3) the approach to handling student transgressions. In this chapter, we will examine the role of school and classroom rules in relationship to students' moral development. In the following chapter, we will take up approaches to what is traditionally referred to as "discipline" that are conducive to moral and social development and social justice.

Schools and classrooms present students with social experiences and a cultural context that may be very different from the student's own family and immediate neighborhood. Indeed, it was this very basic fact of school as a social institution that led the pioneering sociologist Emile Durkheim to propose back in the early 1900s that the school should be the *primary* social institution for moral education. The family, Durkheim argued, was too limited in variety and breadth of social experience, and could not reflect the values and norms of the broader society or engender the emotional commitment to society that Durkheim viewed as hallmarks of mature morality. Durkheim was writing at a time of waning authority of the Church in Western Europe. One can argue with his conclusion about the exclusive role of the school in forming a set of broader common values among students, and his dismissive view of families and their role in cultivating strong ties to cultural identities. Nonetheless, his sociological orientation alerts us to the powerful role that schools play as social environments that impact the development of children.

At home, students and their families or communities may engage in practices that are at odds with practices or rules established at school. Some students are placed in a position of "code-switching," or learning to alternate between home/community and school practices. These students can become fluent in both sets of practices, and even create unique blended practices that change the culture of school. We draw our views of culture from Gutiérrez and Rogoff (2003), who argue that "culture" is not a trait, or a way of being or thinking that resides within an individual, but consists instead of repertoires of shared practices that lead to commonalities between people, as well as variance. We are wary about assumptions regarding how students of various racial and ethnic backgrounds will interact with school policies and procedures, as each individual embodies and engages with their multiple intersecting identities differently.

It is also important to keep in mind that not all school rules are in fact concerned with morality. While it is the case that some school rules deal with matters of morality, and also true that the manner in which even trivial rules are enforced can have moral consequences, it is a mistake to equate school norms with moral standards. This is because the differences among convention, morality, and personal discretion discussed in previous chapters also hold within the micro-society of the school. As teachers and administrators wrestle with how best to establish and maintain educationally constructive school rules and discipline, they are constantly confronted with the different ways in which students at different ages react to those different types of norms. For the most part, teachers and administrators are unaware of the systematic way in which these types of norms vary. Nor are they generally aware of the tacit ways in which their own classroom interactions are often guided by these qualitative differences. Let's examine what has been learned about how children and adolescents think about moral and nonmoral school rules, and then consider the implications for moral growth and social justice in school settings.

CHILDREN'S CONCEPTS ABOUT SCHOOL RULES

Rules and Morality

Children and adolescents expect schools to have rules governing moral transgressions such as hitting and hurting, or stealing personal property (Thornberg, 2010). They argue that it is wrong for schools or teachers to permit such behaviors because they result in harm to people. Researchers have found that elementary school children apply these expectations to evaluate the legitimacy of teacher authority. Elementary school children accept instructions from teachers that would prevent harm to another child, but reject the instructions of teachers to engage in such things as hitting, which if followed would result in harm to another child (Laupa & Turiel, 1993). This finding is entirely consistent with the basic research indicating that children do not view such things as hitting as wrong because there is a rule. Instead, they argue that the rule should be there because *hitting is wrong.*

It is possible, and perhaps even likely, that a child would follow a teacher's command to hurt another out of fear of the teacher's power. Nonetheless, the research suggests that children might not view such a teacher as a legitimate authority. The one caveat that must be added to this conclusion, however, is that because teachers are presumed to have greater knowledge than children, they have great potential to alter the ways in which children read the meanings of people's intentions and actions. As was covered in Chapter 2, the informational assumptions people bring to social situations can radically alter their reading of events. Teachers who perpetuate biased and prejudicial accounts of people along racial, ethnic, and gender lines have the capacity to alter the ways in which children view the actions of others. The impact of such teacher bias, particularly when enacted within the context of a shared community-wide viewpoint, has been the subject of recent research indicating that children are aware of racial and gender stereotypes by as young as 5 years of age (Bigler & Liben, 2006). As we will discuss in the following chapter, students are influenced by adult bias, but also negatively judge teachers who display such discrimination (Spears Brown & Bigler, 2004).

Classroom Social Conventions

If we move from the moral domain to consideration of classroom convention, we see a very different pattern regarding children's acceptance of teacher authority. Studies have shown that with respect to conventions, students acknowledge that school authorities may legitimately establish, alter, or eliminate school-based norms of propriety (e.g., dress codes, forms of address), and the rules and procedures for academic activity (Blumenfeld et al., 1987). Schools may vary widely in terms of these conventional and procedural norms, while sharing a common set of core moral rules.

The scope of the school's legitimate authority in establishing conventional norms is limited from the child's point of view by whether they encroach on areas of activity perceived by children as within the personal domain. Smetana and Bitz (1996) found that children in elementary school are consistent in claiming personal jurisdiction over such issues as with whom to associate, how to spend lunch money, and choice of hairstyle. In adolescence, students are even less likely than 5th-graders to grant legitimacy to teacher authority regarding personal or prudential areas of conduct. This holds true even for students in urban China (Liu, 2018).

As was noted in Chapter 2, the definition of what counts as personal is not, however, solely a matter of individual decisionmaking. Schools are social institutions that place different sets of constraints on personal behavior than might exist in other social settings such as the family and the general outside environment. The majority of students in middle school and high school acknowledge these institutional differences and are somewhat more willing to accept conventions regulating conduct within the school setting such as public displays of affection (kissing in public) that would be considered personal in nonschool contexts (Smetana & Bitz, 1996). Students who defy these school-specific constraints on personal conduct tend to exhibit more general problems with social adjustment. Thus, schools represent a rather unique context within which children must learn to negotiate and accommodate their own personal freedoms in relation to the organizational conventions imposed by the varying institutions of general society. As we will discuss below, this becomes problematic when school and classroom conventions limit the personal expression of students from marginalized groups and students who do not conform to binary gender norms.

Developmental Factors and School Conventions. There are also developmental factors that enter into students' expectations regarding school conventions. Before 4th or 5th grade, children don't generally view the conventions of schools to be their business. Young children rarely if ever respond to another child's violation of a conventional school norm (e.g., talking without raising one's hand) (Killen & Smetana, 1999). This is not to say that young children are unaware of, or uninterested in, social conventions in general. While young children have a sense of convention, they have a difficult time making a connection between themselves and the arbitrary conventional norms established by adults. In particular they seem to maintain a distance between themselves and what they perceive to be the adult-generated rules that run schools as institutions.

One implication of these developmental trends in young children's conceptions of convention is that the responsibility lies with teachers to establish responsible school conventions and procedures that create safe, equitable spaces. Young children are not likely to push back on the legitimacy of adults in creating routines and procedures for the normal school day. As we will discuss in the following chapter, however, teachers can engage young children in helping to construct some of the conventions and classroom procedures as a way to encourage them to take personal responsibility for their actions, and also to help them construct a sense of the classroom as a community (Watson, 2018).

As was described in Chapter 3, the development of social convention follows an oscillating pattern in which children shift between phases when they affirm the purposes of convention and subsequent periods when further reflection leads them to conclude that conventions don't really matter. First grade tends to be a period of affirmation of convention as consistent with the "natural order." Around 7 or 8 years of age (2nd grade), however, children start paying attention to the situational inconsistencies in the application of social conventions as evidence that conventions are not describing a "natural order." Such things as using abbreviations in text messages instead of full sentences are now seen as evidence that full sentences don't really matter in other contexts either. As you might expect, there are behavioral correlates of this period of negation, though not as pronounced as what one sees in early adolescence.

In our observations of classroom social transgressions, we noted that the rates of conventional transgression are higher in grades 2 and 7 than they are in grade 5. In grade 5, children are about 10 to 11 years old. This age corresponds to the modal age for Level 3: affirmation of the functional value of conventions as serving to keep social order. School rules keep things from turning into chaos. As one 5th-grade student put it: "We need rules or everybody would be running in the hallways." In contrast, both grades 2 and 7 correspond to modal ages at the front end of phases of negation of convention. The main tool that teachers possess to help students constructively deal with the negation of convention maintained by 2nd- and 3rd-grade and middle school children is the relationships that they establish with students. In the next chapter, we will discuss the establishment of a climate of *trust* between students and teachers as critical to a developmentally positive approach to student violations of classroom conventions.

One natural question that arises is whether the amount of time teachers spend on dealing with violations of classroom conventions is partially a function of having more conventional rules than necessary. In our observations of classroom interactions, we have found that teachers are responding to a fairly large number of repeated violations of the same norms. The vast majority of classroom conventional transgressions committed by elementary school children fall into a few categories: cross talking, being out of one's seat, talking without raising one's hand, and being out of line to enter the classroom. Over half of the classroom conventional violations we observed were labeled cross talking. If a norm is violated at a fairly high level across grades, including 5th grade when children are at their most compliant, then there may be reason to reconsider the appropriateness of the convention.

Let's consider the issue of talking in class for purposes of illustration. Second-grade and 5th-grade children differentiate between disruptive talking, which prevents others from hearing the teacher and doing their work (a moral harm), and merely chatting quietly with a neighbor. During our interviews, children expressed the view that rules against disruptive talking were good ones. In our observations, however, we witnessed teachers responding punitively to children's talking that was neither disruptive to others, nor interfering with the overall learning of the children being reprimanded.

There is a difference between chaos and conversation. Even in the most interactive and well-organized classroom, there is bound to be "downtime" in which children will want to simply talk to one another. This is particularly the case when children finish their seatwork ahead of their classmates, and during periods of classroom transition from one activity to another. We would mention here that the educational neuroscientist Mary Helen Immordino-Yang (2016) has noted the importance of periods of "downtime" and even "daydreaming" for optimal cognitive functioning. In addition, children (and our university education majors) often find it pleasant to occasionally chat with a neighbor while doing their work. In none of the above examples are educational goals being compromised. Reprimanding children in such situations would seem to add little to their education, or their love of schooling. A far better way to make use of the children's desire to socialize is to integrate it into instruction through the uses of discourse and group activity as instructional methods. A simple suggestion that we would offer is that teachers and school administrators reduce conventional regulations to those that are actually instrumental to the operation of a school or classroom.

Research by Gutiérrez and colleagues (1995) describes the consequences of teachers attempting to control too tightly student discourse and participation in a classroom. They describe how teachers are in a position to control the primary *script* or format of participation in a classroom, which often reflects dominant sociolinguistic and cultural conventions and values. While some students may join in this legitimized script and engage in "appropriate forms of participation," others who may feel alienated develop a *counterscript* that involves unsanctioned peer discussion and may integrate local forms of knowledge that are not as valued in academic settings. Students engaging in counterscripts are often interpreted as being off-task. These researchers suggest that teachers should seek a *third space* in their classrooms, where "students and the teacher can work together outside of their own scripts and achieve a productive social heteroglossia in the classroom. . . . As long as the teacher does not permit an underlife to challenge the monologism of his own script, there is little room for true dialogue in this classroom" (1995, p. 467). This analysis helps us make the link between patterns of responding to classroom conventions and a classroom culture of marginalization. We discuss the importance of dialogue and discourse in moral education for social justice in more detail in Chapters 7 and 8.

School Conventions and Adolescence. Early adolescence is a second phase of negation of convention. This is coupled with an expansion of what students at this age consider to be personal, rather than under the jurisdiction of adult authority. The developmental double whammy of the early adolescent negation of convention along with the expansion of the personal is associated with an increase in parent–child conflicts (Smetana, 2011). As we noted in Chapter 2, this is a dynamic that holds across diverse cultures and reflects the normal process of development. It also makes teacher–student relations more challenging. School norms that were annoying to 5th-graders become highly objectionable to some adolescents in grades 7 through 9. Issues of appearance, manners, tardiness, and talking in class may become a blur of personal choice and arbitrary adult dictate.

These adolescent behaviors often give a false impression of self-centeredness, and the resistance to authority is sometimes mistakenly responded to through harsh control. This approach by schools and teachers to imposing control results in declines in junior high students' intrinsic motivation and interest in school (Eccles et al., 1998). Through it all, these middle school students are still children in need of affection and structure. Schools are social institutions that require compliance with certain norms in order to function. The key, then, in terms of positive social climate is to construct a conventional system that allows for personal expression. As with young children, a positive approach to this age group is for teachers to make a distinction between norms needed to operate the school and to protect student safety and those behaviors that constitute a "minor threat" to the social order. For example, marking a student tardy for being next to his seat rather than sitting in it as the bell rings may make the adult feel powerful, but it does little to enhance the student's appreciation of the norm of promptness. Without reducing things to a cliché, this really is a phase that will pass, and some adult patience is called for. Most students who were "good kids" in 5th grade still view teachers as people worthy of fair treatment. For example, a student will call teachers by titles in order not to needlessly offend the teacher, even though the student is clueless as to why using the teacher's first name is offensive. Firm and fair enforcement of rules with a dash of humor will work better than rigid requirements.

Eventually, junior high school students and high school freshmen reach the point (14–17 years) where they construct an affirmation of convention as basic to the structuring of social systems. As one would expect, this developmental shift is associated with a marked decline in classroom misconduct. It is also a period in which students fully comprehend that the array of school conventions structures the high school as a societal system. Even as students move within their own particular crowds and cliques, the larger conventional culture of the high school with its norms, rituals, and traditions provides many students with a sense of belonging.

WHEN WORLDS COLLIDE: SCHOOL RULES AND SOCIAL JUSTICE

The broad developmental trends make it clear that students are actively evaluating and responding to school norms in terms of their underlying understandings of the organizational function of social convention along with their moral judgments of the fairness of those same school rules. The oscillating pattern of emerging understandings of convention means that students are not seamlessly being socialized into the dominant "mainstream" culture as envisioned by school authorities at least since Durkheim. Instead, each generation of students is evaluating the legitimacy of the norms and conventions of school against their own criteria of fairness and respect for persons. From a social justice perspective, we might ask, what happens when students conclude that school-based social conventions are devaluing the conventions of their home communities? What happens when school norms and rules effectively erase the gender identity of students who do not conform to the binary of male and female? What happens when the normative expansion of the personal domain in adolescence is met with school rules that disallow forms of dress and hairstyle that express the ethnic identities of students? As the feminist theorist Marion Young explains, the everyday practices that reinforce the marginalization and powerlessness of a social group constitute a form of oppression. She wrote, "*Oppression in this sense is structural, rather than the result of a few people's choices or policies* [emphasis added]. Its causes are embedded in unquestioned norms, habits, and symbols, in the assumptions underlying institutional rules and the collective consequences of following those rules" (2011, p. 41). As was said earlier, not all conventions are moral. But conventions that deal with mundane content may have moral consequences in how they are implemented.

When students are punished because their forms of personal and cultural expression go against school conventions, research tells us that students either withdraw from full participation in academics through disidentification with school (Griffin, 2002), engage in active resistance in the form of disruptive behavior (Gregory & Weinstein, 2008), don a facade of conventional mannerisms concordant with the dominant culture while distancing themselves from their disruptive or disinterested peers (Rogers & Way, 2018), or less commonly, take an active stance of resistance toward mainstream enculturation while participating in the academic aspects of school (Rogers & Way, 2018).

Let's consider some actual recent cases in which school rules ran into resistance from students. In 2008, Becca Bloch, a graduating senior from Oak Park and River Forest High School in Illinois, refused to march with her classmates at graduation. Bloch, who was also the editor of the student newspaper, elected to skip the graduation ceremony in opposition to the school's longstanding dress code of white dresses for girls and dark suits for boys. Girls also traditionally carried a dozen red roses as part of their graduation attire, a tradition the high school had adopted in 1877. In speaking to the district administrators, Bloch argued, "For me, the focus is to have a dress code that reflects equality and uniformity among graduates. It doesn't have to be caps and gowns. The focus is to make it not separate but equal, but that you are a graduate. You are not a female graduate. You're not a male graduate" (Dean, 2008).

In 2020, DeAndre Arnold, a senior at Barbers Hill High School in Mont Belvieu, Texas, was told that he would not be allowed to graduate unless he cut his dreadlocks because they exceeded the length allowed under school policy (Beachum, 2020). Moreover, Arnold faced in-school suspension for failing to comply with the school dress code. Arnold's father is from Trinidad, where the wearing of dreadlocks is an aspect of that culture. He told a local radio station, "I really like that part of Trinidadian culture. So, I mean I really embrace that." The school rule stipulates that hair not extend on male students, at any time, below the eyebrows, the ear lobes or the top of a T-shirt collar. During the Christmas break, the rule was revised to include the overall length when let down. Prior to this revision of the dress code, Arnold had been in compliance by keeping his hair up.

In 2017, Fresno mother Erika Paggett got a phone call from her son's school informing her that he'd been pulled out of class (Solé, 2018). Her 8th-grader hadn't been disruptive or gotten into a fight, but the teacher said his new haircut was a distraction to other kids. Her son had recently gotten crisscross lines shaved into his hair, but the school dress code prohibited razor cuts. "It's common practice in the African American culture to get what's called a lineup, and that's done with a razor," Paggett said.

These actual cases of students running afoul of school polices regarding dress and hairstyle are not isolated, but reflect a subtle battleground where school conventions intended to impose a level of order cross over into imposition of dominant cultural standards on a diverse student body. In at least two of these cases, the school rules and legal system were altered to protect student diversity. In 2020, Oak Park and River Forest graduates wore standard cap and gown. Also in 2020, the state of California began enforcing a law that forbids schools from punishing students for wearing their hair in Afros, braids, twists, and locks—styles that have been targeted by school disciplinary codes.

How Should Schools Respond?

The challenges presented by these examples can be transformed into opportunities for social justice and moral education in two ways. The first is to enlist students as resources and allies. The second is for teachers and school administrators to proactively anticipate and address inequities produced through existing school rules and norms that may not be evident to students, especially children in elementary school. As an illustrative example, we will refer to how schools may address injustice and harm resulting from rules and norms sustaining the gender binary.

Enlisting Students as Allies

The traditional approach is to simply ignore any resistance or protests of school rules and policies from students and treat them as the "normal" noise to be expected from immature and developing children. This approach interprets the developmental research as providing teachers and administrators with an age- and grade-related road map for anticipated periods of misbehavior. The social justice issues implicated in student resistance would be viewed as inappropriate and misguided in the school context. The role of the school would be seen as standing firm in defense of order and discipline in the service of students' socialization and academic achievement.

From our reading of the research literature, the traditional approach to school rules stifles moral growth and character formation, and lends institutional force to the recapitulation of existing social injustice. The traditional approach engages in what we refer to as *immoral* education. The alternative is to engage with students at the school level in the same process of evaluating and updating school rules as has been long advocated at the classroom level (Watson, 2018). This would have two components. The first would be for the teachers and administrators to monitor recurring sources of student misconduct and resistance toward school goals. Such recurring points of resistance through active defiance or passive nonparticipation should be viewed by school authorities as indicators that the rules or norms are at odds with the goals and/or developmental needs of students. Rather than simply standing firm around such issues (as was the case for both boys described above whose hairstyle was "nonconforming"), the school should enlist students as allies to identify these points of contention, and as collaborators in modifying school rules to reduce or eliminate these points of conflict.

This is not a new idea, and has roots in American education that date back to John Dewey. We will say more about this in the next chapter when we discuss classroom and school climate. The developmental research we reviewed in the first part of this chapter indicates that schools could enlist the input of students at points of affirmation of convention beginning in upper grades of elementary school. Most schools in the United States and Europe have student councils or similar mechanisms for enlisting student input. However, to make these into vital aspects of school governance instead of pro forma activities with little authority, students would need to be taught how to engage in effective forms of collective discourse to move toward viable solutions and to engage the teachers and school administrators in shared solutions. We will outline the nature of such discourse and how to teach children to employ it in Chapter 8.

Teachers and Administrators as Proactive Agents of Social Justice: Addressing the Gender Binary

We started this chapter with the words of a 5-year-old kindergarten student who expected her school to have a lot of rules to protect children from being hurt by the actions of others. While some forms of harm, such as hitting, are obvious to young children, other forms of harm that result from existing social norms and standards are not. In such cases, it is the obligation of teachers and administrators to review school norms and policies with an eye toward identifying and adjusting those rules and norms when they are the source of harm. As an illustrative example, we point to the increased awareness educators today have of the damage traditional gender norms and rules impose on children who do not identify with the categories of male or female. Schools have historically been gendered institutions. Every aspect of school life has been defined by gender, from practices as minor as lining up by gender to enter school, to as personal as the use of lavatories or restrooms.

Solutions adopted by schools to resolving the gender binary, such as nongendered bathrooms, have been a source of controversy bordering on panic (New York Times Editorial Board, 2016). Our suggestion regarding these sorts of issues is that schools supplement their internal deliberation and discussion with available research. For example, researchers from the leading pediatric hospitals in the United States have called for schools to take a *gender-affirming* stance that differentiates sex, and sexual orientation from gender expression, and asks that schools adopt policies that allow students to engage in forms of gender expression that allow them to live as they are most comfortable (Hidalgo et al., 2013). As a practical matter, this means reducing as much as possible the degree to which school-based activities are defined by gender. This broad moral and practical principle would inform everything from school rules, to the language and pronouns used by teachers and administrators, to the nature of high school homecoming, and as we saw in the case of Oak Park and River Forest High School, attire for high school commencement. As was the case with that high school, schools would be wise to include students at appropriate developmental levels in fashioning such rules and policies. In our view this would be most effective when combined with moral education based in critical pedagogy of the form we outline in this book. In the absence of such preparation, there is no guarantee that students will not simply impose a new set of biased policies. The goal would be to coordinate the necessary organizational function of social convention with moral principles of welfare and fairness.

In this chapter, our focus has been on the nature of school rules and norms in relation to social justice and students' moral and social development. In the following chapter, we extend this discussion to consider broader issues of school climate and student discipline.

CHAPTER 6

Promoting Moral Wellness and Social Justice Through Classroom Management, Climate, and Disciplinary Policies and Practices

In Chapter 5, we looked at how classroom rules help to structure schools as cultural and moral institutions. We also considered how students' concepts of morality and social convention enter into their willingness to follow school and classroom rules, as well as their evaluations of teachers as legitimate social authorities. In this chapter, we will continue to explore how the social life of the classroom can contribute to students' social, emotional, and moral development. Our approach will be guided by the goals of social justice education, with attention to the developmental needs of children and adolescents. Much of the foundation of what we refer to as "moral wellness" is supported by wise school policies that foster the development of emotion recognition, empathy, emotional and behavioral self-regulation, and basic moral judgments. The social and emotional climate of the classroom and school, and how teachers and school authorities address behavioral issues through classroom management and discipline, are core elements of how teachers and schools contribute to social justice and to these areas of social–emotional development, moral growth, and character formation.

Our discussion will be in the spirit of what is being referred to as *transformative* social and emotional learning (SEL) (Jagers et al., 2019). These researchers argue that social–emotional learning (specifically the five components of CASEL's model: self-awareness, self-management, social awareness, relationship skills, and decisionmaking skills) is not value-neutral. For example, when promoting self-management or emotion regulation, schools may hold students accountable to social norms and practices that stem from dominant, White, middle-class expectations, causing extra acculturative stress for students from non-White backgrounds (Jagers et al., 2019). Additionally, in promoting self-awareness, schools and teachers may fail to include ethnic and racial identity as important components of students' sense of self, making non-White students feel like a part of them is less important. Our focus will be on making classrooms and schools positive experiences for the development of all students with particular attention to equitable and just classroom functioning and school discipline policies, as well as the overall school climate. We do not endorse particular SEL programs. Instead, we favor using the academic curriculum, and naturally occurring classroom and school social interactions, as the context for SEL. This affords the benefits of SEL and moral education without the loss of instructional time, and the artificiality of decontextualized SEL activities (Hart et al., 2020). For example, emotion recognition and empathy can be supported through teacher feedback during peer interactions, as well as reflections on the feelings of characters appearing in texts. We will offer examples of how to gain this "two for one" benefit of integrating SEL and moral education through the curriculum and regular classroom activities in this chapter and the ones that follow. We begin with general issues of classroom climate. The second part of this chapter will be devoted to classroom management and disciplinary policies that address the issues of social justice we raised in the first chapter of this book.

THE BIG 5: BASIC ELEMENTS OF A MORAL CLASSROOM CLIMATE

Students' social–emotional and moral growth in schools and classrooms builds on five basic needs of children and adolescents. These are: autonomy, belonging, competence, mutual respect, and fairness. Attending to all five of these basic elements produces an environment in which students are able to care for others, and importantly, be able to also accept care *from* others (Noddings, 2002). The elements of justice and mutual respect also allow students to create relationships with peers and teachers that are based on trust (Watson, 2018). This overall sense of relatedness with peers and teachers is associated with both academic engagement and prosocial conduct (Furrer & Skinner, 2003).

Autonomy

Without a sense of autonomy, there can be no sense of personhood. Without personhood, there can be no engagement as a member of a moral community. This does not mean that a child needs to exist apart from their community, relationships with land or elders, or social history, but that in addition to collective sense-making, each person is an agent over their own thoughts and actions. The need for autonomy is expressed in two ways. The first is through the construction of the personal domain of prerogative and privacy. A student's sense of themselves as an individual with a unique social identity is gained through control over activities, friendship choices, personal expression, and privacy (Nucci, 2014). In the classroom and school setting this translates into providing students some space for decisionmaking both in the social arena and, where appropriate, over academic issues. The examples we discussed in the last chapter over student hairstyles are illustrations of the dysfunctional restriction of aspects of autonomy of expression that emerge when schools impose a single cultural standard for what counts as legitimate zones of the personal.

The second component of autonomy is the child's exertion of self-control and self-determination. Moral autonomy refers to a commitment to doing what is right based on moral judgment, rather than social pressure or social convention. It also means doing what is right for one's own reasons. There are two basic ways in which individuals are motivated to do something. One is to respond to external incentives in the form of punishments and rewards. The second is to engage in actions because of their perceived intrinsic value to the individual (Ryan & Deci, 2017). It is obviously much easier for teachers and schools to manipulate external rewards and punishments than it is to somehow connect with or influence students' intrinsic reasons for doing something. Yet it is the connection with intrinsic, non-pragmatic motivation that is the most effective and enduring way in which to link up moral reasoning with action.

An effective way to enhance the development of self-regulation is for teachers to scaffold students' social problem solving rather than imposing adult solutions. We will take this up again later in this chapter. There are also techniques for helping students to gain control over their feelings by having them check in with their feelings at the start of the school day, and engage in periodic emotional "system checks," as our Oakland middle school teachers referred to them, throughout the day. Practices such as mindfulness that allow students to recognize and identify their thoughts and feelings as well as the physiological states that signal the onset of anger have been found to help students reduce their engagement in aggressive responses, and to more generally engage positively with peers. Readers who are interested in learning about these practices and techniques can find many examples on the Greater Good Science Center website: greatergood.berkeley.edu/.

Belonging

The need for belonging is built into human beings from the time we are born. Our first expression of this need is in the attachment we establish as infants with our caregiver (Watson, 2018). The need for belonging does not end in infancy or early childhood, but extends throughout the life span. Classroom teachers cannot be expected to replace parents and family as basic sources of love and belonging. However, the classroom and school can go a long way toward supporting children's sense of connection, and their beliefs about their own self-worth and the trustworthiness of others. Belonging does not function in opposition to autonomy. On the contrary, a strong sense of autonomy allows the student to feel connected with others without being subordinated to them. Likewise, a strong sense of belonging allows the student to be themselves as an autonomous agent without feeling isolated, uncared for, and without group membership.

Historically, and currently in the United States and broader world, students with disabilities, LGBTQ+ students, Black and Brown students, female students and nonbinary students have been made to feel unwelcome in schools. This act of exclusion is in itself a moral harm (Gaffney, 2019). Official school policies and norms as we discussed in the previous chapter can contribute to a community of openness and belonging. Beyond that, however, schools and teachers can proactively foster a welcoming sense of community. This can include simple symbolic things such as classroom decorations and posters that reflect the ethnic, racial, and gender composition of the student body. But it can also mean teachers and administrators taking steps to combat social exclusion, harassment, and bullying.

Social exclusion is a ubiquitous problem that stems from a legitimate personal domain claim by children to select their friends and associates. It is made harmful when social group membership and prejudice combine to define children as unworthy of inclusion based on gender, racial, or ethnic group or other feature not relevant to a shared activity (Killen, 2019). According to the Southern Poverty Law Center, K–12 schools are the most cited locations for discrimination and bias-related harassment. Although the vast majority of children and adolescents will state that it is wrong to exclude or harass another student, they will sustain social exclusion on the basis of traditions ("we have never mixed before"), stereotypic expectations ("Girls aren't good at science"), and group identity ("They don't belong to our group"; "He won't fit into our group") (Killen, 2019). In a focus group that we conducted with 5th-grade children, we learned that the primary source of conflicts at their school was peer exclusion. An interesting sidelight of these discussions was the spontaneous tendency of the children to recognize that it was the act of exclusion that was the primary problem, and not just the characteristics of the children who instigated the fights or arguments that followed.

Although we will not endorse specific programs for reducing social exclusion, we will briefly mention one here, developed by Melanie Killen (2019) and colleagues at the University of Maryland, that holds particular promise for combatting social exclusion in the elementary school. *Developing Inclusive Youth* (www.diy.umd.edu) is an interactive in-classroom activity that has two components to it: a web-based curriculum tool that engages individual students in considering realistic instances of possible peer exclusion, followed by a teacher-led classroom discussion session that immediately follows students' use of the tool. The discussions follow the format for responsive engagement and transactive discourse we will outline in Chapter 8. These discussions evoke students' accounts of their own similar experiences of exclusion, and generate shared solutions for how to eliminate or minimize exclusion within their classroom and school. Students who have participated in this program are statistically more likely to desire to play with peers from different ethnic and racial backgrounds and more likely to feel a sense of classroom support from their peers.

Exclusion based on sexual orientation is especially pernicious at the middle and high school level. Although considerable progress has been made on these issues in recent years (Russell & Horn, 2017), in many schools the climate for gay and lesbian youth is negative. Students who identify as gay, lesbian, or transgender frequently report hearing negative comments from other students and school staff, and a high number of students report that they are harassed on a daily basis by other students because of their sexual orientation (Bochenek & Brown, 2001; Russell & Horn, 2017). This type of victimization can lead to multiple negative developmental outcomes for youth, including such things as depression, substance abuse, and suicide. Research by Stacey Horn (2003) has shown that there are some positive factors in adolescents' views about homosexual peers that could be used as the basis to offset this negative situation. She has discovered that a large majority of those high school students who have objections to homosexuality also believe that it is wrong to tease or harass fellow students simply because they are gay, lesbian, or transgender. This rather positive finding that has been replicated in several settings indicates that adolescents, including those who hold negative views of homosexuality, are open to moral arguments that would deter peer harassment and teasing of LGBTQ+ classmates. Schools can build on this latent tolerance by doing such things as allowing students to construct gay–straight alliances in which students collaboratively work to improve school climate. Schools that have such alliances not only improve safety for LGBTQ+ students, but raise the overall sense of safety of the heterosexual population as well (Li et al., 2019). However, we recognize that gay–straight alliances may be more accessible to some students than others. Researchers have shown that Black and Brown students can feel alienated at gay–straight alliance meetings, or may hesitate to participate at all (Mayo, 2015). Mayo (2015) suggests extending the work of gay–straight alliance groups to off-campus, community spaces that might be more accessible to Black and Brown students who feel judged and uncomfortable attending meetings on school grounds. At a more basic level, we would argue that schools should work toward disrupting hetero-gender normativity as the backdrop against which all forms of gender expression are to be measured (Russell & Horn, 2017).

Competence

The need for competence is expressed in children's curiosity and efforts to solve puzzles, master skills, and get along with others. Competence is enhanced when students succeed at academic tasks, and when they are successful in making friends and sustaining relationships. Moral education does not occur in a vacuum. It is connected to the entirety of the academic and social life of the classroom. The same classrooms that reduce social exclusion and increase a sense of student belonging are those that enhance the likelihood of a sense of competence within students, and respect for the competence of their classmates. A consistent finding in the educational research literature is that attending to moral growth and social–emotional learning contributes to the academic achievement of students (Hart et al., 2020).

Fortunately, recent research in cognitive psychology, education, and neuroscience has provided the basis for structuring classrooms and teaching practices that foster and sustain a *growth mindset* (Dweck, 2015). In a nutshell, classrooms that foster a growth mindset focus on student growth and progress rather than on comparisons with others. Students are helped to set challenging, attainable goals; treat failure as an opportunity to learn; accept constructive criticism; and celebrate success. In essence, these are classrooms that build competence. In the words of Carol Dweck (2015), the core theorist and researcher in this area, "In a growth mindset, people believe that their most basic abilities can be developed through dedication and hard work—brains and talent are just the starting point. This view creates a love of learning and a resilience that is essential for great accomplishment."

Respect

Teachers and school administrators expect students to treat them with respect. Respect, however, is a two-way street. Teachers and administrators derive their power from the state. Their authority, however, comes from the students who grant authority based on their perceptions of the teacher as a competent instructor and person worthy of respect. Teachers undermine their authority when they appear to exercise arbitrary, harsh, or discriminatory power. There is considerable evidence that the use of teacher power through disciplinary referrals in middle school and high school is much higher for male students of color than for other groups. The Civil Rights Project at UCLA documented this phenomenon in a report called "Out of School and Off-Track: The Overuse of Suspensions in American Middle and High Schools" (Losen & Martinez, 2013). Black and Brown students and students with disabilities are disproportionately suspended and expelled from school, leading to a higher likelihood of dropping out and eventual incarceration.

These suspensions are frequently in response to what schools have defined as "willful defiance" on the part of students. The definition of willful defiance, however, is itself subject to criticism. Maisha Winn points out in her book on restorative justice (2018) that the South Carolina "Disturbing Schools" statute makes it unlawful, among other things, for any person "to act in an obnoxious manner" (p. 2). She asserts that this vague language allows for "ambiguous interpretation" of any action in the classroom, and unfair punishment of students from marginalized backgrounds. In September 2019, California took steps toward eliminating racial disparities in suspensions and expulsions by banning public and charter schools from using "willful defiance" as a justification for suspending students in grades K–8. Willful defiance is a disciplinary category that was targeted in UCLA's Out of School and Off-Track report as contributing to disproportionate suspensions. "The broader ban comes in response, in part, to criticism that the willful defiance category of suspensions was a too-broad and arbitrary catchall for any behavior that a teacher finds objectionable, such as repeatedly tapping feet on the floor, refusing to remove a hat or failing to wear a school uniform," reports the *Los Angeles Times* (Agrawal, 2019).

Research by Gregory and Weinstein (2008) sheds some light on the teacher–student dynamics behind these statistics. They found that the primary reasons for disciplinary referrals fall into two categories of "disobedience" and "disrespect" (Gregory & Weinstein, 2008). In a systematic study of students who received referrals for defiance, 86% were referred by just one to three adults—their behavior was inconsistent from teacher to teacher (Gregory & Weinstein, 2008). The students, who had received disciplinary referrals, self-reported an awareness that they behaved differently with some teachers in comparison with others. A basic position maintained by the boys who received disciplinary referrals for defiance was that the teachers who were the object of their defiance did not respect them. These same students reported more trust in and obligation to cooperate with the teachers who were nominated by themselves and by their peers as worthy of respect over the teachers who were involved in disciplinary referrals. The characteristics of such teachers were that they were more trusting and caring as well as academically demanding than the teachers who were the source of referrals. As stated by one of the 9th-grade students in the study regarding one of these nominated teachers, "she doesn't disrespect us in any kind of way. It's not like, 'I'm the teacher and I'm the authority and I am gonna use it however I want to.'" A 12th-grade student stated, "Well, actually, it is not that he enforces his rules cause he don't have to because all the students respect him . . . if he ask the class, you know, be quiet so that we could get our class discussion started, they automatically be quiet" (Gregory & Weinstein, 2008, p. 469). Our point here is that respect is a basic prerequisite for moral interactions. Mutual respect is foundational for moral reciprocity and trusting relationships. It is imperative that teachers convey respect and model it for their students irrespective of ethnicity, race, gender, or other group characteristics.

Fairness

Fairness is what ties autonomy, belonging, competence, and respect to morality. Children construct their sense of fairness in early childhood, and employ their understanding of fairness to evaluate teachers and schools as valid institutions. Fairness emerges in relationships based on reciprocity. Children expect and seek fairness from adult authority (Smetana, 2011). As we stated above, teachers who treat students with respect receive respect in return. Students are quite sensitive to teacher displays of unfairness. For example, children are aware of discrimination based on gender and race at early ages and by 3rd grade are able to form expectations that a teacher who was discriminatory in one context is likely to show preferential treatment toward members of a particular gender or race in other situations (Spears Brown & Bigler, 2004). Finally, as we saw in Chapter 5, children and adolescents expect schools and teachers to protect them from harm and exploitation by other students. This protector role of teachers extends from basic safety on the playground to the fair treatment of students through classroom procedures and grading of students' work.

FACILITATING MORAL AND SOCIAL DEVELOPMENT THROUGH CLASSROOM MANAGEMENT: THE ELEMENTARY GRADES

Establishing an overall school and classroom moral climate extends beyond the emotional tone of the school to include methods of classroom management and discipline. All approaches to classroom management have two goals in common: control and efficiency. With variations in underlying theory and recommended practices, their primary intent is to make academic instruction run smoothly. Developmentally oriented educators have generated approaches to classroom management that have the additional goal of fostering students' social and moral competence (Watson, 2018). There are some differences in the underlying theories that support the work of these newer developmental approaches. However, they share enough in common that we will borrow from Marilyn Watson (2018) and refer to them collectively as *developmental discipline*. These developmental approaches are also in synchrony with the goals of social justice education and *restorative justice* (RJ) practices as a replacement for zero tolerance and school suspension. Historically, developmental discipline has been aimed at elementary school, while restorative justice emerges in middle school and high school. We will describe these approaches in this developmental sequence. However, an astute reader will readily recognize the overall continuity and blending that exists between these two approaches.

Developmental discipline is aimed at having the student do what is right for their own reasons rather than to receive external rewards or to avoid punishment. The particulars of developmental discipline adjust according to students' age and grade level. There are, however, four central strategies that characterize developmental discipline across grade levels.

1. Focus on building the classroom and school community by:
    a. establishing caring, trusting, respectful, and fair relationships with each student;
    b. building respectful, caring, and fair relationships among students.

2. Teach students the social knowledge and skills they need in order to act in ways that are kind, fair, and responsible.
3. Attend to the antecedents of misbehavior by
    a. examining teacher-generated procedures and policies that make student misbehavior likely;
    b. examining school policies and procedures that make student misbehavior likely;
    c. examining student needs and motives that are contributing to misbehavior.
4. When external control is needed, keep it "light." When possible, choose ways that are non-coercive or punitive. Respond to misbehavior in ways that effectively stop the behavior, but that also:
    a. help the student learn from their mistake;
    b. minimize the pain or shame that they will experience;
    c. minimize the harm to their relationship with the teacher or their peers;
    d. minimize the loss of autonomy or sense of competence.

In this chapter, we have already addressed many of the elements of establishing a moral classroom community. What we will take up now are some suggestions for how to respond to misbehavior in ways that foster students' moral and social development. We will begin with a discussion of how to handle moral conduct through social problem solving. We will then explore how to appropriately employ positive feedback and consequences for misbehavior.

Facilitating Moral Developmental Through Social Problem Solving

The great moral achievement accomplished by young children is the construction of an understanding of fair reciprocity. Because young children generate their initial understandings of morality out of their direct experiences in social interactions, the primary contribution that schools make toward young children's moral development is through the framing of these direct moral experiences. Teachers do this by helping children focus on the effects of actions and their reciprocal implications. For example, a teacher might respond to moral transgressions in the following way:

"Demarcus, Alejandro needs some clay. Please give him some."

"Veronica, Madelyn hasn't had a turn on the swings. Please let her have one."

In both cases, the teacher statements focus on the needs of the other child, and not simply on the power of the adult. But even these domain-appropriate moral statements lack the element of reciprocity. While they do connect with the young child's concepts of morality, they do not explicitly direct the child's attention to the reciprocal nature of turn-taking or distribution of goods.

There are two ways for a teacher to do this. One is for the teacher to do all of the thinking, and lay out the reciprocal implications in statements to the children:

> "Demarcus—how would you like it if Alejandro had all of the clay, and you didn't have any? He needs some too. So, please share with him."

This is a reasonably efficient way for a teacher to handle the situation, and makes sense in contexts where the teacher's time is at a premium. The teacher's response is domain appropriate, it does not dwell on social rules (conventions), and it lays out the reciprocal nature of morality and moral justification. However, it does not engage the students in active problem solving, and is therefore not an optimal way for a teacher to make use of this situation. A better use of this teachable moment is for the teacher to assist the children in conflict resolution.

The value of engaging children in conflict resolution is that it engages them in recognizing the contradictions that exist between their own initial ways of looking at things and what is necessary for their own needs and those of others to be met. This is a slow process that is helped along by the child's inevitable experience of being on more than one side of these prototypical childhood disputes. One day's owner of the clay or the swing is the next day's child on the sidelines. In Piaget's terms, what takes place is the gradual disequilibration of the child's current way of thinking, and its gradual replacement by a more adequate re-equilibrated form that resolves the contradictions arising from the initial way of looking at things.

From this viewpoint, an argument can be made for allowing the children to solve such problems on their own. Allowing children to solve their own problems has the advantage that the solutions generated are "owned" by the children, and the process contributes to the child's autonomy and social efficacy. In fact, teachers cannot enter into every conflict situation that arises among children, and observational studies have indicated that teachers allow a fair number of social conflicts among preschool and early elementary children to be resolved without adult intervention. In many cases, young children handle these disputes quite well. Approximately 70% of preschool children's disputes during free play are resolved by the children themselves either through reconciliation by the instigator or through compromising and bargaining.

While this may seem impressive, the value of allowing children to solve their problems on their own can be overstated. Adults have the developmental advantage of being able to see both sides of a moral dispute in ways that young children cannot. Moreover, children look to adults to provide protection from exploitation and harm, and to help them work through social problems. As was stated before, adults impede moral growth when they reduce moral situations to ones of social convention and adult power. Adults contribute to moral growth when they engage children in moral reflection. With respect to conflict resolution, adults contribute to young children's moral growth by assisting them in identifying the sources of the conflict, by helping them to consider the perspective of the other, and by helping them to arrive at mutual solutions. This approach also provides children with experiences that counter the tendency to conclude that the use of sheer power and intimidation are the only methods by which one can achieve personal goals. Finally, adults can serve as honest brokers, bringing in the contributions of ideas from peers who may have witnessed a conflict or dispute. This peer strategy serves as a precursor to responsive engagement we will outline in Chapter 8 and the restorative justice practices we will discuss below. Scaffolding children's social problem solving also engages children in the development of SEL skills of emotion recognition, empathy, and emotion regulation within real life.

An excellent example of a teacher intervening in a dispute between two young children can be seen in a short video available on YouTube called "Two Boys One Chair" (www.youtube.com/watch?v=nR-n7FMixtM). The video is from a real incident that took place in Linda Rayford's kindergarten class in Hayward, California. Two boys, Rayshawn and Paul, are competing to take possession of the same chair in order to complete a class assignment to create a drawing on a paper plate. Ms. Rayford walks by and sees the two boys trying to sit in the same chair and says to them, "Here's one plate. You guys figure it out." Rayshawn picks up the plate and tells Paul to find another chair. However, Paul insists that he was there first and refuses to leave, saying, "I am the one who got here first." To which Paul replies, "I am." The two boys then take turns saying, "I am."

Ms. Rayford returns and asks: "How are you two doing? Did you come to any conclusions?"

> *Rayshawn:* I have a plate.
> *Ms. Rayford:* What about Paul?
> *Rayshawn:* He has to go to another table.
> *Ms. Rayford:* Why does he have to go to another table?
> *Rayshawn:* I have the plate and I'm going to draw my name on it.
> *Ms. Rayford:* If you have two people and one plate, what could you do?
> *Rayshawn:* Say, please can Paul move to another table?
> *Ms. Rayford:* Have you asked him?

Rayshawn then turns to Paul and says, "Please Paul, could you move to another table." Paul then begrudgingly starts to get up from his chair.

Ms. Rayford then asks, "Is that okay with you, Paul?" He shakes his head no. Ms. Rayford stops him from leaving and says, "Okay, then, let's work it out." Paul sits down again on the same chair with a frown on his face.

Ms. Rayford says, "He doesn't like that solution." Another boy, Mark, at the same table says, "He didn't like that solution." Ms. Rayford turns to Mark, "Could you come up with another solution?" He offers, "They could share." He elaborates that they could get another chair and share the plate. Ms. Rayford paraphrases the solution and says, "you work it out." Paul turns to Rayshawn and, pointing to the plate while drawing his finger down the middle, says, "Rayshawn, we will both do one side okay?" Rayshawn nods his head and says, "okay." The two boys then get another chair, draw a line down the center of the plate, and energetically set to work on their drawings. Ms. Rayford comments to the boys, "You worked that out very nicely."

For most teachers this would be the end of things. However, Ms. Rayford allowed the two boys to talk about this incident in the class community meeting. In the context of the meeting, the two boys acknowledged the help that they received from a third boy at their table. Ms. Rayford responded to both boys, "Very good. I am glad you listened to Mark's suggestion. It was a good suggestion." This incident ended a few days later when the decorated plates were to be taken home. Each boy decided to take home the half of the plate the other boy had drawn.

In looking at this incident, some teachers may wonder why the teacher didn't simply tell the boys to share the plate, or resolve it in some other way rather than take up the time to have this set of conversations. (The total amount of time these conversations took was about 5 minutes.) From the perspective of classroom order and efficiency, a teacher-imposed solution would make sense. We acknowledge that there are times when those goals of order and efficiency should take priority. Also, children do not always engage in cooperative resolutions of conflicts. In such cases, the teacher will need to make a judgment as to whether sufficient harm or injustice is being perpetrated as to warrant a direct intervention by the teacher.

However, as we noted above, this incident illustrates the utility of integrating moral and social–emotional developmental goals through naturally occurring classroom events rather than relying on formal SEL programs to get at these same ends. In this case, the two boys were required to engage in perspective taking, empathy, emotion recognition, emotion regulation, and their understandings of fairness. These children were in the process of taking ownership of their own social and moral actions, which is the ultimate goal of all efforts at socialization. Moreover, by incorporating the input from other students, these children (with the support of their teacher) were creating a moral classroom community and anticipating the processes of restorative justice for handling moral transgressions in middle school and high school contexts.

Facilitating Social Development Through the Judicious Use of Consequences

There are some situations in which consequences for misconduct are clearly called for. The goal of all effective classroom management is to anticipate problems and to avoid the need for consequences. In Chapter 5, we discussed the wisdom of eliminating unnecessary classroom conventions that are guaranteed to generate high levels of noncompliance. Managing the antecedents to misbehavior would also include attention to the academic demands of the classroom that might tax the ability of a student to stay on task. This can be as simple as making sure that all students have access to materials at their reading level. However, even when a teacher attends to students' needs for attention and power, and does all that is reasonable to address academics and school norms, children will still act in ways that are counterproductive to group learning. This should come as no great surprise to teachers who have brilliantly taught an academic lesson and nevertheless see mistakes on tests. Making mistakes is part of the process of growth and development.

Supporting Positive Behavior. One way to avoid discipline problems in the classroom is to provide feedback that supports children's positive behavior. This feedback can come in the form of tangible rewards, but most often comes in the form of adult praise. Providing positive feedback from adults is at the heart of a widely used and often state-mandated approach called positive behavioral instructional support (PBIS). The intent behind PBIS is to shift the emphasis from punishment to attention to positive behavior. Within our own university school leadership program, PBIS is viewed as a school-wide, proactive, positive approach to classroom behavior, and an alternative to disciplinary actions such as detention and suspension. We do, however, urge careful attention to the ways in which positive rewards and feedback are employed.

While the use of positive feedback and rewards can help sustain and guide a child's developing morality, an over-reliance on rewards and positive adult feedback can backfire and actually undermine the child's moral motivation (Ryan & Deci, 2017). The limitations of external reinforcement are most readily apparent with the case of offering children tangible rewards for their good behavior. There is substantial research literature indicating that providing external rewards to children, such as gold stars or stickers, reduces their tendency to spontaneously engage in the rewarded behavior. In other words, children shift from engaging in the behaviors for their own intrinsic reasons toward doing things simply for the "money." PBIS advocates agree that rewards can be used poorly in the classroom—for example, when they are delivered ambiguously—or the reward is not actually desirable from the learner's perspective, or when rules for getting a reward create physiological pressure (Horner & Goodman, n.d.). However, they strongly advocate the use of rewards for building new skills or sustaining desired skills, and cite evidence that rewards can increase task interest and intrinsic motivation, especially for tasks that the learner has little initial interest in.

Marilyn Watson (2018) strenuously argues that any use of rewards is antithetical to her conception of developmental discipline. We would argue in contrast that one can distinguish between the use of rewards that serve to *validate* what the student is already motivated to do, from the use of rewards as a means of "shaping" the student's behavior to conform to the wishes of adults (Ryan and Deci, 2017). For example, a student who has consistently treated classmates with kindness and generosity might well respond to a "citizenship" award as reflecting social validation for her actions, rather than as an effort to shape her behavior. On the other hand, the routine awarding of pins or other emblems, and the weekly public listing of the names of students who have displayed "virtue" or "character" as advocated by some neo-traditionalist programs (c.f., Character Counts), exemplify how *not* to support children's positive behavior. In such cases, the rewards become overt sources of competition, and commodities in and of themselves. While they may temporarily serve to mold and shape students' conduct, they also undermine the very motives such programs seek to instill.

Similarly, in providing praise to a student, we need to differentiate between positive statements that validate the child and encourage their efforts at moral action, and "controlling praise" that serves the adult's desire to mold and shape the student. Controlling praise focuses attention on the child rather than the child's actions, is nonspecific in content, and often employs terms that are superlative in nature. Examples of such praise are: "Aisha, you are such a good student"; "Alejandro, you are the nicest child I have had in class in years." The effect of controlling praise is to give the child a momentary boost in self-esteem, but at the cost of setting the bar at an unrealistically high level. Is it realistic to assume that Aisha and Alejandro are always going to be so superlatively well behaved? Second, the feedback to the child says little about what it is that warranted being labeled "such a good student" or "the nicest child in years." Any reasons that the children might have had for doing the behaviors that won them their accolades are lost in the focus on the evaluations of the children themselves. Thus, one risk associated with controlling praise is that it fosters an ego-oriented focus on one's own perceived social status, instead of a desire to engage in a specific behavior. The moral self that is constructed on this basis may be superficially oriented toward behaving morally, but not for moral reasons. The child who needs to always be "such a good student" in order to fit social expectations is not operating out of moral motivation, but in order to sustain external approval.

In contrast, praise that takes the form of encouragement uses moderate language and focuses on the specifics of the action. Such praise lets the student know that his actions are appreciated, and also indicates that it is the actions that are being evaluated and not the child himself. Examples of validating praise would be: "Tatiana, that was a kind thing that you just did. I am sure that Marcy appreciated the time you spent with her when she wasn't feeling well." "Mike, thanks for helping clean up the room. It makes everything better for everyone. I really appreciate it." Encouraging praise is especially effective as a response to what we might refer to as "everyday acts of character." In the previous example, Mike might have been one of the children who never helped with cleanup time. For him to have done so might well have taken considerable personal effort. Acknowledgment from the teacher in the form of thanks would let him know that his efforts were recognized and his contribution validated. The teacher might even add a word of encouragement to "keep up the good work." In any case, praise should be used sparingly and directed at specific acts rather than at the characteristics of children.

Responding to Misbehavior. An essential aspect of all learning is making mistakes. It would be nice to believe that moral education is a matter of guiding children down the "right" path, but the fiction of "error-free" learning has even less to do with morality than other aspects of education. While children are rarely, if ever, motivated to purposefully make mistakes in academic areas, the very nature of moral misconduct is that it often involves actions that the child knows to be wrong. Correcting errors in the moral area is not simply a matter of pointing out mistakes, but also helping the child to choose to act in ways that are not always concordant with their immediate desires.

Helping the child to want to do the right thing is in part a function of teachers' responses to children's behavior. Consequences provided to students in response to their misbehavior should not take the form of expiatory punishments designed solely to inflict discomfort or cost to the student (Watson, 2018). A classic example of an expiatory punishment is spanking. A classic example from school would be detention. Expiatory punishments are to be avoided since they do not provide the student with any reason beyond the pragmatic goals of punishment avoidance as a motivation for action. Since students associate expiatory punishments with the person meting them out rather than with their own misconduct, such punishments invite revenge and provide students with a sense that they have the right to retaliate. In other words, the morality of the situation is turned on its head as the student, guilty of misconduct, now becomes in their own mind the aggrieved party. An example that some readers might relate to would be getting "grounded" by your parents for some misbehavior. We can invariably recall examples from adolescence when this happened to us. Often, we may have difficulty even remembering the specifics of our misbehavior. However, we have no problem whatsoever in conjuring up the sense of outrage we felt toward our parents at the time. Frequent use of expiatory punishment by a teacher transforms the emotional climate of the classroom into an environment of "ill will" that supports students' self-protective and "selfish" motivations.

Instead, logical consequences should be connected in a meaningful way with the nature of the transgression (Watson, 2018). Logical consequences include such things as restitution, depriving the transgressor of the thing misused, and exclusion. Because of the non-arbitrary, reciprocal nature of morality, it is somewhat easier to envision logical consequences for moral transgressions than for violations of social conventions. For example, if a child takes something away from another child, a logical consequence would be for the child to have to replace it. However, even conventions, once in place, have a logic associated with their function. A student who talks disruptively during story time might be asked by the teacher to leave the story area until they are able to rejoin the group and sit quietly. If this sanction is coupled with a domain-appropriate statement of the rule or social–organizational function of the norm, the student is likely to see the connection between the rule and the misbehavior. An indefinite or extended expulsion from the story area, however, would shift the consequence away from the behavior and become an arbitrary, expiative punishment rather than a logical consequence.

Teachers can increase the likelihood that students will accept the logical consequences of misbehavior by engaging them in group discussions about patterns of misbehavior occurring in the classroom, and seeking their advice on how to avoid or reduce such problems in the future (Watson, 2018). In Chapter 5, we explored the use of group discussions as a way of engaging children in the consideration of what rules should be in place to regulate or help guide students' conduct. In this case, the discussion concerns what to do about behaviors that the children agree are problematic. Through group discussion, the teacher can guide students, especially in elementary and middle school, to generate ideas about what would constitute appropriate logical consequences. Part of the teacher's role is to help the children focus on prevention of misbehavior. By engaging children in such discourse, the consequences of misconduct are moved from a top-down, adult-imposed act of power to autonomously constructed, logical outcomes reflecting values shared by the children.

Finally, an ethical response to students' misconduct must allow for the student reentry and acceptance into the social group. Once the logical consequence has been met, the child must have the opportunity to move forward as a class member. Otherwise, the logical consequence is transformed into expiatory punishment with all of the negative ramifications already discussed. This is a fairly easy requirement to meet when it comes to typical transgressions of social convention. It is not always so easy when the transgression involves moral consequences to other classmates. While the teacher may be willing to move forward, the students may be unwilling to risk interactions with someone who had caused them pain or injustice. In such cases, the teacher needs to help the transgressor understand the connections between aggressive conduct and the responses of their classmates. The teacher must also help the other students to recognize that they would not want to be permanently excluded either. This requires patience and persistence on the teacher's part, and is helped or hindered by the overall moral and emotional climate of the school and classroom. However, it is not always clear in social conflicts between peers *who* is the victim and who is the perpetrator; conflicts are complicated, and harm can be done by multiple parties. Restorative justice, described below, allows for this complexity to surface and for harm to be addressed and needs to be met.

RESTORATIVE JUSTICE

We have noted several times in this book that the rates of school suspension and expulsion are much greater for Latinx, Native American, and African American students and students with disabilities. For example, a recent longitudinal study of students in the Texas public school system reported that African American students (26.2%) were more likely to receive out-of-school suspension in response to a first infraction compared with Latinos (18%) and Whites (9.9%) (Gregory et al., 2016). These statistics have serious consequences. After accounting for demographics, attendance, and course performance, each additional suspension further decreases a student's odds of graduating high school by 20%. As we noted in the first chapter, this trajectory is also associated with later incarceration and referred to as the school-to-prison pipeline (Wald & Losen, 2003).

Disrupting this negative pattern is not something that can be achieved through a school program. Instead, it requires rethinking the entire way in which schools and classrooms interact with students. Developmental discipline represents such a shift at the elementary school level. Restorative justice practices (RJ) are an example of this developmental community approach to school discipline being used primarily at the middle and high school level. The basic premise of RJ is that members of a community are worthy of respect, that people on all sides of a conflict deserve to be heard and listened to, and to the extent possible, everyone involved should be welcomed back into the community. The three pillars or defining characteristics of RJ include: harms and needs, obligations, and engagements (Zehr, 2015). Harms and needs refers to an initial exposition of who has been harmed and what their needs are. In addition to working through interpersonal harm, restorative justice scholar Maisha Winn (2018) urges us to think about the broader social harm and needs of both educators and students. She writes that students who often cause harm in schools have also *been harmed* by policies including discriminatory discipline. "If teachers are prepared to think about access to languages, literacies, the sciences, history, art, music, and mathematical reasoning as both civil and human rights, it might be possible for them to think about the moral and ethical obligations of addressing harms and needs that stem from education debt" (Winn, 2018, p. 20).

The second pillar, obligations, refers to the centrality of accountability and responsibility in RJ. If students or staff do not want to participate in RJ circles, they are not forced to; participants have to engage willingly. This concept also affirms the principle of autonomy and self-discipline mentioned earlier in the chapter. Finally, engagement or participation is the opportunity to "practice justice and freedom while cultivating participatory democracy" (p. 21) through discourse, listening, sharing, and constructive dialogue. This feature directly aligns with a key facet of moral education— that of responsive engagement (Laden, 2012).

As is the case with developmental discipline, the most effective RJ includes steps to make community building effective. This includes opportunities for students, teachers, administrators, and staff to engage in "proactive circles" in which they can openly discuss their shared concerns about academics and school life. In a sense, circle conversations extend the practice of the morning meeting common to life in elementary school into the upper grades. The Oakland Unified School District, for example, suggests having proactive circle conversations about race and gender equity at school sites, even during staff meetings, in order to a) analyze existing data and identify racial disparities in current discipline practices, and b) create safe spaces to talk about topics that make people uncomfortable. In this way, restorative justice is not simply a set of procedures, but is meant to shift schools toward adopting a social justice lens. Winn emphasizes that restorative justice is not a program but a paradigm shift.

Restorative justice circles can also be instituted reactively, in response to conflicts that arise in school. During a restorative justice circle, each participant takes a turn holding a talking piece and sharing their thoughts. Circles are usually made up of the parties involved, a facilitator—either a student circle keeper or adult RJ circle keeper—and an advocate or support person for each party. If other stakeholders wish to join, they may. Student circle keepers (SCKs) as described by Winn are students who have received RJ training and are called on to mediate conflicts within their school community. The facilitator poses an initial question or prompt and then walks participants through exchanging stories, histories, context, and explaining their actions. This allows each participant to share how they have been harmed, or how they feel. It is important for each participant to get to define themselves and their story, because students are often involuntarily defined by labels such as "troublemakers" or "at-risk" in school contexts. Winn describes this sharing time as a potential "restorying" process. From the perspective of moral development, "restorying" is akin to the idea of *narrative moral agency* (Pasupathi & Wainryb, 2010)—or the opportunity to construct a narrative of oneself that reconciles one's actions with one's beliefs and emotions.

A set of values and guidelines are predetermined before RJ circles begin. In Winn's ethnographic research studying restorative justice in Madison, Wisconsin, student circle keepers used cards as props. Some cards had value words, like honesty, respect, and inclusion, written on them, and others had specific guidelines like "listen with an open mind" written on them. These cards helped the SCKs moderate and facilitate an open conversation among all participants, with the goal of all participants coming to deeper understandings of each other.

When such practices are employed, student conduct improves and student disciplinary suspensions decline, along with student perceptions of respect from their teachers and student respect for their teachers (Gregory et al., 2016). According to a 2014 report, the impact of RJ in Oakland, California, went beyond reducing suspensions and expulsions, and included improvements in students' abilities to resolve conflicts and building "developmental assets" such as empathy, emotion management, and how to sustain positive relationships (Jain et al., 2014). Winn's research in Madison also attests to the potential of RJ to foster leadership skills and agency in SCKs, and provide opportunities for unexpected student leaders to emerge. Agency, empathy, emotion management, and positive relationships are all goals of moral wellness and transformative SEL.

More serious incidents that entail moral transgressions such as fighting or harming another student, theft, or property damage may be addressed in "restorative conferences." These are scripted meetings run by trained teachers or administrators that employ a structured meeting protocol. The goals of such meetings are accountability by the parties that caused harm, a deeper understanding on all sides, and the reintegration of participants into the school community, rather than stigmatizing or expelling anyone. The student who is the focus of the meeting is able to bring a supportive person to the conference. In order for this process to go forward, the student must accept responsibility for their actions, and when possible work toward making amends. In the case of property damage, for example, help to repair the damage. In the case of harming another student, offer a sincere apology and establish a plan so that the harm does not recur. Key to this process is to avoid humiliating the student and to offer entry back into the school community. (An example of guidelines for establishing RJ practices can be found at this website: www.ousd.org/Page/1054).

Success with restorative justice, as with developmental discipline, rests with teachers, administrators, and students who receive appropriate training and approach all members of the school community with respect. Winn (2018) argues that in order to enact a true paradigm shift—one that goes beyond equity in discipline and moves toward creating *humanizing,* democratic cultures in schools—all teachers and staff should be paid to attend RJ training. She also argues that learning the procedures is not enough; teachers need pedagogical stances that support them in transitioning to RJ. These pedagogical stances are: History Matters, Race Matters, Justice Matters, and Language Matters. In sum, while RJ can be used as a tool for social justice and equity, it also provides a platform for transforming relationships between adults, adults and students, and students with their peers, and fostering moral development. Making cognitive connections among history, race, justice, and language in our everyday circumstances is part of what Paulo Freire calls developing a "critical consciousness" (2005). In the next chapter, we will consider Freire's framework of critical pedagogy, which also envisions the classroom as a potentially *humanizing* and liberatory space, where understandings of systemic and societal oppression lead students to "read the world" in a nuanced, critical way and take collective action toward justice. Next, we will tackle how an underlying lens of social justice, in terms of critical pedagogy, affirms the goals of domain-based moral education and offers helpful directions and adaptations for an effective framework.

Part III

MORAL EDUCATION AND CRITICAL PEDAGOGY ENACTED

The Curriculum, Digital Media, and Praxis

CHAPTER 7

Critical Pedagogy and Domain-Based Moral Education

Complementary Frameworks for Comprehensive Social Justice Education

In this chapter, we shift our attention from the social context of school to begin examining ways in which the academic curriculum and classroom-based interaction can be used as a central tool for moral development and social justice education. It is through the curriculum that students can connect their direct social and moral experience with great literature, history, and the treasure trove of factual information that comes from the natural sciences. It is through the academic curriculum that students can learn how to question existing beliefs, develop the skills to create new knowledge, and gain the capacity to express themselves in writing, speaking, and the arts. It is also through the curriculum that students can learn to take a critical moral perspective toward their own conduct and values, as well as the social norms, beliefs, and institutions of society. Classroom-based interaction allows for students to encounter diverse perspectives on issues they may have taken for granted, and apply new lenses to personal, everyday conflicts. Some of the examples we provided in the preceding chapters of students engaged in resistance to existing sexist or racist school policies illustrated how students' awareness of the historical context and cultural meaning of such customs as hairstyle or gendered forms of dress informed their protest and moved it from being an individual complaint toward powerful collective moral argument.

We begin our discussion of how to link moral education with the curriculum with a focus on *critical pedagogy*. Critical pedagogy is a key framework that complements and aligns with the goals of moral education and moral development from a social–cognitive domain theory perspective. We offer a general outline of critical pedagogy, and then describe points of alignment between moral education and critical pedagogy in the following areas: a) a focus on constructivism and cognitive development, b) the potential for reasoning transformations, c) an orientation toward informational assumptions, and d) pedagogical strategies. This section reflects theoretical work that we have also been engaging in with our colleague Sarah Manchanda at UC Berkeley. Finally, we consider the issues surrounding the blending of these two frameworks as they pertain to young children, and we take up a question posed by Kelly and Brooks (2009), "how young is too young?" when it comes to enacting social justice education. It is worth noting that critical pedagogy was originally conceived of as a liberating strategy to work toward freedom and democracy for students living under social oppression and hardship. We view critical pedagogy as a useful framework for engaging students from all backgrounds, including those who identify with marginalized and oppressed groups as well as those who do not, in transformative critical education.

OVERVIEW OF CRITICAL PEDAGOGY

Critical pedagogy falls under the larger umbrella of social justice education. According to Hytten and Bettez (2011), critical pedagogy belongs to a theoretically specific category of social justice education literature. Other categories of social justice literature include philosophical or conceptual, practical, ethnographic/narrative, and democratically grounded. Theoretically specific social justice education frameworks "provide inspiration and resources for educators who connect their personal and pedagogical commitments to the goal of transforming oppressive social systems and structures" (p. 18). From our perspective, the features, foundations, and vocabulary of critical pedagogy align it particularly well with findings from the field of moral development and have the potential to expand moral education in important directions.

Critical pedagogy is attributed to Paulo Freire, a Brazilian activist, educator, and scholar who revolutionized literacy education for adults in poor areas of Brazil. His framework, outlined in *Pedagogy of the Oppressed* (2005) and in subsequent texts by other scholars, suggests that education should facilitate a "waking up" to structural and systemic inequalities that play a role in the everyday circumstances of students. Freire conceptualized this awakening as a developmental process of learning to see the world through a critical lens and to connect local struggles with larger social, historical, and political movements against oppression. These new perceptive abilities, which include the capacity to work toward rectifying contradictions and inequalities, is called a *critical consciousness*, one goal of critical pedagogy. We will elaborate on this later in the chapter.

Freire strongly advocated that students remain at the center of the learning process and that instruction revolve around the everyday circumstances and problems that affect students and their ability to live and flourish. Education should facilitate shifts in how students perceive the world around them, and should foster an ability to identify contradictions in society—or elements of the status quo that run counter to justice—and then organize and engage in collective action to fight injustice and oppression. Students, according to Freire, must view their current circumstances involving oppression "not as a closed world from which there is no exit, but as a limiting situation which they can transform" (2005, p. 49).

Education should take the shape of *praxis*—a cycle of inquiry, action, and reflection. One component of this cycle without another is not sufficient for bringing about critical shifts in thinking. Freire wrote, "It is only when the oppressed find the oppressor out and become involved in the organized struggle for their liberation that they begin to believe in themselves. This discovery cannot be purely intellectual but must involve action; nor can it be limited to mere activism, but must include serious reflection: only then will it be a praxis" (2005, p. 65). Freire was a strong critic of what he called the "banking" model of education, or traditional learning environments in which teachers impart knowledge to students who are expected to absorb it. Instead, he suggested a "problem-posing" form of education in which students and teachers wrestle with questions about their worlds; use culturally relevant texts and social resources to illuminate elements of history, struggle, power, and privilege that are pertinent to their questions; and then develop action plans to change these circumstances. In the following sections, we make connections between critical pedagogy and moral education.

ALIGNMENT IN CONSTRUCTIVIST, COGNITIVE FOUNDATIONS

Critical pedagogy and domain-based moral education both seek to encourage *updates* in how students think and reason about the world. These updates ultimately depend on two things according to both frameworks: a) the building of cognitive capacities over time that allow for the critique of specific contexts, and b) opportunities to apply those skills or capacities to their own circumstances while engaging in dialogue with others. Critical pedagogy is constructivist in nature, meaning that educators who adopt this framework purport that these updates happen through a process of students actively making sense of and interpreting the world around them. This process of active interpretation and re-equilibration, as developmental psychologist Jean Piaget referred to it, contributes to our cognitive development and our ability to think and reason in complex ways.

Freire's focus on moving away from the banking model of learning toward a problem-posing model is part of enacting a critical pedagogy in which students are active agents in their development. He emphasized the importance of students intervening in their own histories and contexts. He wrote, "By predisposing [people] to reevaluate constantly, to analyze 'findings,' to adopt scientific methods and processes, and to perceive themselves in dialectical relationship with their social reality, that education could help

[them] to assume an increasingly critical attitude toward the world and so to transform it" (Freire, 1973, p. 30). This dialectical relationship with one's surroundings and social reality that Freire describes is echoed in cognitive developmental theories.

Adams and Bell (2016) elaborate on the ways that both structuralist cognitive developmental theories and sociocultural theories of cognitive development are helpful constructivist frameworks that can inform social justice education. Cognitive assumptions, like cognitive dissonance that leads to dissatisfaction with one's current worldview, support the intentions of critical education that aim to lead students to more complex, critical ways of thinking. They write, "Social justice education can be seen as a 'pressure cooker' for cognitive dissonance which, presented in ways that are not overwhelming, opens opportunities for more abstract, complex, and critical thinking" (p. 34). These authors also elaborate on Vygotsky's sociocultural model of cognitive development, which views learning as a process that is mediated by historical and cultural contexts. Meaning-making is a process that depends on opportunities to interact with peers at different skill levels, as well as cultural tools and artifacts. For social justice education, it is helpful, they argue, to consider the historically and socially constructed nature of cultural systems—for example, language—because meanings, then, are readily revisited and revised. They sum up by writing: "Developmental theory offers explicit ways for facilitators to recognize the 'cognitive dissonance' that participants experience, model new ways of thinking that can incorporate the dissonant material, and provide the mediation and scaffolding that supports the process" (p. 35).

As described in previous chapters, social cognitive domain theory has a constructivist lineage as well, and attributes key changes in reasoning within domains and coordination across domains to both age and interaction with the physical and social environment. Social cognitive domain theory moves beyond the metaphor of stages (used by Piaget and Kohlberg) as a way of describing a developmental trajectory. Moving forward, we build on this common cognitive developmental heritage to envision a kind of pedagogy that capitalizes on children's cognitive skills (such as coordinated reasoning, tolerance for uncertainty, perspective taking, reflecting, and deliberating), as well as children's constructivist instincts, in order to facilitate a process of becoming a critical moral agent that works toward overturning injustice. Critical moral agency is the motivation and awareness to engage in society and work with others to transform one's own oppressive circumstances and work for justice in the world. Moreover, this common constructivist link determines what moral education and critical pedagogy do *not* entail; that is, moral education, from our perspective, is not about teaching students a decontextualized set of values or learning to *always* prioritize moral concerns on principle. Likewise, critical pedagogy is not about perpetuating static truths about the world and groups of people in it. In both frameworks,

Critical Pedagogy and Domain-Based Moral Education

questioning and reconstructing knowledge is a more powerful form of education that requires students to apply evolving social and moral reasoning to always-changing scenarios.

ALIGNMENT IN FOSTERING REASONING TRANSFORMATIONS

Both moral education and critical pedagogy are frameworks that advocate for building cognitive capacities through active learning. As such, they expect changes and transformations in how young people view, understand, and reason about the world around them. But what kind of changes and transformations are critical pedagogues and moral educators looking for? What *types* of shifts, or what *direction* of change, do they seek to foster?

As we described in Chapter 3, social cognitive domain theory tells us that through our everyday interactions within our social worlds, we will construct increasingly sophisticated forms of social and moral reasoning. In the moral domain, for example, as we grow older we move from thinking about fairness in terms of equality to thinking about equity. In the conventional domain, we move from affirming social conventions based on ideas of uniformity and conformity to negating them because we notice exceptions to uniformity. We also go through age-related changes in how we coordinate multiple domains. For example, middle schoolers are more likely to prioritize personal concerns over moral concerns in situations of indirect harm than are high schoolers who do the opposite (Nucci et al., 2017). These changes are in a promising direction—toward being able to draw on more than one domain in a moment of judgment and think outside of oneself to consider social systems and the concerns of others.

The purpose of moral education from a social domain theory perspective is to urge students to go one step further and *apply* our evolving moral understandings of equity to social conventions that maintain social order in order to identify social norms and conventions that cause harm. Similarly, moral education urges us to apply our moral understandings to our conceptions of personal rights and freedoms and consider when these two domains are in conflict with each other; for example, wanting to buy a fancy sports car, but considering its effects on the environment by way of carbon emissions. Moral education seeks to foster this type of critical coordination across domains. In previous writing about this pedagogical framework, we advocated for the development of a *critical moral perspective*: "Students will apply their moral understandings to evaluate the morality of existing social norms, institutions and practices. This goal moves moral education beyond the task of fostering conventionally moral, nice people toward encouraging the development of citizens who can contribute to the moral growth of society" (Nucci, 2009, pp. 93–94). An evolving critical moral perspective signifies a type of critical reasoning transformation in the learner.

As part of critical pedagogy, Paulo Freire also outlined specific types of reasoning transformations—a process he referred to as consciousness-raising or an awakening of critical awareness. This developmental process progresses toward a *critical consciousness*. A critical consciousness, "allows people to make broad connections between individual experience and social issues, between single problems and the larger social system" (Shor, 1992, p. 127). Shor detailed four qualities of a critical consciousness: power awareness, critical literacy, permanent *desocialization* (e.g., questioning power and inequality in the status quo), and self-education (e.g., knowing how to seek out information and engage in dialogue). Desocialization, he explained, is a process of *unlearning* "truths" about the world that we have internalized through status quo messaging, such as what teacher–student relationships must look like, what a syllabus must look like, or harmful stereotypes about people who are different from ourselves (Shor, 1992, p. 114).

Freire noted that some changes in our thinking occur naturally, by way of interacting with different groups of people and engaging in a complex social world. However, moving from what he calls *naïve transitivity* to *critical transitivity* would require "an active, dialogical educational program concerned with social and political responsibility, and prepared to avoid the danger of massification" (Freire, 1973, p. 15). We can see similarities here between this framework and moral education: While some developmental changes in reasoning occur naturally due to cumulative experiences in a social world over time, others do not—and these require proactive education.

Freire used the term naïve transitivity to describe an orientation toward the world that attempts to simplify problems. He explained this state as being disinterested in investigation, and emotionally tied to beliefs with "magical" explanations for the way things are (1973, p. 14). In contrast, a critically transitive consciousness is "characterized by a depth of interpretation of problems; by the substitution of causal principles for magical explanations; by the testing of one's 'findings' and openness to revision" (p. 14, 1973), in addition to a propensity for dialogue. This reasoning transformation includes a movement away from relying on "common sense" explanations and toward inquiry and investigation. Feminist scholar and critical theorist bell hooks reminds us, however, that for Freire, a critical consciousness without a commitment to meaningful praxis (action and reflection) was incomplete. The connection between thinking differently and acting differently is an essential part of this reasoning transformation.

Therefore, similar to how moral education seeks to foster a critical moral perspective through which students can *apply* complicated understandings of morality to their immediate contexts, Shor described the process of developing a critical consciousness as learning to apply new lenses to one's immediate circumstances—including aspects of the school day. He wrote, "It involves critically examining learned behavior, received values, familiar language, habitual perceptions, existing knowledge and power

Critical Pedagogy and Domain-Based Moral Education

relations, and traditional discourse in class and out" (1992, p. 114). We can see how both frameworks seek to build on naturally occurring developmental trajectories, and then urge students beyond—to foster *critical* reasoning transformations that allow students to apply their moral concepts of justice, equity, and rights to their social worlds.

ALIGNMENT IN TARGETING INFORMATIONAL ASSUMPTIONS

Both pedagogical frameworks addressed in this chapter attend to the role that informational assumptions play in the critical reasoning transformations described above. In our previous writing on moral education (Nucci, 2009), we have argued that academic lessons should help students examine the unwritten or unsaid factual assumptions that are embedded in social and moral judgments. Research by Wainryb (1991) and others has shown that the factual assumptions that people hold to be true about nature, reality, and other groups of people can significantly alter their interpretation of the moral and social implications of certain actions and behaviors. For example, Wainryb (1991) reported that parents who previously endorsed spanking their children changed their interpretation of the action when they were shown scientific research that spanking was not more effective than other strategies. These parents became attuned to the moral harm of the action of spanking itself. In another illustrative example, Killen and her colleagues (Killen et al., 2002; Killen et al., 2013) have identified how children's factual assumptions about the abilities and preferences of their peers of different races and genders can lead them to socially exclude peers that are different from them, in order to maintain the perceived integrity and identity of social groups. From the perspective of moral education, before students engage in small-group dialogues about an issue, teachers should provide enough background information or allow time for research and inquiry, so that students can make informed judgments and contribute in a meaningful way (Nucci, 2009).

Critical pedagogy aims to disrupt harmful informational assumptions about marginalized and disenfranchised communities that students may have internalized. Critical pedagogues challenge students to consider the historical and social reasons that certain people have more power, wealth, and influence than others, and aim to disrupt the version of "normal" perpetuated by the mainstream media. Freire wrote, "The more accurately [people] grasp true causality, the more critical their understandings of reality will be. Their understanding will be magical to the degree that they fail to grasp causality. Further, critical consciousness always submits that causality to analysis; what is true today may not be so tomorrow" (1973, p. 39). In his vision for critical education, he advocated a process of constantly re-evaluating facts, and subjecting facts to analysis.

In their book *The Art of Critical Pedagogy*, Duncan-Andrade and Morrell (2008) illustrate this aspect of critical pedagogy through units that made use of research and the evaluation of facts. For example, their students identified major discrepancies in school funding between their own school and a nearby wealthy school. Students conducted research into school spending policies, interviewed policymakers, administrators, and students to advocate for a more just distribution of resources. Other critical pedagogues, such as Soep and Chavez (2010), have written about the use of journalistic production processes that include fact-checking, interviewing, editing, and research to facilitate constant reevaluation of information. Critical pedagogy and moral education align, therefore, in their prioritization of research, the process of inquiry, and an overall mindset of openness toward new information.

ALIGNMENT IN CLASSROOM STRATEGIES

Both moral education and critical pedagogy emphasize discourse and dialogue as crucial to fostering reasoning transformations and inspiring collective action in the classroom, as opposed to didactic, lecture-style pedagogy. Moral education, specifically from the perspective of social cognitive domain theory, has argued for allowing students the opportunity to have regular small-group discussions related to moral and social dilemmas that pertain to academic content. Within these small-group discussions, teachers should be fostering *transactive discourse* (Berkowitz & Gibbs, 1983), a form of discourse in which students operate on each other's reasoning—offering critiques, contradictions, elaborations, juxtapositions of their peers' ideas, in order to collaboratively find a resolution to the dilemma at hand. Previous research has shown that the frequency of high-level transacts (speech acts in which students offer reasoning critiques of other students' ideas, e.g.) corresponds to more nuanced and complex coordination between domains in short-answer moral reasoning assessments (Nucci, 2014). This strategy will be elaborated on in upcoming chapters.

In order to engage in transactive discourse, students need to have the necessary background information (mentioned above) to offer fact-based arguments and counterarguments, and actively listen to and engage with their peers. We draw on philosopher Anthony Laden (2012), who describes a type of interaction he calls *responsive engagement*, which entails genuinely inviting your conversation partners to adopt your ideas as their own (and vice versa), being willing to change your mind, and listening to others without judgment. Drawing from Habermas et al. (1991), Laden makes the distinction between debate (a competitive form of discourse) and deliberation—a type of discourse brought on by joint goals. Giving students in classrooms the chance to deliberate and build these responsive engagement skills, we argue, may lead to transactive discourse and support the general social–emotional and cognitive competencies entailed in a critical moral perspective (Ilten-Gee & Nucci, 2018). The content for these classroom discussions is inspired by traditional academic content; for example, science teachers might present dilemmas over the ethics of conducting animal research. Teachers would craft a question, scenario, or dilemma that takes into account the relevant domains of the conflict (moral, conventional, personal) and then engage students in deliberation. Specific examples of this academic/moral integration strategy will be presented in Chapters 8 and 9.

Classroom dialogue and discourse is seen from the perspective of critical pedagogy as a component of developing a critical consciousness as well as a means of ensuring that students are not left out of the knowledge construction process. Students must *own* their journey toward critical awareness; a teacher cannot bestow this on them from a place of privilege. "Critical and liberating dialogue, which presupposes action, must be carried on with the oppressed at whatever the stage of their struggle for liberation" (Freire, 2005, p. 65). There is an emphasis on shifting the power from the teacher to the students in what Freire called "co-intentional" education.

Critical pedagogues advocate for engaging in problem-posing dialogue. Academic content still serves as a foundation for curriculum, but students' everyday experiences and relevant texts (in a broad sense of the word) are integrated into class activities and valued as knowledge. Duncan-Andrade and Morrell argue that "meaningful links" should be made between students' worlds and the content of their curriculum (2008). Similarly, Shor wrote:

> [Problem-posing education] does not mean that students have nothing to learn from biology or mathematics or engineering as they now exist. . . . As long as existing knowledge is not presented as facts and doctrines to be absorbed without question, as long as existing bodies of knowledge are critiqued and balanced from a multicultural perspective, and as long as the student's own themes and idioms are valued along with standard usage, existing canons are part of critical education. (1992, p. 35)

Duncan-Andrade and Morrell (2008) shared examples of integrating the canon with students' own experiences from their work with urban high school students in California. Students read texts like *Savage Inequalities* by Jonathan Kozol and considered the economic disparities between their own school and wealthy schools in their district. In class dialogues about race and justice, students shared experiences of being harassed by campus security and feeling like prisoners in their own school. This collective dialogue resulted in the creation of a student-published magazine dedicated to starting conversations about the material and social conditions of their school.

In both moral education and critical pedagogy, educators seek to adapt the traditional academic content in a way that makes space for dialogue and dilemma. Moral education research has documented specific aspects of student dialogue that lead to complex reasoning. Critical pedagogy advocates for using students' everyday experiences as motivation for class discussion in conjunction with academic content.

We would be remiss not to include scholarly critiques of relying solely on discourse and dialogue as a primary method of critical education. These critiques are important to consider as we try to evolve these frameworks for the future. Ellsworth (1989) wrote that relying on rational dialogue in her social justice university course exposed the fact that not all opinions voiced by students are always equal. Some voices came from positions of privilege and power. Speech by oppressed groups was "constructed within communities of resistance and is a condition of survival" (p. 310). She argued that power dynamics—between students of different backgrounds, and between teacher and student—can distort dialogue, as well as always deferring to rational, logical arguments. Without tuning into these imbalances, one risks perpetuating *the opposite* of an empowering or emancipatory environment. This critique, while leveled at critical pedagogy, applies to moral education as well. When students are discussing moral and social dilemmas, how are we helping them navigate identity? Emotion? Personal experiences? The content of our courses may feel personal to each student in a different way—perhaps because they have been adversely or acutely affected by the topics at hand, or perhaps because they are left out of the story entirely. In one sense, classrooms are ideal settings for these dialogues to take place, precisely because of the diversity of perspectives potentially present. Still, Ellsworth's critique must influence how teachers structure these dialogues. We advocate that classroom dialogue creates space for the multifaced and intersecting identities and positionalities of students, and that teachers consider their own voices in these dialogues as partial and not without bias. Additionally, educational practices should incorporate strategies *in addition* to dialogue, that highlight nonverbal strengths and literacies that students bring to the classroom. Critical pedagogues, for example, have written about the practice of making and remixing media (films, podcasts) as an example of rich, problem-posing learning. In Chapter 10, we will examine the potential of making media to facilitate both a critical consciousness and a critical moral perspective.

CRITICAL CONSCIOUSNESS AND CRITICAL MORAL EDUCATION: EVEN FOR YOUNG CHILDREN!

Both frameworks outlined in this section are applicable to the education of young children in addition to older ones. As Kelly and Brooks (2009) point out, preservice and inservice teachers can be hesitant to engage in critical pedagogy and social justice education because they fear the topics are "developmentally inappropriate." Likewise, moral educators often focus on social–emotional learning for young children instead of tackling social and moral dilemmas. However, Kelly and Brooks argue that for many elementary teachers, "developmentally inappropriate" becomes a fallback excuse for avoiding topics like race, gender, and class, even when the children themselves bring them up. As Brown and Anderson (2019) argue:

> Children *see* identity. They see it on their skin, their hair, their clothes, their voices. They talk about it, experience it, and interact with others based on race and gender. As such, we suggest, based on the literature that does exist and our own areas of expertise, that it is never too young to talk about race and gender, and it is important to teach children—even young children—to have a critical understanding of how race and gender affect their lives and the lives of others. (p. 1)

Instead of trying to explain an entire societal complex to young children, they recommend keeping conversations inquiry based and asking children what they notice, who is affected, and why it is important? From the perspective of social cognitive domain theory, children from the age of 3 understand moral concepts of harming and helping others. Children in preschool have an understanding of fairness, and notice that certain social conventions dictate behavior. These broad concepts can be used in conversations about race, gender, disability, and class inequality. Young children may not understand the idea of societies as systems, but that does not mean these important topics are off-limits. An episode of National Public Radio's *Life Kit* podcast from 2019 interviewed experts about how to talk about race with young children. They suggest: (1) Don't sweep children's questions about race under the rug, or ignore them; (2) Don't wait for children to bring up race; (3) Be proactive to help children develop a positive sense of diversity; (4) When a child experiences prejudice, "address the feelings and fight the prejudice"; and (5) Don't avoid topics like slavery or the Holocaust, but instead, provide children with facts and focus on allies and resistance.

Critical pedagogues also advocate for consciousness-raising at a young age. Shor (1992) cites an example from Ooka Pang's book *Teaching Children About Social Issues: Kidpower* (1991). Pang noticed children's eagerness to call out "that's not fair!" in school. She drew their attention to the word "justice"—included in the Pledge of Allegiance that was part of their morning routine. She asked students to think about synonyms for justice, and students said things like "playing fair." She then asked them to think about instances of justice on the playground. She also wanted her students to think about justice in the context of a social system—she chose the health care system. Pang discussed first what it meant to care for people in your own home, and then to visit the school nurse. She was able to help children connect their understandings of welfare and fairness in a local context to a societal context. She assisted them in generalizing beyond the walls of their school and constructing a larger meaning for the word justice.

Another example of content aimed specifically at young children that tackles systemic issues of class, gender, and race is the children's television show *Sesame Street*. *Sesame Street* created a series of videos and resources for parents and teachers about helping children with incarcerated parents (Sesame Street, n.d.). Some of these videos involve a muppet, Alex, whose father is in jail. They explain the word "incarcerated" and break it down: "someone breaks the law—a grown-up rule." The episode reminds Alex that he is not alone, and that others have experienced the same thing. This episode connects children's ideas about rules to a larger social system. It also addresses children's developing personal domain and the things that make us all special or different from our friends and peers. The episode also addresses some of the social–emotional skills that are important to moral education at this age, such as recognizing and sharing our feelings with others and forming close relationships.

Critical pedagogy is integral to our vision of moral education for social justice. We turn in the next chapters to implementation within the academic curriculum. We begin in the next chapter with a more explicit examination of how educators can construct lessons taking the domain of reasoning into account, and how to structure moral dialogue as a core aspect of those lessons.

CHAPTER 8

Using the Academic Curriculum for Moral Development with a Social Justice Orientation
The Basics

In this chapter, we will go over the basic process for using the academic curriculum to facilitate moral development within a social justice framework. A central premise of this approach is that each lesson will generate a 2 *for 1* set of benefits. A successful lesson or unit should serve *both* academic achievement and moral development for social justice. Adopting this 2 for 1 approach allows teachers and schools to engage in social justice education and contribute to students' moral development and character formation *without sacrificing instructional time*. More importantly, evaluation research has demonstrated that programs for emotional or moral development that are implemented in isolation have little long-term effect on children, and tend to be short-lived (Greenberg et al., 2003). Thus, the 2 for 1 approach is not only the most efficient way to go; it is also the most effective.

The use of the curriculum should go hand in hand with establishment of a socio–moral atmosphere and practices of classroom management and discipline as described in Section II. This will result in a holistic approach to academic teaching that benefits academic achievement as well as addressing issues of social justice along with emotional and moral development. Robert Jagers and colleagues (2019) cite research showing that transformative SEL is associated with academic achievement. Likewise in our own research, we have demonstrated that adopting the approach outlined in this chapter not only contributes to students' social and moral development, it also increases student engagement and sense of academic learning (Nucci et al., 2015). An indication of the value that teachers find with this 2 for 1 approach is that the teachers we have worked with reported continuing to use the lessons created during our work with them, and constructing new lessons during the years after our research team had left their schools. As one of our Oakland middle school teachers put it:

> Lessons that do include discourse surrounding an issue of morality always produce the highest levels of engagement I have ever seen in my tenure as a social science teacher. For this reason I will continue using and developing lessons that allow for student engagement into issues of morality.

As indicated in the above quote, this holistic and integrated approach to teaching is consistent with the intuitions and practices of many successful teachers. The practices described in this chapter and the ones that follow should be seen as extensions of good teaching, rather than a radical departure from what good teachers have been doing in their classrooms. What will be novel is the intentional focus on connecting curricular content and instructional practices with social justice and moral educational goals. In our work with classroom teachers, we have found that there is an initial adjustment period as teachers reanalyze existing materials to identify moral, conventional, and personal issues within their academic lessons (Midgette et al., 2018). It also takes some time and practice before constructing lessons addressing the elements of cross-domain coordination becomes a facile process. Teachers who work in middle and high school STEM content areas are initially at sea in trying to envision how their math and science courses afford opportunities for investigation or discourse around morality and social justice. In the following chapters, we will provide some examples of lessons that accomplish the 2 for 1 goal of advancing academic achievement and moral development within math and science classrooms.

As we will describe in detail below, a core element of this approach to moral education is the engagement of students in discourse around matters of controversy. Most teachers will already be familiar with ways to generate class discussion. What will be novel to many teachers are the specifics for student discourse that takes the form of *responsive engagement* (Laden, 2012). This aspect of moral education requires that teachers shift away from a "banking model" of moral socialization in which there are correct answers known by teachers that are to be transmitted to the students. It requires an understanding of the necessity of an active process of discourse, reflection, and construction for students to generate genuinely moral positions. It takes some time to help students develop the listening and discussion skills needed for effective moral lessons. Finally, the approach that we outline assumes the involvement and engagement of all students within the school and classroom. A core component of social justice education and responsive engagement is that *all* members of a discourse community, including students with disabilities and students from marginalized backgrounds, have a seat at the table.

GOALS

In addition to having the 2 for 1 goal that lessons intended to address moral development and social justice contribute to academic learning, there are eight other basic goals for use of the regular curriculum to address moral development for social justice. Some of these goals need to be further specified by grade level in relationship to normative patterns of moral development. What follows is a description of the general goals for use of the curriculum for moral education for social justice that cut across grade levels. These goals allow for an analysis of the particular aims of a given lesson. Not all lessons will address all of the goals listed. Collectively, however, the lessons that students experience within a school year should cover all of the goals listed. Goals 1–4 refer to social and moral development. Goals 5–7 integrate those four goals within the overarching aim of employing the curriculum to promote moral education for social justice. Goal 8 refers to the extension of the curriculum to the critical theory component of praxis. We will take this up more explicitly in Chapter 10.

Goal 1. *Moral domain*. Students will develop their concepts of fairness and understanding of their obligations with respect to the welfare and rights of others. This goal means extending students' prevailing concepts of fairness to begin to question their assumptions about what it means to be treated fairly, and to reevaluate their moral obligations toward others. As noted in Chapter 3, this also entails guiding students through the early adolescent transitional period toward the capacity to coordinate personal goals and moral obligation in complex or ambiguous situations.

Goal 2. *Conventional domain*. Students will develop their understandings of the functions of societal conventions in everyday life. In middle school and high school, students will coordinate their concepts of convention with an understanding of societies as rule-governed systems. Although Goal 1 is included in all developmentally based programs of moral education, fostering of concepts about convention is not generally included as an aspect of social developmental education. This is because traditional moral education programs based on the work of Kohlberg and Piaget have regarded social convention as an inferior basis for structuring morality. Research demonstrating that convention and morality are different conceptual frameworks contradicts those older assumptions. Goal 2 stands as recognition that a constructive member of society must have an understanding and appreciation of the functions served by convention if they are to function within society, and if they are to be able to navigate and contribute to worlds outside of their own social and cultural framework. The latter is an essential component for membership in a pluralist democracy in which respect for the culture and traditions of others is needed. It is by first understanding the functions of conventions that students can apply morality to evaluate conventions that perpetuate social inequalities and address the structural inequalities within the existing social system.

Goal 3. *Personal domain.* Students will develop an understanding of the role of a zone of personal choice and privacy for maintaining a sense of autonomy, individuality, and the capacity to create a self that is consistent with one's own sense of identity. Development within the personal domain is tied to the student's developing understandings of self and personhood. This is an essential aspect of establishing the ability to function as a competent person. It is also critical to the person's ability to appreciate the rights and needs of others.

Goal 4. *Coordination across domains.* Students will develop their capacity to employ knowledge from more than one domain to reason about and evaluate their own social behavior and the conduct of others. They will also develop in their capacity to apply knowledge from more than one domain in evaluating the norms of social groups, social institutions, and general society. This goal directly ties into the critical pedagogy aim of moving students toward perceiving the contradictions within the norms and values of their own community. Such contradictions could be, for example, noticing discrepancies between what a policy promises it will provide for low-income residents and what actually gets provided. Identifying and acknowledging these contradictions involves applying moral standards of fairness and rights to the social rules or dictates of authority that conflict with morality. Perceiving and wrestling with these conflicts is part of developing a critical consciousness.

Goal 5. *Factual assumptions.* Students will develop the skills and attitudes consistent with an inquisitive and critical orientation toward the factual assumptions associated with social and moral value judgments. This will involve connecting the personal experiences students may have had with the particular social or moral issue under consideration. As mentioned in Chapter 7, critical pedagogy also places an emphasis on reevaluating long-held factual assumptions and embracing new logic and scientific facts.

Goal 6. *Critical moral perspective/critical consciousness.* Students will develop a critical moral perspective. Goals 4 and 5 should combine to result in students who approach their own personal moral positions with humility and willingness to change in the face of new information or a more compelling moral argument. This is also referred to as a dialogic mindset (Ilten-Gee & Nucci, 2018), a term that comes from Mikhail Bakhtin (1981) and means living in a state of constant dialogue with other perspectives and voices, and being willing to reevaluate one's own perspective. Goal 6 also means that students will apply their moral understandings to evaluate the morality of existing social norms, institutions, and practices. This includes developing the capacity and tendency for "responsive engagement" through dialogue with others to seek shared moral positions. Additionally, students will develop the ability to examine their own unique circumstances through a lens of social, historical forces and make connections between their own lives and societal struggles. This entails transitioning from interpersonal explanations of injustice and inequity to structural explanations. This goal moves moral education beyond the task of fostering conventionally moral, nice people toward encouraging the development of citizens who can contribute to social justice and the moral growth of society.

Goal 7. *Character development.* Students will connect moral and social knowledge to their sense of themselves as moral agents. This goal is tied to the development of character as an aspect of the self-system as we described in Chapter 4. The aim would be to connect the processes of *responsive engagement* embodied in reflection, discussion, meaning-making, and reasoning to the student's core personal values and sense of self. The assumption is that genuine moral development will result in not simply a surface change in moral language, but a deeper shift in the student's moral perspective and worldview. Unlike traditional character education, however, there are no particular virtues that would be presumed to attach to all students as they construct themselves as moral beings. Nor would the goal of connecting to the moral components of the self be aimed at attaining a decontextualized "good person" whose conduct would always be guided solely by moral considerations.

Goal 8—*Praxis.* Students will apply the insights gained through curricular analysis, reflection, and discourse into actions that provide a "real world" test of those insights, and provide feedback for further moral and practical growth. In social justice education, embracing collective strategies for change is encouraged. Collective action first requires engaging in dialogue and reasoning, in order for everyone to understand why the action is expected to produce results.

BASIC PRINCIPLES OF LESSON PLANNING

There are four basic educational principles for constructing lessons to attain the moral and social development goals listed above. In addition to these social development aims, however, a successful lesson should also be evaluated in terms of its connection to the academic standards and goals of the subject matter. Thus, each lesson should be consistent with principles of sound academic instruction as well as social development in order to meet the 2 for 1 objectives of academic and social and moral development.

1. *Generate reflection and construction of knowledge.* Lessons that facilitate moral development engage students in actively figuring out increasingly more adequate ways of understanding and reasoning about the social world. This principle draws from the basic premise of all constructivist teaching. Genuine understanding and the ability to reason can only result from the active efforts of students to recognize and resolve contradictions, build from the hints and suggestions of others, and generate novel insights through personal reflection. These processes map onto Piaget's notions of cognitive equilibration, Vygotsky's ideas about co-construction and the zone of proximal development, Bruner's concept of scaffolding, and Freire's rejection of what he called the "banking" method in favor of problem-posing education. Teachers will recognize that this principle means that simply memorizing rules, maxims, and definitions has little effect on students' development. Successful lessons are those that generate controversy, pose problems to solve, and require the student to come up with ideas and solutions rather than simply model the views and behaviors of others.

2. *Employ age/developmentally appropriate activities, terms, and discourse.* This principle acknowledges that students at different ages and points of development will process information differently, and provide different resolutions to social and moral issues as a function of their level of understanding of the social and moral world. Teachers must select issues that align with the developmental levels of their students, and frame questions and activities that will generate productive student reflection. This reflection should be geared toward helping students wrestle with their contemporary ways of thinking, and expanding and challenging these ways of thinking. This principle fits the intuitions of most teachers and has been supported by a generation of research. We will provide general guidelines for constructing lessons to fit developmental level in the following chapters.

3. *Employ domain-concordant issues, terms, and discourse.* This principle states that the tasks assigned to students in a social and

moral development lesson need to be in sync with the domain of the focal issues. We will provide examples of how to identify and select curricular issues by domain in a later section of this chapter. Research has indicated that attention to domain is essential to achieving the goals of social justice education (Nucci et al., 2015). Treating all social issues, including matters of morality, as determined by social convention impedes the development of students' construction of moral reasoning. Similarly viewing all social norms as having moral meaning hampers students' construction of their understandings of the functions of societal convention. Instead, the discourse and terminology should change depending on the domains that are relevant to the lesson. More importantly, taking a singularly "progressive moralistic" or "socially conservative" approach to all social norms reduces the likelihood that students will develop the capacity to coordinate morality and convention when considering complex social issues.

4. *Embrace a bidirectional relationship between curriculum and students' own personal experiences, feelings, and sense of self.* This principle advocates that teachers should make connections between the academic content and students' experiences, which is consistent with the accepted educational practice of integrating students' prior knowledge and interests in the classroom in order to maximize student learning and motivation. It also refers to the critical pedagogy principle of engaging students in the creation of the curriculum by integrating external factors that are impacting students' lives into the course content. This encourages students to connect their social understandings and moral judgment to their own experiences with social injustice—to engage students in more than a rational exercise and connect with the emotions associated with outrage and positive emotions of care that come with genuine engagement with morality.

PUTTING THIS INTO PRACTICE

Identifying and Categorizing Issues by Domain

In order to construct lessons that effectively impact moral and social development, the teacher needs to be able to identify the domains of the issues that are to be the focal point of the lessons. The primary reason for doing this is to ensure that the discussions and activities of the students are concordant with the type of issue being considered. The other reason is to insure that students confront issues from several domains rather than focusing predominantly on either morality or convention, or only considering complex multifaceted issues without the opportunity to hone their concepts and reasoning within each particular domain.

One factor that enters into domain classification of issues is that most real-life events occur in contexts that include some elements from more than one domain. For example, using titles and surnames to address teachers is a matter of social convention. However, respect for other people that can be conveyed through convention does have an element of morality. What follows are criteria that a teacher can use to identify issues by domain.

Morality

- Does the act affect the welfare of others? If yes, the act is likely to be a moral issue.
- Would a transgression still be wrong if there were no rule or norm about the act? If yes—because it affects others' welfare—the act is an issue of morality.

Social Convention

- If there were no rule or norm about the act, would the act still be considered a transgression? If no, the act is a matter of convention.
- Could things be set up differently so that the purposes of the norm could be achieved through a different arrangement? For example, students could show approval by snapping their fingers instead of clapping. If yes, the norm is a convention.
- Is the primary purpose of the norm to coordinate the interactions of people or to organize the system in some way? For example, we walk on the right-hand side to allow efficient movement through the school hallway. If yes, the norm is a convention.

Personal

- Do the effects of the act fall primarily on the actor? Are the effects on the actor benign? If yes to both, the issue is personal. If yes to the first question and no to the second, the act is a matter of prudence. Children and younger adolescents generally view prudential issues such as whether to eat healthy foods as matters that parents and teachers can influence or control. Older adolescents and adults generally treat even these latter issues as personal.
- Is the act a matter of privacy? If yes to this question and to the first question above, the act is personal.
- Is the act an aspect of constructing autonomy and a unique sense of identity? If yes to this question and to the first question above, the act is personal.

Overlapping or Multifaceted Issues

The above criteria can be used to identify complex social issues that have elements from more than one domain. For example, rules and laws that define who is allowed to vote help to structure how people contribute to governance of a particular social group. Thus, these rules have to do with social organization. These rules can also be changed through social consensus. Voting laws are a matter of convention. On the other hand, voting rules also differentially treat people in ways that give one group of people, voters, more power than other people, nonvoters. Thus, the rules that govern voting have a considerable element of morality to them. A lesson that focused on voting rights and suffrage would, therefore, be one that would address both morality and convention, and how these elements of social life interact with one another. We could do a similar analysis for issues that involve considerable overlap between social convention and the personal domain.

Addressing Informational Assumptions

Each lesson or series of related lessons should afford students the opportunity to connect the topic with their own personal experience, or with their existing beliefs. Working from this grounding in students' personal experience, the lesson or unit would provide contextual information central to the topic. For lessons dealing with issues of social justice, this would involve connecting students' own struggles or awareness of the struggles of their peers with the historical antecedents of present social conditions. It would involve pointing out how structural root causes of inequality, like racism and sexism, affect specific contexts and issues.

In many cases, addressing informational assumptions will entail the teacher providing students with access to original source materials rather than limiting their discussion to the information provided in textbooks. This would most certainly be the case for lessons in the social sciences at 5th grade and above. An excellent example of the use of original source materials for integrating moral education for social justice within the teaching history is provided by the University of Virginia "Educating for Democracy" curriculum. We will be using some of the lessons from this project in the following chapter to illustrate how to construct moral lessons. For example, in the UVA curriculum, the discussion of social and moral issues surrounding the question of slavery includes the Confederate Constitution sections regarding slavery, experiential accounts by enslaved people, information regarding poor Whites in the South who did not own slaves, John C. Calhoun's statement before the U.S. Senate in 1837 advancing the argument that slavery was a "positive good" for Black and White people, and other primary source materials to give a contextualized picture of this complex issue.

The use of original source materials has been the hallmark of honors and AP courses. However, limiting the information of the majority of students to summaries provided in textbooks robs them of the intellectual experience of viewing events firsthand and offers the false impression that knowledge is "fixed" and official. Moral education for social justice requires the elimination of this educational disparity. The Oakland Public School District, which serves as the educational context of the research reported in this book, included the use of original source materials for all students in social science classes in grades 6 and above.

FROM PEER DISCOURSE TO CRITICAL MORAL PERSPECTIVES: CREATING DISCUSSIONS FOR ENGAGED REASONING

The key element for moral and social cognitive development is engaging students in meaningful reflection. This can be accomplished in a number of ways; however, the primary tool for engaging students to think in new ways about moral and social issues is discussion. It is through open discussion that students hear differing perspectives and points of view, and experience challenges to their own positions coming from peers as well as the teacher. We see this at an early level in the arguments and negotiations among young children. Without such argumentation, there would be no reason for a child to assume that others do not hold the same position as they do, and certainly no reason to assume that the other person might be in the right. At an advanced level, discussion can take place through interactive and online chatting, discussion posts on learning management sites, and multimedia platforms. We will say more about that below.

Research on student dialogue has provided considerable insights into the aspects of discussion that lead to conceptual and developmental change. These factors of effective discussion are common to dialogue around moral issues as well as in the sciences (Sionti et al., 2011; Turner & Berkowitz, 2005). This research has determined that the key to conceptual and developmental change is that participants in the dialogue actively take into account statements of others and make use of what the other person(s) has to say when offering a new statement. Transactive statements are of two types: *representational transacts* such as paraphrasing or juxtaposing the statements of another person with one's own are forms of active listening that serve to connect the ideas of members of a dialogue and to insure shared understanding; and *operational transacts*, which, in contrast, are statements that make use of or act on the statements and reasoning offered by the other person or people in the discussion. Research has determined that the ratio of operational to representational transacts that appear in a dialogue is associated with development of both moral judgments and concepts of convention, as well as the greater tendency to coordinate morality with convention or personal considerations when dealing with more complex social issues (Nucci et al., 2015). However, we argue that it is not enough to measure transactive discourse and call it moral education.

Responsive Engagement

Transacts can be used in two fundamentally different ways. We can employ transacts simply for strategic action in which our goal is to somehow get the other person to agree with and go along with our own point of view and our own goals. A great deal of our conversations are of this strategic kind. The prototype of strategic discourse is debate. In a debate, the goal is to win the argument. It doesn't matter whether or not the position we take is the most defensible, but whether or not we are able to convince the other, or convince the judges, that we have been able to outdo our opponent in presenting our case. In contrast, when we engage in a genuine dialogue, our goal is to move toward common ground. Here we draw directly from the contemporary philosopher Anthony Laden (2012), who defines *reasoning* as a social activity that is to be distinguished from individual cognition or thinking. He wrote, "In reasoning, we cannot be engaging in a pattern of reflection that isolates us from others" (p. 145). Instead, Laden proposes that we view reasoning in terms of offering invitations to join one another in accepting a common vantage point. We cannot reason fully if we are alone, but instead need to interact with others to authentically take into account their perspectives. We cannot presume to represent another person or group's perspective without including them in the dialogue.

When others are at the table, we are also forced to consider our own egos. *Engaged reasoning* (Laden, 2012) is a type of interaction or dialogue in which participants actively invite others to contribute to a shared set of information and find a stance that everyone can claim as their own. These interactions are also characterized by participants' genuine efforts to respond to each other's contributions; they are not ignoring, bulldozing, or manipulating the words of others, but attempting to find common ground. Laden refers to this activity of reasoning as *responsive engagement*.

Many aspects of this perspective are similar to the community of inquiry approach within the Philosophy for Children movement. The founder of the movement, Matthew Lipman (2003), wrote:

> When we think by ourselves, rather than in conversation with others, our deductions are derived from premises we already know. As a result the conclusion we infer is completely unsurprising. But when no person knows all the premises, as is often the case in dialogue, the reasoning process has much more vitality and the conclusion can come with considerably more surprise. (p. 179)

Within this framework, dialogue is referred to as mutual exploration and inquiry. Mikhail Bakhtin, a literary scholar and theorist whose work often gets applied to education, believed that "dialogue" is not simply talk (Shields, 2007, p. 65). According to Bakhtin, dialogue is the foundation of relationship and fundamental to cultivating a way of life that is open to change (Shields, 2007).

One of Bakhtin's key ideas is *heteroglossia*, or an embracing of multiple, varied voices. This orientation is in contrast to a monologic mindset that is singular and closed off to different opinions. Through dialogue, we are able to glimpse multiple partial truths that we put together as best we can into a full picture of reality. Shields (2007) explained further, "It is appropriate to say that for Bakhtin dialogue is ontological—a way of living life in openness to others who are different from oneself, of relating to people and ideas that remain separate and distinct from our own" (p. 65).

In addition to remaining open to and engaging multiple perspectives, Bakhtin wrote about the constant push and pull of authoritative discourses (i.e., authority of religious teachings, dominant societal narratives, messages from people in power) and internally persuasive discourses (Bakhtin, 1981, p. 342). In order to discern where we stand ideologically as individuals, we are constantly distinguishing our own discourses from authoritative ones, pulling away from the language of power and status quo in some realms and assimilating it in others. Ideology, for Bakhtin, is a system of ideas that permeates our communication and speech. Engaging head-on with authoritative discourses and interrogating their legitimacy, as well as interrogating our own beliefs and where they come from, is part of this constructive process of ideological development. Bakhtin's theory implies that a process of self-reflection, struggle, and revision of one's beliefs is constant and inevitable as we interact with our worlds.

Laden and Bakhtin have insights for educators working toward cultivating a critical moral orientation in students. They envision the following: a) a kind of social interaction in which each participant is really listening—not just crafting their next point, b) a capacity to find common ground with people who look and sound different than they do, and c) a way of life that promotes actively changing our own assumptions about what is right and fair based on new information and perspectives. When we give students the opportunity to engage in dialogue about issues that are moral or social in nature, not only do students get to practice these skills and mindsets, but researchers and educators can also glimpse the process of students' ideas taking shape by analyzing their discourse. Consider the brief excerpt of the dialogue among a group of 8th-grade students around whether it is all right to destroy property as an act of protest against something that is unfair. This dialogue (from Nucci et al., 2015) was in the context of an American history lesson about the Boston Tea Party and took place at the same time as "Occupy Wall Street" demonstrations were taking place in the city of Oakland. The students, many of whom were students of color from working-class families, were largely in sympathy with the protest. The question before them was whether the actions of some of the protesters, who engaged in damaging small businesses in the downtown area, were justified. In an earlier discussion, the students had differentiated between damage done to corporate businesses and large banks (part of the "1 percent") and smaller family-owned businesses. As one of the students put it, "Big corporations may have more money to spend, but as small businesses, they may be really tight and not have enough money to spend on windows and not even have enough money to have that replaced."

In the dialogue, we have inserted the coding for operational (O) and representational transacts (R). One of the students, Kelly, starts off the discussion by taking the position that damaging property is not a form of moral harm.

> You're only destroying property, which can be fixed. You're not harming a person, which will be physically and actually be mentally and emotionally hurt. And property is just an object. It's not something that can feel or whatever.

A second student, Dante, offers a counter to Kelly's position by asking her to consider whether she would maintain her argument if she put herself in the position of the owners of a "ginormous house." In making this move, Dante is asking Kelly and the other members of the discourse to consider whether or not there would be mental and emotional harm associated with damaging property.

> Okay, so, Kelly you're saying that it's okay to destroy property because it can be fixed, right? (**Paraphrase-R**) What if you're saying . . . what if you're super rich and you live in a really nice . . . like huge, ginormous house and some Occupy protesters came to destroy it, would you feel that's okay? (*Competitive Extension-O*)

Kelly counters Dante's argument by differentiating the destruction of someone's house that would cause harm to people from the destruction of a business, which in Kelly's view is an extension of the economic system that is the point of the protest.

> That's different because that will be . . . that will be where you . . . where you live or your kids will be growing up in. That would be different. But if you do it in, like a building or something, like the whole office or something, that's just your work, that's just your job, that's just where you go. You could still work somewhere else. (*Refinement-O*)

At this point, a third student, Eliana, picks up an aspect of Dante's argument by connecting the destruction of the place of business with the ultimate costs to the employees.

> Destroying property is an indirect way of destroying people I guess because you're . . . you're like . . . if you worked at a building and they had to repair it, they might take that out of your paycheck or something so then you wouldn't be the one to get the money. (*Counter Consideration-O*)

Dante seconds Eliana's position and continues the thread of arguments that damaging property, including a business, has the likelihood of ultimately harming people.

> Kelly, it's not different when you're destroying a . . . you know, your place of work from your home because somebody has to pay for that. And most likely it's gonna be you paying for the repairs. There's no difference between a home and a business because it's all gonna cost you money. It's all gonna take work to fix. (*Reasoning Critique—O*)

Kelly responds by rhetorically asking whether the loss of income to individuals is an actual form of harm.

> *Kelly:* Well, is that, like, be hurting a person physically or emotionally? (Extension—O)
> *Dante:* Yeah. (*Simple affirmation—R*)

At this point, Ciera, a fourth student in the discussion, circles back to the damage done to a person's house to connect property damage with a significant moral harm to persons.

> Um, well, I know this is a little bit extreme, but to some people, their house could be everything to them. So, their house is just like another part of their lives. (*Common-Ground Integration—O*)

As exemplified in the above example, the goal of a discussion based on responsive engagement is to have the argument win, and not an individual student, or elite group of students. In the discourse cited above, we see how representational and operational transacts function to convey an understanding and appreciation of the claims made by others (representational), and seek to move the argument forward by acting on the previously stated positions (operational). The students in this example were actively engaged and responsive to one another's arguments. Although students took different positions, no one's ideas were dismissed out of hand, and there was a genuine effort to find a common ground based on whether damage to property ultimately resulted in damage to people. In our approach to social and moral education, we attempt to engage students in transactive discourse that moves toward *responsive engagement*. The discourse we have cited is moving toward that common ground, but in the example we do not see Kelly embracing the position taken by the other three members of the discourse when the teacher ended the discussion period. This was not uncommon in the middle schools we worked with.

Agree to Disagree?

For many of our teachers, arriving at diverging viewpoints was an acceptable outcome. In their view, it was important to allow students the space to "agree to disagree." For example, middle school teachers in one of our studies (Midgette et al., 2018) purposefully omitted asking students to work toward a common ground out of their concerns that the more socially dominating students would have their views prevail. We also observed that in some cases, teachers provided instructions for discussion that became a simple exercise in learning about the positions maintained by other students and sharpening individual positions. However, these instructions did not encourage engaged reasoning. In the process of writing this book, we raised these issues with Anthony Laden. He suggested that there are richer forms of agreeing to disagree in which members of a discourse do not move from their initial positions, but come to understand how where they stand situates them among reasonable possibilities and what the underlying differences are that generate those positions. In fact, students may have excellent reasons to remain steadfast in their position, even if their group members are employing operational transacts. While consensus may be a useful task for inviting students to find common ground, common ground is not categorically more adequate for moral reasoning. For example, students' personal history or experience with a particular situation might provide a strong basis for disagreeing with the group on a particular historic or ethical dilemma. In such cases the discourse may allow people who disagree to nevertheless forge common policies or ideas about how to move forward, and to go on together. In the discussion we presented above, the students were not debating, but were indeed listening and trying to articulate the basis of their differences, and seeking a space they could share.

Instead of holding common ground as the sole conversation ideal, we propose that students seek a new plane of reasoning that acknowledges the varied perspectives and positions of each discussant, alongside reasons, facts, and information. Some students may enter a discussion with an emotional connection to the topic, while others may bring the perspective of someone who has been harmed by the topic. Still others may enter the discussion ignorant of the potential harm of the topic. All voices must be included, and as discussants, we have to wrestle with how to weight and coordinate the different types of perspectives from our conversation partners. Critical pedagogues like Ellsworth and hooks write that the voices of people who have been oppressed represent something special and important in the context of a discussion. "It is inappropriate to respond to such words by subjecting them to rationalist debates about their validity. Words spoken for survival come already validated in a radically different arena of proof and carry no option of luxury of choice" (Ellsworth, 1989, p. 191). She does not argue that students' words "spoken for survival" are accepted unproblematically, but that they be valued for the truths that they are. Considering a response to the question of whether experiencing oppression gives one special jurisdiction over speaking to that oppression in a discussion, hooks says:

> I would ask them to consider whether there is any 'special' knowledge to be acquired by hearing oppressed individuals speak from their experience—whether it be of victimization or resistance—that might make one want to create a privileged space for such discussion. Then we might explore ways individuals acquire knowledge about an experience they have not lived, asking ourselves what moral questions are raised when they speak for or about a reality that they do not know experientially, especially if they are speaking about an oppressed group. (1994, p. 89)

These authors remind us that each student's unique, multifaceted identity and social positionality will factor into how they engage in discussion with their peers and how they reason through moral dilemmas and academic content. Past experiences with oppression and personal experiences with social conflicts should be welcomed into the classroom discussion arena. When students are seeking resolutions in these discussions, logic and rationality should not be the only factors that influence the outcomes; empathy toward others' experiences, interpersonal connections, and symbolic factors can and should influence students' reasoning as well.

Preparing Students to Engage in Productive Discussion

The use of engaged reasoning contributes to an overall moral climate of mutual respect and cooperation that not only serves moral and social justice education, but academic achievement as well. Over the past two decades, preservice and experienced classroom teachers have incorporated domain-based discussions across a range of content areas. In working with teachers and students, we have come up with suggestions for how to implement discussions that generate responsive engagement. We are aware that most teacher training programs endeavor to prepare teachers to lead whole-class discussions and to set up small-group discussions. The following guidelines should be viewed as recommendations based on our experience and not as prescriptions. Middle school teachers at the start of one of our projects were engaging in whole-class formats at a 2:1 ratio with small-group discussion, and shifted to a 1:1 ratio once they became committed to promoting responsive engagement as an educational goal (Nucci et al., 2015). Perhaps more impressive is that these same teachers reduced the amount of whole-class instruction that was didactic by two-thirds and increased the amount of organic discussion by a similar amount.

As part of one of our projects, we worked with teachers and 5th- and 6th-grade students to come up with the following guidelines for how to structure a good classroom discussion. These guidelines incorporate elements of transactive discourse and translate the basic notions of responsive engagement into language readily accepted by students and teachers. Although these guidelines are the handiwork of elementary school students, they have also been embraced by students across grade levels to frame their discussions. We offer them here as a starting point for concrete suggestions for how teachers might introduce the basic ideas behind responsive engagement.

9 Rules for a Good Discussion

General Principle. The purpose of a good discussion is to work with others to come up with the best set of ideas or ways to deal with a situation. In an argument or a debate, only one side wins. In a good discussion, everybody wins!

1. Think before you speak.
2. Listen carefully to what others have to say.
3. Do not interrupt when someone else is speaking.
4. Make use of what others have to say when it is your turn to speak.
5. Only say what you truly believe.
6. Do not remain silent. Make sure to contribute to the discussion.
7. Let other people speak. Do not hog the discussion. Once you are done speaking, let other people talk before you speak again.
8. Support good ideas that other people have, even if they are different from your own.
9. Search for the best solution even if it is different from the way that you thought at first.

In working with teachers, we have found that implementing the above nine rules works best when students have an opportunity to discuss what these rules mean and then to consider which ones they would find difficult to put into practice. We have found that elementary school students from grade 4 through middle school take this discussion very seriously. High school teachers may or may not feel the need to have this list of rules, though as we have mentioned, students across grade levels have found them useful. This list of rules should also be viewed as a starting point as students may wish to alter, delete, or add new ones to reflect their own approach toward responsive engagement. For example, Rule 5: "only say what you truly believe," is intended to discourage students from offering statements simply to score points, or in order to not be an outlier. However, this rule may be suspended during practice rounds in which students try to generate the best pro and con positions for a given issue prior to the actual discussion. As stated in Rule 9, the purpose of engaged reasoning is to move toward consensus on the issue under consideration based on the best argument rather than to win a debate. As we discussed above, there may be situations in which students in a discourse may come to a principled disagreement in which a sincere effort to come to consensus was simply not possible. In those cases, it would be the effort to genuinely hear the positions expressed, to sincerely try to find common ground, and generate mutual respect for the members of the discourse that would serve as responsive engagement.

Implementing a discourse of the sort described by the above nine rules requires skills that not all students have developed as part of their linguistic repertoire. What follows are some suggestions for how to prepare students to effectively engage in moral discussion. Students and teachers find these exercises fun. They should be used early in the year to prepare students for later work. They may be used sporadically thereafter, as a way to develop discussion skills, but shouldn't be overdone. These games are intended to help students develop their capacity for generating representational and operational transacts. They are *not* intended to serve as actual discourse protocols.

Warm-Ups: Learning to Listen. In order for students to discuss one another's ideas and points of view, they need to be able to listen to what each other has to say. There are many exercises that teachers have developed over the years as ways to help students learn to listen. Place students in groups of five seated in a circle facing one another, and ask them on the count of three to say their names out loud all at once. A brief follow-up discussion with students will quickly reveal that it was very difficult to make out anyone else's name under those conditions.

This second activity is intended simply to address the tendencies among some students to listen to others only to tell when they have stopped talking so that they may begin. This sort of parallel conversation is common among very young children, but it is an affliction that many older students

Using the Academic Curriculum for Moral Development   135

and adults share as well. The purpose of the game is to get each player to accurately paraphrase the statement of another speaker. It is similar to the game "telephone" except in this case, the goal is accuracy.

> Place students in threes. Player (1) tells something brief about himself to player (2). Player (2) restates it as accurately as possible to player (3). Player (3) then evaluates whether or not the paraphrase was accurate. Player (2) then tells something brief to player (3) with player (1) as the "checker" until all players have had a turn at each role.

Transactive Discourse: Elaboration Game. One of the simpler transacts is to extend the arguments made by a previous speaker. This game may be used directly after the listening game since it extends the use of paraphrase. In this game, the student must take into account what the previous person said and elaborate on it. Prior to play, the teacher models a simple elaboration of a previous statement. The teacher then gives the class an interesting issue to discuss. In one of our Oakland classrooms, the issue was "Should the city of Oakland put a tax on sugary drinks?"

> Place students in circles of up to six players. Player (1) begins by expressing a point of view. Player (2) paraphrases the statement made by player (1) and elaborates or extends it. Player (3) does the same with the statement made by player (2). This continues until all students have had a turn at extending the argument. With elementary-aged children, the teacher should circulate from group to group to hear whether or not children are accurate in providing elaborations, and help out when this doesn't occur. With junior and senior high school students, the teacher can assign one member of each group to serve as "checker."

Transactive Discourse: Rebuttal Game. The rebuttal game is an extension of the elaboration game and uses the same procedure except that each student must paraphrase and offer a refutation of the argument advanced by the previous speaker.

Establishing a Discourse Protocol: Some Common Questions Asked by Teachers

Over the years, we have learned that it is essential to allow enough time for students to get the basic arguments on the table, considering pros and cons or differing points of view, and then to have the time to work toward common ground. We have seen teachers translate the above discussion games into a discussion protocol. This can make for a very stilted discussion rather than an organic search for common ground. We will close this section by reviewing and providing answers to some common questions teachers have raised about how to use discussions for social and moral lessons. We do so with humility. Teachers are educational professionals. What we are offering here are suggestions that have emerged from our experience.

- *How do I structure groups?* Research on small-group discussion indicates that for students in grades 4 and above groups should have five or six students. In younger grades, children can work in pairs or triads. In general, groups should be *heterogeneous* with respect to gender, ethnicity, and academic ability. This is to ensure that all voices are *at the table*. For dilemma and conflict discussions, groups should include children who hold opposing views with at least two members on each side of the issue (in grades 4 and above).
- *Do I also use whole-class discussion or only small groups?* A pattern employed by many teachers is to have a small-group discussion followed by a whole-class discussion. This allows everyone the benefit of hearing a range of solutions or positions. Generally, students participate at a greater level in small-group rather than large-group discussions.
- *Should I have students generate a list of pros and cons before engaging in the open discussion?* This is generally a good idea, and can be done in two rounds by first having each student in a small group put the pro side on the table and a second round listing the counter position. This allows students to get a good sense of the issue and helps to provide ideas for their own arguments during a third open round of conversation aimed at finding common ground. Also, initially going around the circle giving each student a chance to contribute to the pros and cons will help to engage everyone in the open discussion.
- *Should I begin the lesson by having students write out their thoughts before going into the discussion?* Some teachers want to do this in order to let students get their thoughts in order. Our recommendation is to allow the discussion to unfold before asking students to do any writing. This is to avoid fatigue given that the lesson should end with a written product, and to avoid having students take hard and fast stands prior to hearing the ideas and perspectives of their peers.
- *Are there some sentence starters that I can give to help students to offer their arguments?* The following are sentence starters that teachers have put together to help students frame their statements: "I agree with you because . . ." or "I heard you say. . . ." "That doesn't make sense to me because. . . ." "If that were true, then. . . ." "Can you say more about that?" "I see a connection between. . . ."

- *Can I use this type of discussion with young children?* The short answer is yes, especially with regard to moral dilemmas or moral conflicts. However, these discussions should be integrated into reflective "pairs" reading or other academic activity. Teachers can effectively lead small-group and whole-class discussions with young children to accomplish what older children can in groups on their own. Generally, young children do not have much to say about social conventions. Discussions about conventions are more fruitful in relation to classroom rules or in the context of understanding a story plot than in trying to get young children below grade 3 or 4 to try to figure out the social functions of conventional norms through academic content.
- *Can I take a moral position as the teacher?* The short answer is yes, but with this caveat. Every time a teacher provides an answer, it robs the students of the opportunity to construct their own understanding and to come to hold a moral position firmly on their own. The better role for the teacher is to ask the provocative questions, and to prod students into looking for solutions beyond easy answers that will cause them to grow in their moral and social understanding.
- *Should I connect the discussion to some other academic assignment?* Yes, link an assignment to the discussion. This will increase the likelihood of on-task behavior, and will help students to deepen their understanding and knowledge through reflection.
- *How can I help ensure that students make use of the ideas of other students in the discussion?* One tactic that teachers have taken is to require that students quote at least one of their peers when generating the written assignment that follows the discussion. This requires students to take notes during the discussion. This has the negative side effect of slowing down the discussion due to copying notes and handwriting.
- *Can engaged reasoning discussions take place online?* At the time that we were writing this book, much of the world was practicing forms of social distancing in an effort to control the spread of the COVID-19 virus. In the United States, schools were closed and all instruction took place through virtual distance learning. A question readers may have is whether discussions that have the qualities of responsive engagement can take place online. Fortunately, the answer is yes. These discussions can take place via online group conversation through media such as Zoom. In addition, we have found in our own teacher education courses that text-based discussions generated through online chatting are as effective in producing transactive discourse as face-to-face conversation, and written products following the discourse are of equal quality.

CHAPTER 9

Lesson Plans for Moral Development and Social Justice
Some Examples

In this chapter, we will look at examples of lessons using the regular academic curriculum to stimulate reflection and discussion to promote moral development and social justice. These lessons will illustrate how to address issues that fall predominantly within the domains of morality, social convention, and the personal, as well as issues that include elements across domains. The lesson topics were also selected for their incorporation of issues related to in/justice within social systems. We provide examples designed for students in the elementary grades as well as at the middle school and high school level. These examples will include questions designed to encourage deliberation and engaged reasoning. Our goal is to provide a clear picture of how a teacher working at any grade level can construct lessons that achieve the 2 for 1 goal of contributing to academic growth along with moral development for social justice. In Chapter 11, we will present examples of action projects and community engagement, continuing Freire's cycle of praxis. The focus in this chapter is on the incorporation of attention to moral development and social justice more broadly across the curriculum.

Nearly all of the lessons come from work that we have done with classroom teachers through our research collaborations and lessons that have been created and implemented by our preservice teacher education majors. With each lesson we will spell out the moral and social development goals of the lesson, and describe the academic goals in more general terms. In the work we have done with our students and collaborating teachers, we have required them to indicate which specific learning standards each lesson addresses. However, since learning standards vary by state, that information will not be included here. The lessons for younger students often start with a "Do Now" activity that asks them to think of situations they have experienced that are related to the subject of the lesson.

MORALITY

The Primary Grades (2-4)

The great achievement in the moral development of the young child is the construction of the concept of fairness as just reciprocity. The goal of curricular lessons for moral development in the primary grades is to help children read the emotions and intentions of the protagonists in stories or historical events, and to take them into account when judging what would be the moral or fair outcome of a situation. Lessons should direct children to try to work out solutions that take both sides of a dispute into account. As children develop, we would expect them to search for moral resolutions that go beyond strict equality or tit-for-tat solutions to conflicts. The first step in a moral lesson with young children would fall under the rubric of social and emotional learning (SEL). This initial step involves getting children to identify the feelings and motivations of the protagonists.

The following example is based on the story of "Bimbo the Big Bully" from the book *Nine True Dolphin Stories* (Davidson, 1974). The central issue is the fairness of different ways to respond to a bully. It also raises the consciousness of bullies to let them see what happens when they act as they do, and also allows the other children to have empathy for what may motivate the bully. The goal is to engage children in seeing perspectives from both sides and to try to bring those perspectives together. The tendency for children at this age is to view a tit-for-tat response as a fair way to deal with an aggressor. The dolphins in the story, however, respond differently. This opens up space for children to consider other ways to handle similar situations from a moral perspective.

"Bimbo the Big Bully"

This story presents an actual incident in which the directors of an oceanarium in San Diego introduced a pilot whale into a tank with several dolphins. At first things went well. But then Bimbo, the pilot whale, began ramming the dolphins with his nose. The director decided to intervene by draining much of the water from the tank so that the dolphins could still swim, but Bimbo could not. When that happened Bimbo became very scared and made sounds that showed how scared he was. The dolphins, hearing his cries, came to comfort him. After that, the director raised the water level, and Bimbo no longer rammed the dolphins.

Lesson Goals

1. Identify feelings and motives of characters in the story.
2. Consider what is fair in dealing with someone who harms you by taking into account the perspective of both the character who is harmed and the character doing the harm.

Procedure

1. Do Now (5 minutes, in pairs): Have you ever had to deal with a bully? How did that make you feel? Have ever been without friends? How did that feel? Why do you think some kids act like bullies sometimes?
2. Pairs reading: Have students read the story in pairs, or for nonreaders, the teacher could read the story out loud.
3. Discussion: Following the reading, work with students in small groups of up to six children for discussion. Then open things up for a whole-class discussion.

Questions to Guide Discussion

1. Do you think Bimbo was trying to hurt the dolphins? Why do you think he would do that?
2. How do you think the dolphins felt when Bimbo kept trying to ram them with his nose?
3. Do you think it was wrong or all right for Bimbo to do that? How come?
4. The director of the oceanarium drains the tank so there isn't enough water for Bimbo to swim around. That scares Bimbo. Why did the director do that?
5. Do you think it was fair for the director to do that to Bimbo?
6. Bimbo was hurting the dolphins. Suppose the dolphins got together and hurt Bimbo back. Do you think that would have been okay? Do you think Bimbo deserved that?
7. When Bimbo was scared, the dolphins came to help. What do you think of that? Do you think that the dolphins should have helped Bimbo? After all, Bimbo had hurt them.
8. In this story, Bimbo was scared because he was the only whale in the aquarium and was without any whale friends. Have you ever been somewhere without friends? How does that feel?
9. Did the dolphins help Bimbo not to feel afraid anymore?
10. Do you think if Bimbo is less afraid he won't act like a bully anymore?

SEL Supplements. This lesson provides several opportunities for children to offer emotion or feelings terms to account for the behaviors of the characters. One way to supplement this and other moral lessons is to add these feelings terms to an emotions dictionary that the children can generate as part of their language arts curriculum. Beyond using the curriculum to help young children construct their knowledge about feelings and their concepts of fairness, language arts can also be a good context within which to work on children's fears and help them to generate a sense of trust (Watson, 2018). One of the very common outcomes we have seen in the discussions about "Bimbo the Big Bully" has been the open identification of some children with Bimbo, and their perception that Bimbo was just trying to play and make friends. These early emotional patterns are important for the construction of morality. Teachers we work with in urban school districts have supplemented their classroom practices with stories that deal with some of the sources of their fears and concerns. There are now considerable resources online for teachers interested in making use of what is referred to as "bibliotherapy," the use of children's literature to help children address social and emotional issues.

Middle School and High School

As we saw in Chapter 3, the transition through middle school into high school is associated with shifts in moral reasoning from a tit-for-tat, strict equality view of fairness toward incorporation of considerations of equity. This adolescent period is also marked by an increasing attention to moral complexity, with a transitional period in middle school in which moral decisionmaking around complex issues is characterized by vacillation. With development, adolescents display the capacity to coordinate moral and nonmoral considerations in arriving at judgments about the right course of action. Lessons presented to adolescents should reflect this emerging capacity to deal with moral complexity.

John Brown's Raid

Goals. This lesson engages students in weighing the ethical and moral implications of the use of violence to achieve a moral good. This lesson addresses the themes of justice versus vengeance raised in "Bimbo the Big Bully." However, the issues raised in this particular lesson open up questions as to whether violence is ever justified as a means to address a moral wrong. The central focus of the lesson comes from the antebellum period leading up to the Civil War, content often designated for 8th-grade American history. The issue itself, however, and many aspects of the following lesson, can be readily adapted for students in high school American history. The focus of the lesson is on a retaliatory raid led by John Brown and his sons against a settlement in Missouri.

Procedure. Students are asked to read about John Brown from original source material if possible. Following their reading, the teacher presents the class with the following summary for small-group and subsequent whole-class discussion.

> In May 1856, a border raid from Missouri, a proslavery state, devastated the antislavery town of Lawrence, Kansas. Within a few days, John Brown, who strongly opposed slavery, together with his sons and a few companions, retaliated by attacking a settlement at Pottawatomie Creek, Missouri. The raid killed five settlers. John Brown hoped that his actions would spark a slave rebellion. However, that did not occur.

Questions for Discussion and Homework

1. Was John Brown justified in leading a retaliatory raid against the proslavery settlement? How come?
2. How far should a person go in retaliation? Is it right to hurt others as much as they have hurt you or the people that you care about? How come?
3. Is there a difference between vengeance and justice?
4. Brown had hoped that his actions would set off a slave rebellion. If that had taken place, would it have justified the raid? Why/why not?

Expanding the Lesson. The John Brown saga poses a series of rich moral questions. Indeed, while some would argue that what John Brown did was morally wrong, others would make the case that he should be seen as a hero. There are people who pay homage to John Brown each year by visiting his gravesite on his birthday, May 9.

You may wish to take the discussion in several directions. One is to bring the issue closer to home and discuss acts of retaliation adolescents take against people who have harmed them in some way.

Another route is to connect the John Brown raid with modern acts of political retaliation and violence such as abortion clinic bombers who believe their actions serve to protect the innocent unborn. With older high school students, you might bring in the argument advanced in defense of terrorism (which most people view as abhorrent and unjustified) as an act of self-defense used by less powerful political groups against a more powerful oppressor.

One of the most effective extensions we have employed has been to follow up the discussion and homework around the John Brown incident with the writings of Dr. Martin Luther King Jr. and Malcolm X on the issue of violence as a means for social change and self-defense in a context of fighting racial oppression. This discussion is placed within the context of the civil rights struggles of the 1960s. Our approach has been to introduce two quotations that students can also find at the end of Spike Lee's movie *Do the Right Thing*:

> Violence as a way of achieving racial justice is both impractical and immoral. It is impractical because it is a descending spiral ending in destruction for all. The old law of an eye for an eye leaves everybody blind. It is immoral because it seeks to humiliate the opponent rather than win his understanding; it seeks to annihilate rather than to convert. Violence is immoral because it thrives on hatred rather than love. It destroys community and makes brotherhood impossible. It leaves society in monologue rather than dialogue. Violence ends by defeating itself. It creates bitterness in the survivors and brutality in the destroyers. —Martin Luther King Jr.

> I think there are plenty of good people in America, but there are also plenty of bad people in America and the bad ones are the ones who seem to have all the power and be in these positions to block things that you and I need. Because this is the situation, you and I have to preserve the right to do what is necessary to bring an end to the situation, and it doesn't mean that I advocate violence, but at the same time I am not against using violence in self-defense. I don't even call it violence when it's self-defense, I call it intelligence. —Malcolm X

The teacher asks a student to read each passage aloud. Students are then instructed to discuss in small groups what they think the author meant and then share their interpretations with the entire class. Once this has been done with each passage, the teacher directs the students to discuss the following questions in small groups and then share their ideas during a whole-class discussion. These questions then form the basis for a written homework assignment.

Questions for Discussion and Homework

1. Which of these positions do you favor? Why?
2. When, and in what circumstances, is violence justified? In cases of extreme racism or oppression, is violence justified?
3. Can you integrate these two positions? How would you do it?

Expanding the Lesson and Connecting with Recent Events

Colin Kaepernick and Non violent Protest

(Adapted with permission from Johari Harris, University of Virginia, "Educating for Democracy" project)

The issues raised in the above set of lessons can be connected to more recent struggles over police treatment of African Americans. The actions of professional football player Colin Kaepernick present an example of nonviolent protest that was met with a great deal of resistance by some Americans, including President Donald Trump. In 2020, Kaepernick's form of protest took on added significance with the murder of George Floyd by a Minneapolis police officer who knelt on Mr. Floyd's neck for more than 8 minutes. The lesson begins by having the students read the following passage and the quotes below:

> In August 2016, professional football player Colin Kaepernick began to protest against the surge of police brutality and racism primarily against Black males seen throughout the country. Over the span of several years, dozens of innocent Black males and females were murdered by police throughout the country, with relatively little repercussions for the police involved. Kaepernick's protesting came immediately after the deaths of unarmed Black males like Jamarion Robinson, Alton Sterling, and Philando Castile. On top of the deaths of these men, implicated police officers continued to receive little to no punishment for their actions, with many receiving paid leave while internal investigations continued. As a way of protesting against the unjustness of discriminatory police practices, Kaepernick began to sit during the national anthem prior to kickoffs and shortly after began kneeling during the anthem. Many found his protesting method disrespectful to the American flag and, by implication, to the country as a whole. Anti-kneeling protestors boycotted NFL games, protested at games, and demanded the termination of his contract. Other athletes across sports and citizens nationwide recognized the message behind his actions and supported him by also kneeling and protesting the increasing number of racially charged police killings.

> "I am not going to stand up to show pride in a flag for a country that oppresses black people and people of color. To me, this is bigger than football and it would be selfish on my part to look the other way. There are bodies in the street and people getting paid leave and getting away with murder." —Colin Kaepernick, NFL quarterback

"I disagree, I wholeheartedly disagree. He can speak out about a very important issue. But there's plenty of other ways that you can do that in a peaceful manner that doesn't involve being disrespectful to the American flag." —Drew Brees, NFL quarterback

1. Given what you have read, including the quotes above, do you think kneeling during the national anthem is an effective and appropriate way to protest police brutality in America? (C)
2. In what sense does the flag represent America? How does that work? Why should people stand during the playing of the national anthem? (C)
2a. What do you think of the arguments that kneeling during the playing of the national anthem is disrespectful to America as a country?
3. In reading the quotes above from Colin Kaepernick and Drew Brees, whose position do you most agree with? Why?
4. The actions of Colin Kaepernick were part of a larger movement called "Black Lives Matter." It spread beyond the borders of the United States to other countries dealing with issues of racial injustice. What personal responsibility if any do individual Americans have to take action to achieve racial justice? (M/P)
5. Thinking back to the words of Dr. King and Malcolm X, what do you think is the best way for individuals to contribute to the achievement of social justice? (M)

(C = conventional, M = moral, P = personal)

SOCIAL CONVENTION

The lesson described above about kneeling during the national anthem requires that students coordinate their moral understandings of fairness and justice with the functions of social conventions, such as standing during the playing of the national anthem. Indeed, nearly all efforts at social justice education involve reflections on the morality of existing societal conventions. As noted in Chapter 3, students have a great deal of trouble understanding the functions of social convention. What follows are examples of lessons directed at middle school students to stimulate their understanding of conventions as constituent elements of social systems and social organization.

Middle school is the critical transition period during which young adolescents construct their understanding of the role conventions play in coordinating the interactions of people within a social system. In 6th and 7th grades, the majority of students perceive conventions as simply the arbitrary dictates of authority. By late 7th and 8th grade, students begin to construct an understanding of conventions as a constituent component of social systems.

The lessons below were designed to engage students in that conceptual shift. For about half of students in the United States, this transition is not completed until the freshman year of high school (9th grade). Thus, the lessons presented in this section may be adapted for use with young high school students as well.

Ancient Egypt: Forms of Address

Goals. This lesson focusing on convention comes from middle school world history. The lesson focuses on the use of titles to differentiate among people of differing social status or social class.

Procedure. This lesson has two components: one focusing on the abstract issues from history, the other connecting to students' everyday use of titles at school. Some teachers prefer to introduce the lesson by starting first with the everyday issue. In this example, we begin with the topic addressed in the history lesson. Please note that even in the case of this abstract history lesson, the questions connect to present-day experiences by linking the use of titles to contemporary use of titles to refer to the president.

The lesson begins by placing the students in groups. The teacher then asks a student to read the following passage aloud followed by small-group and then whole-class discussion.

> Throughout most of its history, Egypt was ruled by kings. These kings were thought to be representatives of the gods. Using the king's name directly was considered disrespectful, so people referred to him by his residence. They called him the "per aa," or pharaoh, which meant "great house" in Egyptian.

Questions for Discussion

1. Why do you think the people of ancient Egypt had a special title for their ruler? Explain.
2. Do you think it would have been okay for a regular person to greet the pharaoh by saying "Hey Tut, how's it going?" Why not?
3. What is the "proper" way to greet the president? Why don't we just call the president by the first name, Joe? Why are people expected to call him President Biden, or Mr. President? Explain.
4. Suppose an individual, such as a news reporter, doesn't like or respect a particular president. Would it be okay to express his lack of regard by addressing the president without using a title such as Mr. President? Why?

5. Some people would argue that not using the president's title is disrespecting the country and not just the person. How does that work?
6. Could we have a society that doesn't use titles for people in different positions such as Dr. or your honor for judges? How would that change society?

The following questions link the issue to students' everyday experiences.

1. How about at school? Why do we use titles here for teachers (Mr. & Mrs.) but not for students?
2. What do these titles tell us about how school is structured?
3. Suppose we did away with titles at school. What would change?

Homework or In-Class Writing. Following the discussion, students would be asked to provide individual written responses to the following questions.

1. Why do you think the people of ancient Egypt had a special title for their ruler? Explain.
2. What does that tell us about how Egyptian society was structured?
3. Some people would argue that it is disrespectful for a regular person to address someone like the president by their first name. What makes that disrespectful, when a president's first name *is* their name after all?
4. Some people would argue that not using the president's title is disrespecting the country and not just the person. How does that work?

Expanding the Lesson: Use of Gender Pronouns. A social justice expansion of the above lesson on titles would ask students to consider the uses of gendered titles, Mr., Mrs., Miss, Ms., followed by a discussion of the pronouns used to signify someone's gender (he, she, they, etc.). Students will consider how these pronouns structure social organization, and how they may also harm people who do not fit within the binary categories of male and female. The latter aspect of the lesson asks students to coordinate morality with social convention.

This lesson set is designed with middle school students in mind. However, the following exercise can be used with younger children. When used with younger children, the question that refers to how society would be affected should not be included given that students younger than 5th grade may not be able to address such questions. In this example, we are expanding a lesson from social studies to consider how we address people in our everyday lives as well as in formal letters.

Procedure

Titles and Pronouns Part 1

1. Do Now. Students are asked to analyze the format of a formal cover letter and practice writing a cover letter to an employer of their choice. Students take time to look up the person in charge of the business or organization they wish to work for and compose their letters addressed to this person. Teachers pause here to discuss traditional ways of formally addressing people we do not know and who are in positions of authority, including titles such as Mister (Mr.), Missus (Mrs.), Miss, or Ms. The teacher can point out that these traditional titles rely on assuming the gender of another person.

Introduce Vocabulary and Resources. Teachers can make explicit the connection between assuming someone's gender identity in formal letters and doing it unconsciously everyday with our peers and people we don't know. Teachers can point out that gender labels are everywhere, and specifically binary labels are often forced on people who have to choose which restroom to use, or how to identify on a driver's license, which leaves some people out. To provide groundwork context for discussion, teachers can establish common vocabulary for students (e.g., the Gender Snowperson: assets2.hrc.org/welcoming-schools/documents/WS_Lesson_Gender_Snowperson.pdf), for example, sex assigned at birth, versus gender expression, vs. gender identity, vs. sexual orientation. Teachers could also read a short story with their class that introduces a variety of gender pronouns and addresses the issue of identity in society (sample resources can be found at www.welcomingschools.org/resources/lesson-plans/transgender-youth/transgender-with-books/).

2. Small-Group Discussion Questions:

1. What is the purpose of using gendered titles? (C)
2. What are some consequences of assuming another person's gender? How might they feel if you get it wrong? How might you feel? (M)
3. What are some titles that do not imply gender? (C)
4. Do teachers/parents/adults ever refer to you as Mr. or Ms.? How does it make you feel?

Pronouns Part 2

Students read this piece, "I'm Just Drawn This Way: Teen Finds Gender Identity Through Art" by Desmond Meagley, who was a 19-year-old reporter for YR Media at the time of publication (Meagley, 2016). Another possible article is "The Gender Spectrum" by Carrie Kilman (Kilman, 2013).

Questions for Discussion

1. How are gender identity and gender expression different?
2. What are some ways in which Desmond felt pressured to fit in?
3. Desmond identifies as transgender, but do we know what pronouns Desmond uses from this article?
4. What is the purpose of using gendered pronouns? (C)
5. Consider the idea of adopting pronouns that do NOT identify gender, like they/them. What if we did away with all gendered pronouns, and always used they/them/theirs? How would this change society? (This last part should only be used with students in 6th grade or above.) (C)
6. Many people are choosing to list their pronouns on their business cards or on their name tags. What is the purpose of this? (C)
7. Who should get to decide what pronouns people use when addressing you? How come? (P/M)

This lesson starts conversations about the purpose of social conventions, and aims to complicate the purpose of conventions for this age group through an issue that is relevant to young adolescents: identity. However, the issue of gender identity/expression, and sexual orientation, and creating welcoming and equitable spaces for all people, should be a topic that is taken up year-round through a moral lens as well. Multiple sources for curricular resources around this topic for students of all ages can be found online (e.g., bc.sogieducation.org/sogi3).

(C = conventional, M = moral, P = personal)

What Does It Mean to Be "Civilized"?

Adapted with permission from Nicolas Miller

This lesson is from 8th-grade American history, but can be applied at the high school level. It uses events surrounding the forced removal of Indigenous peoples from land that is now the southeastern United States to explore the meaning of the term "civilized." In the 1800s, five groups of Indigenous peoples were officially designated by the U.S. government as "civilized." Among them were the Cherokee people living in the region of present-day North Carolina. Despite this designation, the Cherokee and other "civilized"

Indigenous groups were threatened, and forced to give up their land and walk to what is now the state of Oklahoma, an event now referred to as "the Trail of Tears." The goal of this lesson is to encourage students to consider what the word civilized implies, and challenge assumptions (subconscious or conscious) that globalized, modernized, and "Westernized" ways of life are inherently superior. "Civilized" is a complex concept that requires coordinating an understanding of conventions as constituent of social systems with moral evaluations of social practices and norms. In 8th grade, this understanding of conventions is just emerging. This lesson helps to stimulate construction of the notion of societies as normative systems. In high school, most students have an understanding of the relationship between convention and social systems, allowing for an even more coherent and critical approach to the issues raised in this lesson. (Note: Although this lesson focuses on conventional reasoning, the obvious moral aspects of this *topic* were not ignored in the classroom.)

Procedure

1. Lesson Introduction. The teacher introduces the lesson with a definition of "civilized":

civilized: when a place or people become more advanced socially, culturally, and morally (ideas about right and wrong).

2. Group discussion and analysis of three practices in relation to the following question posed by the teacher: "Did the Cherokee become more or less civilized after adapting to European American culture?" In small groups, students discuss the following items with 10 minutes for discussion for each issue.

A. Forms of Dress

The Cherokee began to use spinning wheels to produce clothing similar to European Americans.

1. Did the Cherokee become more or less civilized after adapting to European American clothing? How come?/Why not? (C)

B. Adoption of a Written Language and Formation of a Constitution

In 1821, Sequoyah, who was half-Cherokee, introduced a written Cherokee alphabet after studying his language for 12 years. After this development, the Cherokee began to produce a newspaper in both English and Cherokee. They also created a constitution modeled after the U.S. Constitution.

1. Did the Cherokee become more or less civilized after adapting a written language? How come?/Why not? (C)

C. Adoption of Farming Instead of Hunting and Adoption of Slavery

In the 1700s, the Cherokee began to farm their land as opposed to hunting. Some wealthy Cherokee even practiced slaveholding. In 1811, a census was taken: The Cherokee population numbered 12,395 people, while enslaved people of African descent numbered 583.

1. Did the Cherokee become more or less civilized after adopting the European American system of agriculture? How come?/Why not? (Pr)
2. Did the Cherokee become more or less civilized after adopting the practice of slavery? Why/why not? (M/C)

(C = conventional, M = moral, P = personal, Pr = pragmatic)

D. Land Ownership

Originally, the Cherokee viewed their land as owned by everyone and usable by any member of the tribe. They did set up boundaries with other tribes. Then they adopted a European American model of landownership in which a single person or family could own a plot of land.

1. Did the Cherokee become more or less civilized after adopting the European American system of land ownership? How come?/Why not? (C)

3. In-Class Writing and Homework Assignment. *Based on what we have discussed in class*, did the Cherokee became more or less civilized after they adapted to aspects of the European American lifestyle?

1. On a separate piece of lined paper, write a well-written claim/evidence paragraph that includes:
    a. a claim,
    b. at least two reasons to support your claim,
    c. evidence from class,
    d. analysis of that evidence, and
    e. a conclusion.

Make sure to reference your definition of *civilized* and your list of criteria.

THE PERSONAL DOMAIN

The personal domain accounts for students' psychological concepts of persons and personhood. Attention to development within the personal domain is critical to students' construction of moral concepts of rights as freedoms. For young children, personhood is defined by external appearance and actions. Choice about those behaviors is essential since they collectively reflect the "true" self. This leads to the possibility that a child's choice of behaviors will be at odds with cultural or gendered expectations as held by the family or society. It also leads to the possibility that others will gain an incomplete picture of the person from a sampling of observed behaviors. In the following lesson, this notion of layers of self is achieved through a concrete representation that children construct after reflecting on the events depicted in a well-known children's story. It allows for children to also consider that their peers may have aspects of themselves that do not fit within the confines of group conventions, or that are beyond the actions that they display at school.

The complexity of self, and the private aspect of the personal, can be revisited in greater depth at the high school level using literature or media to explore the interior values and beliefs and private thoughts that are at the core of defining "self" and "identity."

The Story of Ferdinand

(Adapted from a lesson created by
Gabriela Casal, Christina Luce, and Zia Manekin-Hrdy)

Lesson Summary (Grade 3)

1. Do Now (5 minutes, in pairs): What is something you think most people really like to do that you don't like to do? Why don't you like doing it? Have you done it anyway, and why? How did that feel? How do you feel about being different from other people in this way?

2. Pairs Reading. In pairs, students read *The Story of Ferdinand* by Munro Leaf. This well-known story is about a juvenile bull who instead of engaging in aggressive acts with peers, prefers to sit peacefully and smell flowers. When Ferdinand grows up, he is very large and strong, but still peaceful. One day, five men come to the pasture to choose a bull for fights in the bullring. Ferdinand is again on his own, sniffing flowers, when he accidentally sits on a bumblebee. Upon getting stung, he runs wildly across the field, snorting and stamping. Mistaking Ferdinand for a mad and aggressive bull, the men rename him "Ferdinand the Fierce" and take him away to Madrid. However, when Ferdinand is let into the ring to fight the matador, he is delighted by the flowers in the ladies' hair and sits down in the middle of the ring to enjoy them, upsetting and disappointing everyone.

3. Discussion (10-15 minutes)

Guiding Questions

- How is Ferdinand different from other bulls? How do you think he feels about being different?
- How does Ferdinand's mother deal with him being different? Is it okay or is it wrong for Ferdinand to choose not to do what all his peers are doing? Why?
- Why was Ferdinand chosen to fight instead of one of the other bulls? Was it okay or was it wrong of the five men to take him away from his home?
- What was expected of Ferdinand once he got to the bullring? What did Ferdinand do instead? Do you think this was the right decision for Ferdinand? Why/why not?
- What do you think was going on in his head? Did Ferdinand want to fight? Why/why not?
- Based on this story, do you think people are always the same on the inside as they seem on the outside? Why or why not?

4. "Layers of Myself" Activity (15 minutes). After watching a short demonstration using a sample portrait of Ferdinand, students will each work on a three-page, three-layered self-portrait using transparency sheets, colored Sharpies, small pieces of blank white paper, glue sticks, and staples. The first page will be a simple sketch of the student's own face. The second page should include two to five things about their inner selves that the outside world might not know. *(For example, on this page of Ferdinand's self-portrait, it says "likes sitting quietly," "loves smelling flowers," and "peaceful.")* On the third page, students will write down two to five things that represent how the out-side world sees them. They will write these down on pieces of paper and glue them to the transparency. *To illustrate, the children are shown Ferdinand's portrait (Figure 9.1). The children will, see for example, that the pieces of paper on the third page of Ferdinand's portrait say things like "big," "strong," "frightening," and "a good fighter."* Once all three pages are complete, stu-dents will place them on top of one another in order and put a staple in the corner, so that it becomes a kind of flip-book. When the flip-book is closed, they see all three layers at once, and some of the "inner parts" may be covered by some of the "outer parts." They won't be called on to share their work with the class, but will have time to do so if they wish.

Figure 9.1. "Layers of Myself" Drawing for Ferdinand

5. Homework. Students will take their self-portraits home with them and write down their responses to the following questions in some form of journal reflection:

1. What is something people *mistakenly* assume about you based on your outward appearance? How does it make you feel?
2. What is something most people *don't* know about you based on your outward appearance? How does it make you feel?

3. Do you know anyone like Ferdinand? Describe them.
4. Have you ever felt like Ferdinand does?

COMPLEX MULTIDOMAIN ISSUES

Many of the issues that arise in everyday life, and within the curriculum, draw from more than one domain of social reasoning, and as described in Chapter 2, require the student to engage in cross-domain coordination. The following two examples, both from the high school level, illustrate how to construct lessons that activate more than one domain. The first is from high school literature; the second is from mathematics.

The Moral Lives of Ulysses Jeffries and Huckleberry Finn: Snoop Dogg Meets Mark Twain

(Adapted from a lesson created by Roy E. Bounds)

Teachers of English and American literature are often confronted with public controversies over the selection of literature for their students. The following lesson uses two controversial pieces to address issues of morality, convention, and the moral growth of individuals within the constraints of their social worlds. The selected works address issues of race and social class from radically different perspectives and time periods. The use of *Huckleberry Finn* in the classroom has come under scrutiny because of how the book treats the relationship between a white adolescent and a runaway slave. In addition, the book includes frequent use of the N-word by White characters. The following PBS website provides ideas and advice for teachers for how to think about the controversial elements of teaching this book, including the use of the N-word: www.pbs.org/wgbh/cultureshock/teachers/huck/howto.html. We recognize that the use of the N-word in the classroom could be traumatizing, anxiety-provoking, enraging, or upsetting for Black students, especially if they are hearing the word spoken by White classmates and sanctioned by teachers. Teachers may decide that neither they nor students will read that word out loud during class. Nobel laureate Toni Morrison wrote that she saw value in intelligent educators leading meaningful discussions surrounding the significance of the N-word, in her 1996 introduction to Huckleberry Finn (www.stjoe.k12.in.us/ourpages/auto/2013/12/10/59680878/Morrison%20Intro%20to%20Huck%20Finn.pdf). The PBS resource above suggests discussing: "Does the use of the word in a 'classic' literary work give it validity outside of the classroom? If so, how?" Both texts in this lesson use the N-word in very different contexts. The two texts juxtaposed could spark a discussion about what words mean to different communities and in different contexts—an issue that draws on conventional reasoning.

Critical pedagogues like Duncan-Andrade and Morrell write, "Studying canonical texts is an important strategy for understanding the values and ideologies of dominant groups at various points in history.... When engaging in these texts, however, it became important to include critical literacy theories and multicultural readings of canonical texts that empowered students as readers and did not defer to the authority of those texts" (2008, pp. 50–51). They also advocate for supplementing canonical texts that may appear on Advanced Placement exams, with popular cultural texts and postcolonial literature.

The character Huck Finn has also been interpreted as exemplifying the ways in which a reflective adolescent struggles with the complexities of morality and moral obligation in the face of powerful societal convention and social institutions (see Turiel, 2015, pg. 559–561 for a comprehensive discussion). The lesson discussed below is excerpted from a larger unit involving an in-depth discussion of both *Huckleberry Finn* and *Love Don't Live Here No More*.

Goals. This lesson engages students in a comparative analysis of the evolution of the morality of two major characters from different time periods. This engages students in constructing an understanding of how personal morality is affected by the conventions of the times and how an individual can transcend those norms through moral self-reflection. The lesson also permits students to compare their own morality with that of the characters from the novels and with the current society's conventional and moral expectations. The characters in both novels are imperfect from a moral point of view. Their imperfections allow students space within which to engage in moral evaluation and comparison with themselves as evolving moral beings. In these ways, this lesson contributes to students' development within the character system as described in Chapter 4. Finally, the lesson addresses social issues of structural racism and social class.

Procedure. Students are assigned to read *Huckleberry Finn* by Mark Twain and *Love Don't Live Here No More* by Snoop Dogg. The PBS.org resource pages also suggest companion readings, poems, and documentaries that can be used in conjunction with *Huckleberry Finn* to provide critical perspectives on the history of racism in America, Black perspectives on the novel, and the history of literary censorship (www.pbs.org/wgbh/cultureshock/teachers/huck/section1_1.html). These supplemental materials will give students a framework through which they can interpret these texts.

Questions for Discussion. The following questions are used to structure discussion of the two books. The questions are followed by letters indicating the domain addressed by the question (M = moral, C = conventional).

Huckleberry Finn

1. Huckleberry Finn and the fugitive slave Jim are both escaping society. Huck because he feels he doesn't fit in and Jim because of slavery. However, throughout the novel Huck appears to be in charge of Jim, even though Jim is a grown man and Huck a teenage boy. Why was that the case? What does this tell us about how American society was structured during the time period this story took place? (C)
2. In various places in the book, Huck is depicted as playing tricks on Jim. Can you provide some examples of where that occurs? What do you think about Huck's behaviors toward Jim in those situations? Would you say that it was okay for Huck to do those? How come? (M, C)
3. In what ways does Huck's behavior toward Jim reflect the conventions of his time period? Explain. (C)
4. Huck does not always appear to agree with the conventions of the times when it comes to his interactions with Jim. Can you identify some situations where Huck goes against the conventions of his era in his interactions with Jim? Explain how what Huck did in your examples went contrary to the conventions of the time. (C)
    a. Using the examples from your answer to the previous question, would you say that Huck was wrong or right to act the way that he did? How come? (C)
    b. How would the society of that time have been different if everyone acted toward Jim the way that Huck did in your examples? (C, M)
5. How would you evaluate Huck's moral position in terms of how he interacts with Jim? Are there things about Huck's actions that you agree with? What would they be and why? Are there things you would disagree with and why? (M)
6. Overall, how would you rate Huck Finn as a person? Explain. (Connection to "moral character.")

Ulysses (Love Don't Live Here No More)

1. Ulysses is an up-and-coming drug dealer in his community. What do you think about that? (This open question may invoke a range of moral and conventional as well as pragmatic responses.)
2. He uses a lot of the money he gains through drug dealing to help his mother and his brother. How does this affect your view of Ulysses? Does it justify his actions as a drug dealer? Why/why not? (M)
3. In what sense do the actions of Ulysses reflect the conventions of his community? Do they also reflect some of the values of the larger society? Explain. (C)

4. In what ways does Ulysses make moral choices that go counter to the conventions of his "street" culture? Can you give examples where that occurs? What do you think about those choices? (C, M)
5. Overall, how would you rate Ulysses as a person? Explain. (Connection to the "moral character.")

General issues

1. Huck Finn and Ulysses are teenagers growing up in different surroundings and in different historical periods. In each case, their behavior is influenced by the conventions of their society. What is also true about both characters is that they make choices to act in ways that go against the expected norms of behavior in order to do what they believe is the right thing in terms of how they treat others. Can you list at least one example for each character that illustrates this point? Explain how your examples illustrate this point. (C, M)
2. Both Huck and Ulysses are on their way to becoming adults. Given the choices they have made and the actions they have taken, what sort of person do you think each character will become when they grow up? For each character, do you think he will become a "good" person as an adult? Why/why not? (Coordination of morality and convention. Connection to character.)
3. Can you think of any conventions from our community or the larger society that direct young people your age to act in ways that are unfair or not in the best interest of other people? How should a person your age handle those things? What advice would you give to someone your age about how to handle those conventional expectations? (C, M; connection to character.)

Essay Playwriting Assignment. This assignment can be written in class or as a homework assignment. It is done in pairs or small groups. The teacher can decide whether or not to select some of the resulting plays to be enacted in class with follow-up discussion.

> For this assignment you are to work together as playwrights. In a stage play, we can make the impossible happen. The premise of this play is that Huck Finn and Ulysses find themselves brought together in a time warp. They are alone and in a room in a timeless setting. A voice speaks to them saying, "Young men, you have been brought here from different times to learn about each other. You will be returned to your place and time in a few hours. In the meanwhile, make yourselves comfortable and get to know each other." Write the dialogue that occurs between Huck and Ulysses.

Lesson Plans for Moral Development and Social Justice

1. In your dialogue, have your characters tell about their lives and what they believe in with regard to what they are doing.
2. Have the Huck character explain about running away with Jim and the things that have gone on. Have Huck explain about the rules and norms about race during his time period. Have Huck also tell about how he thinks about those norms and what he thinks about Jim.
3. Have Ulysses explain to Huck that he is drug dealer, and also what he is trying to do with respect to his family and the norms of the world he lives in.
4. Have each character challenge (in a friendly way) the values and lifestyle of the other person.
5. You will need to decide whether or not your characters will like each other. You will also need to decide whether or not they listen to one another's ideas.

The Use of Child Labor: Profit Optimization in Calculus

(Adapted from a lesson by Daley Stevens and Zach Levine)

This lesson helps to illustrate that addressing issues of morality should not be limited to social studies and language arts. Moral considerations are embedded in many issues covered within the sciences (e.g., climate change, the ethics of human subjects research, etc.). The following lesson illustrates how learning in mathematics may be coordinated with applications to moral problems.

Objectives. The academic goal is to develop students' capacity for solving optimization-based word problems. This particular subset of optimization problems requires the students to understand basic production formulas, derivative rules, and a conceptual understanding of where maxima occur in mathematical functions.

The developmental goal of the lesson is to challenge students' views on the implementation of child labor in production for a business. The students must consider the pragmatic profit motivation of a business with the conventional and moral domain implications of child labor. Students are also asked to consider the personal domain considerations of young adolescents' choice to work even under adverse conditions.

Lesson Summary. Optimization is a calculus topic in which students can use calculus to determine optimal quantities in a given situation. One important application of optimization is optimization of profit, in the business sector. Companies generate models for production, demand, and cost. Optimization can put these models together to figure out what level of production yields a maximum profit. Cost models can be affected by what labor force is producing the units. Older laborers with more experience tend to be paid more, while younger laborers who lack that experience are often paid minimum wage. In some circumstances, employers can even pay their employees below minimum wage, if that illegal behavior simply goes unchecked. The different scenarios with different labor forces provide different levels of maximum profit, which is what the students will examine in this lesson.

Procedure. The teacher will start the lesson by reviewing what optimization is in general, helping students recall that they need to derive the quantity they are looking to optimize and set that derivative equal to zero. The teacher should remind the students that revenue is price multiplied by demand, and that profit is revenue minus cost. The following problem should then be presented, along with an indicator that students may use a calculator.

> Suppose a company, Acme's Knickknacks, produces x knickknacks per month with a demand curve of $p(x) = 3000 - x$, where p is the price and x is the demand. Acme employs laborers at or above the age of 18 in their factories, and they earn roughly double the minimum wage in California. Under current conditions, the cost of producing x knickknacks per month is given by $C(x) = 1000 + 1000x + x2$.
>
> a. What level of production maximizes Acme's profit per month? What is that profit?

The students are given 5 minutes to work through this on their own, and then the teacher takes 3 minutes to walk through the solution. The solution is 500 knickknacks produced per month, which generates $499,000 of profit per month. The teacher will then describe the next part of the problem, which changes the labor situation.

> Acme's Head of Operations, Nicholas Nack, discovers that there are enough 13-year-old children to replace his current staff without affecting production quality or capability. The 13-year-olds get paid substantially less than the current employees, as they would only receive minimum wage working at Acme. With this change, the new cost function is $C1(x) = 1000 + 1000x$.
>
> b. What is the new level of production that maximizes the profit per month? What is that profit?

The students are given 5 minutes to work through this on their own, and then the teacher takes 2 minutes to walk through the solution. The solution is 1000 knickknacks produced per month, which generates $999,000 of profit per month. The teacher will then describe the last part of the problem, which changes the wage situation of the new laborers.

> Seeing the potential profit per month skyrocket in the future, Nicholas Nack focuses on cutting costs even further. Realizing that 13-year-olds might not know about minimum wage laws in California, Nack decides if he offers 13-year-old employees half of minimum wage as their wage, he will cut costs dramatically. He figures the 13-year-olds will be happy to get any money at all. Now the cost function is $C2(x) = 1000 + 500x$.
>
> c. What is the new level of production that maximizes the profit per month? What is that profit?

The students are given 4 minutes to work through this on their own, and then the teacher takes 1 minute to walk through the solution. The solution is 1,250 knickknacks produced per month, which generates $1,561,500 of profit per month. The teacher should now get into the follow-up questions, which get at the moral and conventional problems this question poses.

Follow-Up Questions. (The questions are followed by letters indicating the domain addressed by the question: M = moral, C = conventional, P = Personal):

1. Which scenario (a, b, or c) would be the optimal scenario for the business itself?
2. Imagine you are the CEO of this company. Which of the scenarios would you choose to enact and why?
3. Fourteen-year-olds can work with a permit in California. With that in mind, do you think having 13-year-olds work at Acme is wrong or right? Why? What if it was 10-year-olds instead of 13-year-olds? (M)
4. Does scenario C appear fair to the 13-year-old workers? What makes it fair or unfair? What do you think about paying them below minimum wage? (M)
5. What do you think of Nack's assumption that 13-year-olds will be happy to make any money at all, even if it is below minimum wage? (P) Would you have felt this way when you were 13? (P) Does one have the right to work for a lower wage if that is their choice? Explain. (P)
6. Very often, companies, such as Nike and Zara, outsource labor to regions, such as Bangladesh, where laborers are paid next to nothing, and this cuts costs for these companies. Why do you think this happens so frequently? (C, P) Do you think these companies

consider moral context when outsourcing labor? (M) Or does the pursuit of profit outweigh any moral considerations for them? Do you think companies should focus on profits or weigh the moral impact of their policies? Why? (M)

7. As a class, look up a definition of the word: *exploitation.* For example, teachers could use this definition from the United Nations Refugee Agency: *Exploitation is the abuse of a child where some form of remuneration is involved or whereby the perpetrators benefit in some manner—monetarily, socially, politically, etc. Exploitation constitutes a form of coercion and violence, detrimental to the child's physical and mental health, development, and education.* Teachers could also have students explore a historical timeline showing how rights of children have evolved over the last hundred years (www.unicef.org/child-rights-convention/history-child-rights). Are the labor policies at Acme an example of exploitation? What are some other examples of exploitation you can think of? (M)

Reflective Homework. Consider the following series of questions, and write down a paragraph explanation for each. Try to put yourselves in the shoes of the laborers in question:

1. If a 13-year-old wants to work for Acme, should they be allowed to? (C, M, P) Take this on a case-by-case basis: Case 1 is a 13-year-old who wants to make some money so they can keep up their baseball card collection, and case 2 is a 13-year-old who is desperately trying to help his family members pay medical bills. (P, M)
2. What justifications might Nicholas Nack make about paying 13-year-olds below minimum wage? How might you refute these justifications? (P, M)
3. In scenario A, Acme makes around $6 million in profit in a year. In scenario B, the profit is $12 million, and in scenario C, the profit is about $18.7 million in a year. Does how much profit the company generates influence your feeling on paying 13-year-olds below minimum wage? (P, M)
4. The popular restaurant Chipotle was recently fined $1.4 million by the state of Massachusetts for violating child labor laws. Read this article and identify the arguments made by Chipotle for allowing 16-year-olds to work. Have you had experience applying for jobs? How does this make you feel about applying for a job at Chipotle? (www.nytimes.com/2020/01/28/business/chipotle-child-labor-laws-massachusetts.html).

CHAPTER 10

Critical Digital Pedagogy as a Component of Moral Education for Social Justice

As outlined in Chapter 8, the goals of the moral education for social justice framework include stimulating domain reasoning and domain coordination; engaging in praxis, a cycle of investigation, action, and reflection; and finally, developing a sense of oneself as a moral agent. Previous research in domain-based moral education has sought to accomplish these goals through face-to-face dialogue, discourse, and handwritten reflections. In this chapter, we expand these practices to include media production as a practice that can stimulate the same type of reasoning. This argument has two components: (a) throughout the process of engaging critically with media, teachers can facilitate peer dialogue and discourse about the production process, which can stimulate domain reasoning; and (b) media products themselves such as podcasts films, songs, and so on require producers to design a "dialogue" in the sense that producers collect multiple voices and media elements in order to construct a narrative—juxtaposing opposite viewpoints, sometimes amplifying an argument with a powerful visual or background music track. Producers can engage in transactive reasoning, the process of operating on other arguments, in a way that is similar to what they might do during face-to-face dialogue.

Engaging in media production in classroom contexts has long been a practice of critical pedagogues (Duncan-Andrade & Morrell, 2008; Mahiri, 2011). This chapter outlines Mirra and colleagues' framework for critical digital literacy (Mirra et al., 2018) as foundational to digital pedagogy, and explores the alignment between producing critical media and social and moral development. We will outline ways in which moral decisionmaking, domain coordination, and moral agency show up in media production, as young media makers pursue personal and social justice storytelling projects. Several examples are drawn from YR Media (formerly Youth Radio), a nonprofit media organization in Oakland, California, where Ilten-Gee worked as a youth media producer for five years.

WHAT IS CRITICAL DIGITAL PEDAGOGY?

As we have stated (Nucci, 2009), our position is that character and moral education frameworks that teach students social–emotional skills and virtues of kindness and tolerance are *not enough*. Westheimer and Kahne (2004) call this type of character education a "personally responsible citizen" model, where students are taught "good behaviors" like picking up trash and obeying laws (p. 241). We have argued that these frameworks do not foster young people who are willing and able to challenge systems of power and to go beyond being conventionally "nice" to becoming advocates for justice.

The same challenge has been raised in the sphere of media education. Media, as Stack and Kelly (2006) remind us, can refer to mediums of communication like radio and television, as well as the texts produced within these mediums (television dramas, podcasts, apps, video games). As new mediums and types of texts worked their way into education systems and classrooms, there was a strong tendency to focus on the dangers of exposure to inappropriate content, cyberbullying, identity theft, and so on, which led to what Kellner and Share (2007) termed a fear-based, "protectionist approach" to media education. Vakil (2018) likewise describes ways in which the ethics portion of computer science courses is often largely framed in terms of individual choices and dilemmas, for example, whether to download music illegally in order to support your family. He writes, "Rather, the Internet is presented as ahistorical, apolitical, and neutral, a preferred state that can be maintained if only students make 'informed' and 'appropriate' decisions" (p. 32).

In contrast, the critical media literacy movement (Kellner & Share, 2007) draws on critical pedagogy to urge media education beyond establishing digital codes of conduct and encouraging cautionary Internet usage, to embracing societal investigation, inquiry, problematization, and production.

Many cultural and media scholars point to the work of Marxist theorist Antonio Gramsci and his notion of popular culture as a site of conflict between dominant and oppositional ideologies. Today, popular culture is sustained and created through our experiences with media; we share, publish, reblog, adopt, imitate, and critique what we see on the Internet, television, podcasts, phone apps, video games, and so on. Critical media literacy argues that students should engage with media (including mainstream news media, popular media such as movies, music videos, YouTube channels, advertising, social media campaigns, etc.) specifically to unearth hidden commercial messaging and implicit prejudices within the media we consume. Critical media literacy entails being able to recognize and identify how whiteness, heterosexuality, maleness, able-bodied-ness, and so on are perpetuated as "normal," and develop the capacity to make informed decisions as consumers and citizens. Drawing on Freire's notion of praxis, Kellner and Share (2007) advocated not only for in-depth analysis of media texts, but also active construction and generation of media that disrupted dominant narratives. Mirra et al.'s (2018) four components of critical digital literacy expand on Kellner and Share's theorization and lead us into the realm of digital invention. These four components are outlined here.

Critical Digital Consumption

Critical digital consumption refers to bringing a critical lens to the design, distribution strategies, motivations, and underlying assumptions that are embedded in mass media and popular media, to a) discern fact from fiction, b) avoid dangerous situations, and c) wake up to the ways in which powerful societal forces use media to normalize, perpetuate, and condemn behaviors, appearances, and attitudes. There is a global interest in helping people identify misinformation and become critical consumers and producers of media. And real dangers exist for young people—online hate groups recruit through social media and masquerade as convincing sources of opinion (Kelly & Arnold, 2015; Stack, 2015), and the lines between "fact and fake" on the Internet are often difficult to discern. Critical digital consumption also applies to the ability to question media texts and recognize media artifacts for the human constructions that they are. According to Mirra and colleagues (2018), this requires facilitating student awareness of both genre and theory. In terms of genre, students and teachers should think about the ways in which reading a news article is different than watching a YouTube video or interacting with a digital game. These genres have different affordances and histories, and require different tools and literacies. As Mahiri explained (2011):

> The photography, digital storytelling, blog, and podcast projects were all created by converging an array of multimodal texts as well as written texts. These convergences required the students to understand and appreciate complex, semiotic interrelations across multiple sign systems. Their learning resources, styles, and interests were aided by the multimodal nature and the material intelligence of the digital media that facilitated students actively and critically probing for and producing knowledge and meaning about the world. (p. 48)

The second part of critical digital consumption is theory. Students need access to critical theories in order to frame their analysis of media artifacts. For example, students could read an introduction to feminist theory as it pertains to popular media. Then teachers could introduce students to the Bechdel test (en.wikipedia.org/wiki/Bechdel_test): A movie passes the Bechdel test if it shows two women talking to each other about something other than a man. As a class, students could watch out for these criteria in various movies as they collect data to make an argument about sexism in film. As a follow-up, teachers could introduce critiques of the Bechdel test, which point out that even if a movie "passes the test," it may still feature women who are stereotyped or objectified (Waletzko, 2017: www.huffpost.com/entry/why-the-bechdel-test-fails-feminism_b_7139510).

In addition to critical frameworks, it can be beneficial to bring in alternative, independent news sources to demonstrate alternative journalistic coverage. Mediasmarts.ca is an example of a classroom resource that aims to help educators adopt critical digital consumption practices into their classrooms. For example, there are lesson plans about body image in music, film, and TV, and the ways in which violence is marketed to young people. Stack and Kelly (2006) write, "The media are the primary vehicle through which we come to know ourselves and others. . . . Education plays a central role in providing people with the ability to denaturalize everyday media narratives" (p. 20).

Domain Reasoning Connection. Engaging students in this kind of media consumption activates a very particular domain reasoning conflict: our conventional perceptions of normal media depictions (including representations of body type, gender, skin tone, wealth, archetypes, etc.) vs. the moral concerns of inequity, stereotyping, identity erasure, and shaming embedded in mainstream news media, popular media, advertising, social media, and so on. This conflict requires students to perceive categories that characters are placed into and recognize the implications for their own identity. Mirra and colleagues write, "A critical digital media consumption approach is needed to help students deconstruct the tropes that are used to encourage individuals to identify with particular communities (gendered, raced, etc.) and connect particular products to these identities (Mirra et al., 2018, p. 16). For example, the television show *Cops*, which was pulled from the air in the spring of 2020 after protests over the killing of George Floyd in Minnesota by a police officer, was found to have portrayed African American and Hispanic men as violent offenders at disproportionate rates to their actual crime statistics, and portraying officers as almost always White and male (Monk-Turner et al., 2007). As a class and then in small groups, students could apply critical media lenses to episodes of this show, and consider the messaging about men of color, law enforcement, and why these messages are problematic. For example, Doyle describes how the blurring of civilians' faces as they are arrested by cops in the show dehumanizes them in relation to the police officers, whom you see in their kitchens making tea or with their families (1998).

In this discussion, students will draw on conventional concerns related to their understanding of how information is circulated in society, and how social groups and law enforcement systems operate successfully and unsuccessfully. They will consider genre affordances and design choices, such as blurring characters' faces. They will also draw on moral understandings of fairness and equality of representation, as well as historical and present-day moral harm enacted by police toward marginalized communities. Teachers could facilitate discussions around questions like: What about the cops' behavior surprises you? How do you know who the "good guys" are in this show? Are there aspects of the filming and framing that make an argument for the reader about good vs. bad? In the moral domain, teachers could facilitate discussions around questions like: Are the supposed perpetrators in the show treated fairly? Are both perspectives portrayed equally? Do the instances of force appear justified? Do the supposed perpetrators have a reason to fear the police? To combine moral and conventional concerns, teachers could pose the questions: If someone believes that a law is unfair, should the person obey the law? What if disobeying puts them in danger?

Critical Digital Production

The second component of critical digital literacy is *critical digital production*. Mirra and colleagues (2018) stress that critical digital production is *not* translating written essays into digital ones. It involves developing a new understanding of the affordances of different modes, or systems of communication (Kress, 2003). For example, a digital producer can make use of elements like silence, music, volume, and vocal inflection to design and communicate their message in a podcast in ways they cannot in a written essay. Helping students understand the affordances, limitations, and conventions of a particular digital genre will facilitate intentional digital production.

Production also draws on students' aesthetic sensibilities and technical know-how to design and produce meaningful stories. "A critical digital production involves conceptualizing radical counter-narratives and having the tools and the ability to create these counter-narratives by leveraging the most advanced digital technologies" (Mirra et al., 2018). These counter-narratives will emerge from interaction with critical theories (as mentioned above), and exposure to alternative, independent media sources.

An example of counter-narratives occurred on the platform Twitter in 2014, after 18-year-old Michael Brown was gunned down by a police officer in Ferguson, North Carolina. As the events were being reported, many noticed which photos of Michael Brown were used by mainstream media outlets to report on the events; some used a picture of Brown on his porch making a hand signal and labeled him a "criminal" or a "thug," and others used a picture of him in graduation attire. This sparked the #iftheygunnedmedown campaign, where Twitter users posted a picture of themselves in army uniforms, graduation gowns, and so on side by side with a photo of themselves goofing around. Each tweet was a recognition of the fact that Black victims are portrayed in the media as violent and disruptive instead of accomplished, talented, compassionate. "By posting side-by-side photos and challenging the mainstream media practices, those who engaged in the #iftheygunnedmedown Twitter movement did, in fact, manipulate their own codes, signs, and symbols (through language and photographic representation), and found agency in challenging these common practices" (Jackson, 2016). In terms of moral reasoning, these Twitter users identified structural racism in the media, and were able to use a social media platform to visually create counter-narratives of themselves through imagery. In juxtaposing two dichotomous images of themselves, they reinforced the larger idea that humans are more complex than one moment could ever capture. In the classroom, teachers could use examples of these Twitter posts to facilitate discussions around how students feel they are perceived by others, and how people like them are perceived through the lens of the media.

Ilten-Gee (2020) conducted research that examined 10th-grade students' reasoning about personal conflicts as they transformed handwritten narratives into digital podcasts. The very nature of this study asked students to engage in transmediation (Mills, 2011), moving from written to auditory modes of communication, and therefore risked students engaging in simple translation without fully understanding the genre affordances of the digital podcast. In fact, some participants did simply read their handwritten narratives into a microphone, with little more than a backing track of music to complement their script. Others, however, took advantage of multiple perspectives, scenes, layered voices, humor, existing media clips, sound effects, and the conversational tone of a podcast to transform their stories entirely. For example, Emory (pseudonym) created a podcast about her father, who she believed was homophobic. We hear the following conversation between them:

> *Emory:* Do you know what LGBTQ stands for?
> *Father:* I think so . . . lesbian, gay . . . what?
> *Emory:* B
> *Father:* Bi
> *Emory:* T

And then Emory's father's voice fades into the background, and Emory speaks over him and says, "This is my dad." Emory cleverly uses the affordances of the podcast to portray her father as ignorant, and his views as literally being "behind" the times, as his voice is underneath her own.

Gwen (pseudonym), a 10th-grade participant in this study, made her podcast about the following conflict: "Everyone thinks I'm gay because I have short hair." This is a similar topic to the lesson example in Chapter 9 that considers why we use gendered pronouns and titles, and how this practice requires us to make assumptions about others' identities. Gwen gathered a group of close friends and interviewed them about whether other people have made incorrect assumptions about their sexuality. She asks them, "What does gay look like?" and "What does straight look like?" We hear her friends giggle and stumble in their interviews over answers like, "Straight is like more manly—like not weak and just typical" or "Like rainbows, everything jumping around and being happy. Gay is another word for being happy but we don't see it that way anymore." After these interviews, Gwen reflects, "It got me thinking about how much harder it was to answer what gay looks like. But when they were answering what straight looks like it was so much easier." Her realization implied an understanding of the ways in which conventional forms of dress, appearance, hairstyle become normalized.

Critical digital production can involve having uncomfortable social interactions—whether they are conversations about stereotypes, sexuality, gentrification, identity, or racial injustice. These social interactions heighten the emotional connection producers have to the story they end up telling.

Domain Reasoning Connection. Podcasts are a popular format for critical storytelling (Mahiri, 2011; Soep & Chavez, 2010; Wilson et al., 2012). The four phases of critical podcast production have been theorized to contribute to key principles of critical moral reasoning (Ilten-Gee, in press). These phases are: critical questioning, critical connections, critical construction, and critical conclusion. During the questioning phase, producers are interviewing sources and conducting research. This phase opens up opportunities for living out principles of heteroglossia and a dialogic mindset (Bakhtin, 1981), and encouraging producers to seek out experts and diverse sources, and find corroborating facts that will strengthen their narrative arc. Conducting interviews is an opportunity to cultivate responsive engagement (mentioned in Chapter 8), inviting different viewpoints and remaining open to new information. While not the traditional small-group format of discourse, this interviewing process requires students to operate on their interviewee's reasoning in order to ask follow-up questions and figure out whether they agree or disagree. Soep and Chavez (2010) write that young journalists at YR Media "are not neutral interrogators, but engaged conversationalists."

During the critical connections phase, students have the opportunity to connect their own issue or story with larger societal struggles or narratives that may give their own experiences new meaning or context. This is a chance to begin thinking structurally, instead of interpersonally. They may generate new questions about the roots of their struggle in their own community, or previous iterations of this struggle or conflict. During the critical construction phase, producers have the opportunity to engage in transactive reasoning as they determine what points of view are emerging in their research and in their interviews. Who agrees or disagrees with whom? As the narrator/producer, where do their own opinions fit in? Students have the opportunity to be the architect of a conversation or dialogue between multiple voices/perspectives, organizing them in ways to contradict, juxtapose, affirm, and question each other, creating an argument or arc to frame their topic. This type of transactive reasoning and discourse has been linked with increases in domain coordination (Nucci et al., 2015). Finally, the critical conclusion phase requires producers to coordinate multiple concerns—possibly from multiple domains of reasoning—to take a stance on their issue. This is where producers claim narrative moral agency (Pasupathi & Wainryb, 2010) by reconciling their beliefs, emotions, actions, and new information in a new way. They have a new chance to take a stance on what is good and right.

This cycle of podcasting praxis is inspired by a Freirian idea of praxis, where media makers integrate critical and political ideas of equity, harm, fairness, and justice at each step, and are willing to reevaluate old ideas in favor of new information. The end goal is action—in this case, producing a piece of media and distributing it. Soep points out, however, that when it comes to media production, "Rarely does the process march forward without lots of stopping short, reversing course and circling back to start again" (2014). Teachers should be prepared for a fluid, alinear unit, encouraging multiple versions of media products. Previous domain-based moral education research shows that reflection after-the-fact, with peers and teachers, can help students solidify their points of view, account for other perspectives, and clarify their narratives. We would recommend the same thing with critical digital pedagogy and allow opportunities for classroom gallery walks, where students listen, watch, and experience their classmates' work, and then have time to discuss it in meaningful ways.

Critical Digital Distribution

Recognizing the impact of one's media products and texts on an audience is an opportunity for carrying out social justice, as well as critical moral reasoning. Mirra and colleagues (2018) write that this component of critical digital literacy enables the possibility of authentic engagement with people outside one's own community and sphere. For example, the reporters at YR Media regularly produce videos and podcasts for local and national radio and Internet audiences. They receive comments from strangers who are both sympathetic to and disagree with the youth producers (Soep, 2014). Soep has written extensively on wrestling with audience interaction in youth media production. She has seen young people be targets of discriminatory comments by audience members who do not value youth perspectives on the radio. In an ideal world, the Internet would create a dialogic space for producers and audiences to argue their differences. "The problem with trusting this logic is what happens when there's a significant gap between the author's social values and identities (what Pendarvis calls 'my demographic') and the 'community' he or she reaches through any given media outlet"

(Soep, 2014, p. 179). This is of course something that classroom teachers will also have to consider—balancing the benefits and downsides of letting students have authentic arguments with strangers on the Internet. Young people already do this on social media platforms to some extent, but on those platforms, one often has the ability to curate a specific audience of friends and like-minded individuals.

At YR Media, a lot of time is spent thinking about the future impact of media products. "Under collegial pedagogy, young people work with adults to imagine a life for their work outside themselves and their own personal self-interests, holding themselves and one another accountable to the immediate and longer-term impact of their joint productions (Soep & Chavez, 2010, p. 69). This imaginative exercise is a driving force behind the digital editorial process, guiding reporters and producers to represent multiple perspectives, anticipate critiques, and fact-check their research. It forces them to learn about their potential audiences, in order to communicate across groups, and consider the audience they care about reaching most.

Curwood and Gibbons (2009) conducted research on the ways in which young people create multimodal counter-narratives to construct their identities. They mention a young man who created a digital poem in which he confronted his classmates through humor and comic relief for bullying him. The authors wrote, "We are able to show how he resists racism and homophobia while concomitantly opening a dialogic space with his audience. Digital media production can be a way for youth to explore the master narratives around them, to push back against them, and to tell stories of their lives in an effort to (re)present their identities" (Curwood & Gibbons, 2009, p. 74). Reflecting on the audience for one's media product will affect one's design choices and force producers to think about how their story will be received.

Domain Reasoning Connection. As discussed in Chapter 8, domain-based moral reasoning relies on discourse and dialogue for exposing us to new information and perspectives. Philosopher Anthony Laden argues that reasoning is not an individual activity but a social one (2012). In envisioning a potential audience for one's media products and also attempting to reach that audience, digital producers are asking themselves social conventional questions like, "What platforms are used for what type of media, and why? What design choices am I making that will alienate or attract particular audiences?" They will also engage moral questions like, "What group of people is most likely to have access to my digital text? Is my text presenting a fair version of this story? What harm and what good does my digital text have the potential to do to others? To myself?" And they will entertain personal questions, such as, "How does this story reflect my true self? Does the takeaway of this media product align with how I view myself?" Thus, the distribution component of critical digital production has the potential to stimulate coordinated reasoning among young producers.

Teachers could use the following template with students to stimulate this questioning:

- Who do I want to reach with this product?
- What features of my product will make it easy for people to find? Understand? What features will make it difficult?
- Who will agree or disagree with the argument I am making in my product?
- How might I tell this story differently on a different media platform?
- Will listeners/viewers/readers think this story is fairly presented? Why/why not?

Students could listen/watch/read each other's media products and then discuss these questions in small groups. After discussing their media product with their peers, they might decide to edit or make changes to their media product and expand on an alternative perspective, or include additional sound/visual elements to make their argument more powerful.

Critical Digital Invention

Mirra and colleagues argue that the above three components are not enough—that young media producers come to envision themselves as "not simply masterful and critical consumers, producers, and distributors of digital literacies, but as inventors with the competencies and dispositions needed to dream up digital forms of expression that adults cannot yet imagine" (Mirra et al., 2018, p. 17). This goal encourages teachers to facilitate young people flinging wide the curtain and peering behind the user interfaces that they interact with, to see *who* is creating popular technologies. In considering the *who*, producers can also consider who is *left out* of key decisions. What corporate or government entities fund these platforms? What identities and social positionalities are represented on the boards of technology and communication companies? What algorithms are in place to make decisions about what content is shared widely, what advertisements you see, and what possibilities you have as a digital producer? These questions can lead to considering great divides in the representation of women, LGBTQ people, Black and Brown people in these spaces.

Mirra and colleagues (2018) argue that digital invention must be about equity and encouraging young producers who may not see themselves represented in these worlds, to envision themselves as the creators of next-generation technologies. This means critically analyzing one's own identity and in relation to the world of media and technology. The organization Black Girls Code, for example, provides programming and coding instruction through after-school programs, summer camps, and hackathons with the explicit purpose of increasing the number of women of color in technology jobs, leadership roles, and STEM fields. Mahiri and Sims (2016) used a critical pedagogy approach to develop and study an out-of-school program for male African American middle school students to increase their identification with STEM, their competencies in STEM, and their ability to engage in socially just applications of STEM. Among other things, students built mobile apps to teach others about environmental sustainability. Throughout the program, Sims and Mahiri engaged students in inquiry and discussion about being an African American male in the United States. "So, where STEM had initially been neutral and axiomatic, the students began to ask more critical questions by applying the tools of rhetorical analysis to their STEM learning. They wanted to know: STEM for what, and, STEM for whom?" (p. 67).

Similarly, Vakil writes about a justice-centered approach to achieving equity in computer science education—a learning environment where young people endeavor to understand existing technologies and invent new ones. He advocates for learning activities that focus on the rights and freedoms that come with computer science expertise, critiquing abuses of technological power and focusing on how computer science can be used to achieve social justice goals (2018). "In addition to learning the underlying mathematics and technical features of specific cryptographic protocols, critical educators might also explore the complicated social and political history of cryptography, including its early use by Nazi Germany during World War II (Hill, 2008)" (Vakil, 2018, pp. 38–39).

In these approaches, young people take the critical lenses they have utilized for critical digital consumption, production, and distribution, and turn them toward the technologies and platforms themselves, and to their own social and political identity as a media producer.

Domain Reasoning Connection. There is a specific multidomain conflict embedded in the question of who is able to innovate new technologies. There are the moral concerns of equity and who has traditionally been excluded from high-powered tech jobs. Additionally, microaggressions or stereotype threats (a form of moral harm) from teachers, classmates, and instructional materials in middle school and high school environments are powerful forces of dissuasion for many interested in tech fields. There are the social conventional concerns of what kinds of jobs your family and community expect you to seek out. Finally, there are the personal concerns of developing your own identity. Helping young people wrestle with the epic conflict "what can you imagine yourself to be?" will stimulate critical moral reasoning and contribute to an individual's conception of their moral self.

EXAMPLES OF CRITICAL DIGITAL LITERACY

Production

In Chapter 9, we discussed integrating Colin Kaepernick's "take a knee" protest as an extension to a set of learning activities around civil rights and the use of violence. This set of learning experiences could launch digital media extensions in the classroom. In 2017, YR Media reporter Sasha Armbrester produced a radio piece that aired on National Public Radio's *All Things Considered*, called "Why I Take a Knee" (Armbrester, 2017). She begins this radio piece by telling us about her 16-year-old classmate Teana Boston, who had recently created a remix of "The Star-Spangled Banner" because she had come to realize that America was not the "land of the free" for everyone. We hear some of Boston's new lyrics in the radio piece, including "it happens everyday, lives are taken away." Creating a musical remix is in itself critical digital production. Boston used the frame of the national anthem to form a new message of resistance, in a contemporary context. This layering and interweaving of meanings, beats, and phrases demonstrates Boston's power as a creator and her ability to engage in critical media literacy and digital production.

Armbrester tells the audience that as a high school cheerleader, she is also protesting by taking a knee at sports games. She says that in her ethnic studies class they learned about the shooting of Trayvon Martin, and she was inspired by Colin Kaepernick's actions on the field. "We saw an opportunity to call attention to racial injustice. We began taking a knee, too, but the football players remain standing," she said. Armbrester interviews football players, who, when asked why they kept standing, responded, "I guess it's like, you're just supposed to do it." She even describes getting grief from the coaches. But it was important for Armbrester to take this action. She concludes by saying:

> I think us taking a knee came as a surprise to people, because a lot of people in the school think of cheerleaders as airheads. They think we're oblivious to what's going on in the world. But they're wrong. I got into cheerleading because I wanted to be a role model at my high school. I didn't expect it to turn into this very public protest. But the truth is, I experience racism. I don't want to be treated like a criminal when I walk into a store. I don't want to worry about my younger brother and his safety. So here was this small thing I could do to call attention to racism, and not let it go by. I questioned how I fit into the school and the sport. I decided to take a knee.

This example demonstrates critical digital production, complicated critical moral reasoning, and critical consciousness. Armbrester investigated and conducted inquiry into the Black struggle in America in her ethnic studies class. Questions, contradictions, and resonances were appearing in her daily practices, like singing the national anthem at her sports games. She confronted norms and social conventions as she pursued this investigation: coaches and football players who tell her, *this is the way things are done*. She included these voices in her podcast, engaging in heteroglossia and creating a transactive dialogue with her sources. At the end, she has the chance to take a stance that builds narrative moral agency (Pasupathi & Wainryb, 2010) by reconciling her emotions, beliefs, and actions in a new way. When she says, "But the truth is . . . ," Armbrester is able to bring together multiple considerations: moral ones of experiencing racism and the safety of her brother, conventional ones about the way cheerleaders are supposed to act and behave, and personal ones about her decision to become an activist. This digital piece is now something that Armbrester can share with her own audiences, and that was distributed to a national audience to start even bigger conversations.

Invention

A prime example of critical digital invention comes from Youth Radio Interactive (YRI), a team of young people that works alongside professional journalists, researchers, and developers within YR Media. This team develops interactive tools (apps, websites, multimodal platforms) that allow them to contribute to their social and civic worlds. Lee and Soep (2018) write about a framework of *critical computational literacy* to describe the learning at the heart of this invention process, which includes in their words, "engineering and computational thinking on the one hand, and narrative production and critical pedagogy on the other" (p. 481).

The YRI team at YR Media created an interactive media event commemorating the 60th anniversary of the racial integration of Little Rock Central High School in Arkansas, when nine Black teenagers enrolled at Central High after the ruling of *Brown v. Board of Education*. This digital piece was part of Central High's Civil Rights Memory Project, in which the school solicited youth media projects from all over the country reflecting on this historic moment. YRI decided to host a Twitter event and live tweet the events of that day in September 1957 when the "Little Rock Nine" entered Central High and faced violent protests. This project entailed creating an aesthetically appealing landing page to promote the event.

Lee and Soep (2018) explained that YRI artist "D" wanted to create color portraits (not black-and-white) of each of the nine students for the landing page, to make the graphics look like the event was taking place today instead of in the past. However, D only had black-and-white photos to work with, and the quality was poor. After some research, D and his team discovered that most cameras were not originally designed to pick up dark skin tones. "Traditional photographic technologies were not made to record black skin: narrow ranges of film emulsions were calibrated for white skin; light meters underexposed dark skin; and Kodak's smaller film-developing units or Shirley cards, named after the white model, standardized her whiteness as 'normal' (Cole, 2015)" (Lee & Soep, 2018). This is a complex history lesson to learn; not only was there overt racism in the 1950s, but even household devices were designed to exclude people with dark skin. This is certainly a moment for critical consciousness building, and awakening sensitivities to systemic racism. It was important to D that the portraits were nuanced in skin tone, so he created a "pigmentation scale" from the black-and-white photos he had, and then found contemporary photos of each person to upload into Photoshop and use for reference as he customized the skin tone of each portrait. As Lee and Soep point out, this is an example of bringing a political awareness of the importance of representation to bear on the process of designing and engineering new media texts and tools.

In this chapter, we have scraped the surface of how critical digital consumption, production, distribution, and invention can amplify and complement social and moral development by introducing complex conflicts like equality of representation, audience reactions, and equity in the tech world. In digital production, young people move through a cycle of praxis that often involves in-depth research and interviewing, design, and taking a stance on an issue or topic. These phases present opportunities to engage in heteroglossia, transactive thinking and dialogue, engaged reasoning, and narrative moral agency. However, in order for digital pedagogy to become *critical* digital pedagogy, the experience has to involve a process of critical investigation into historical, political, and societal inequalities, as well as an understanding of the affordances and limitations of the particular technology to be used. Soep and Chavez (2010) wrote about the ways in which media allows literacies to converge, in a framework they call *converged literacies*. They write, "Converged literacy is an ability to make and understand boundary-crossing and convention-breaking texts; means knowing how to draw and leverage public interest in the stories you want to tell; and entails the material and imaginative resources to claim and exercise your right to use media to promote justice" (p. 24). This is how we hope moral educators for social justice will consider the role of media and digital literacy in their classrooms—to start conversations about structural inequalities, generate productive counter-narratives that challenge current representations, distribute these products in the name of achieving justice, and claiming agency as digital makers and inventors.

CHAPTER 11

Integrating Moral Education Within the Cycle of Praxis

with Dr. Johari Harris, University of Virginia

In this chapter, we extend the discussion connecting moral education with critical pedagogy to include other forms of community-based action beyond the production of digital media. At the core of critical pedagogy is the concept of praxis, the process by which teachers and students commit to education that leads to action and reflection on that action. This process has five stages: (1) Identify a problem, (2) Analyze the problem, (3) Create a plan of action to address the problem, (4) Implement the plan of action, (5) Analyze and evaluate the action (Duncan-Andrade & Morrell, 2008). We propose opening the cycle of praxis to incorporate stimulating domain reasoning and domain coordination at the onset of the identification and analysis of the problem, and again as an integral part of reflection at the completion of an action project. The modified cycle of praxis incorporating attention to moral development is as follows:

1. Identify a problem.
2. Analyze the problem; engage in transactive, domain-based moral discourse central to the problem.
3. Create a plan of action to address the problem.
4. Implement the plan of action.
5. Analyze and evaluate the action; engage in transactive moral discourse informed by the action; reflect on the impact of the action on sense of self and moral agency.

An action project moves the process of education from the classroom to the community and back again. In so doing, the educative process is grounded in the students' own reality, and not limited to the official canon. For students who have been exposed to trauma, violence, or circumstances such as poverty that lead to chronic stress, taking action can function as a healing practice, according to critical trauma researcher Shawn Ginwright. "By taking action (e.g., school walkouts, organizing a peace march, or promoting access to healthy foods), it builds a sense of power and control over their lives. Research has demonstrated that building this sense of power and control among traumatized groups is perhaps one of the most significant features in restoring holistic well-being" (Ginwright, 2018). Integrating domain-based moral discourse (what we have referred to as engaged reasoning) within the cycle of praxis deepens the level of moral analysis students bring to their reflection on the social conventions and social structures that sustain social inequalities. Such discourse also merges individual moral development with the shared construction of moral positions. As we discussed in Chapter 4, this dialogic approach to the social world is an essential element in the development of mature moral character that goes beyond basic moral wellness promoted by standard SEL and traditional character education. Including a reflective component at the onset and at the conclusion of the action is key to deepening the student experience as a meaningful transformative event, rather than a one-off activity (Youniss et al., 2001). Finally, engagement in the cycle of praxis contributes toward students' civic engagement and commitment to democratic society (Westheimer & Kahne, 2004).

There are three basic ways in which teachers can approach engaging students in an action project linked with moral education. The first is to build from the domain-based moral discourse emerging from a lesson in the regular academic curriculum to include an action project. The second is to offer students an array of options from which to select a topic for a group action project. In this second approach, the teacher engages students in identifying the moral, societal, and personal domain aspects that may be present in the particular topic area and guides the students to construct a domain-based discourse as the first step in the analysis of the problem. The third is to construct an action project in response to an emergent event in the community.

EXTENDING CURRICULUM-BASED MORAL LESSONS TO INCLUDE AN ACTION PROJECT

In many school systems, the curriculum is mandated by the state. In those contexts, a strategy that teachers can take is to extend domain-based moral lessons within the academic curriculum to include an action project following the principles of the cycle of praxis. This will extend the time spent on a given lesson or unit, but will have the educational payoff of connecting the mandated curriculum with the social lives and experiences of the students. Several of the lessons described in Chapter 9 can be modified to fit the cycle of praxis. For example, the high school calculus lesson examining the use of child labor can be expanded into a deeper exploration of unfair labor practices that are directly associated with the production of products consumed by American teens. This could lead to action projects directed at informing fellow students and local merchants of products from companies that engage in "fair trade" practices and those that engage in the exploitation of their workers. (A version of an action project based on this topic is presented in Nucci, 2009, pp. 179–181.)

What we will turn to now are detailed examples of action projects that illustrate the entire cycle of praxis embedded within units rather than individual lessons. The first is from a lesson designed for 1st- and 2nd-graders to illustrate how this can be accomplished with young elementary school children. The second is adapted from a unit for middle school civics developed by the University of Virginia "Educating for Democracy" project. This unit examines the legacy of racism and oppression against Black Americans, and highlights movements of resistance from the 1960s and 1970s, such as SNCC, leading up to present-day movements including Black Lives Matter. The action project emerges from discussion of the issues related to those outlined in Chapter 9 in the lesson addressing the nonviolent protest of Colin Kaepernick in response to police violence and the Black Lives Matter movement.

Chicano Blowouts of 1968

(Lesson created by Maria Ramos Rojas, Los Angeles Unified School District)

This unit, designed by Los Angeles elementary teacher Maria Ramos Rojas, introduces students to the history of discrimination against Mexican Americans by highlighting a series of youth-driven protests referred to as the Chicano Blowouts. During the 1960s, Latinx students attending school in Los Angeles faced high dropout rates, class sizes of over 40, and high levels of racism and discrimination. There were very few Mexican American teachers, no bilingual education, and no acknowledgment of Mexican American history. Around this time, a solidarity movement around Chicanx identity was emerging in the United States. As Mexican American high school students in East Los Angeles started identifying proudly as Chicanx, they became aware of the inequitable education they were receiving. The Blowouts consisted of a series of student walkouts organized by high school teacher Sal Castro. Through marches, speeches, and artwork, 15,000 students walked out of school to protest unequal education, resulting in occasional police violence. Walkout organizers were arrested. The high school students advocated for school reforms including Chicanx history within the curriculum and college preparatory courses (United Way, 2018).

1. Identify the Problem

In the first three lessons of the unit, students will explore various perspectives of this particular struggle for equality. In the first lesson, students will think about what it means to identify as Chicanx through making posters. The purpose of the classroom posters is for students to critically analyze the social, political, and economic circumstances that made Chicanx students join in unity to protest for social justice during the Chicano rights movements. The second lesson highlights Sal Castro, a Mexican American high school teacher in Los Angeles who helped organize the Blowouts. Students will research his biography and make a classroom poster that details the educational inequalities he hoped to address. The third lesson highlights the student perspective through the eyes of Paula Crisostomo, a Mexican American student during the Blowouts. Students will learn about her life and add to the classroom poster of inequalities that students faced.

2. Analyze the Problem

In lesson four of the unit, students will begin with a moral discourse about the issues Mexican American students faced in the 1960s. These discussion questions will focus less on domain coordination and more on perspective taking and moral ideas of fairness and harm because of the students' age.

Discussion questions include:

1. One day you come to the classroom and your teacher tells you that we can only learn and speak English at school. If you speak a different language in school, then you will get in trouble/punished and will not be allowed to play during recess. If your home language is not English, how would this make you feel? (M) How will your learning be different? (C) What will be difficult? How will you ask for things, like going to the restroom? How would it make you feel if you were punished at school for speaking your home language? Is this fair or unfair? Why? (M)
2. How would it make you feel if your teacher did not think you could do well in school? Is this fair or unfair? Why? (M)
3. Imagine a school district gets three boxes of new science books. There are three poor schools in the district and three rich schools in the district. Which schools would you give the boxes of books to? Why? Now imagine that you attend a rich school. Which schools would you give the boxes of books to? Why? (M)
4. How would it make you feel if I gave you an old science book with ripped and missing pages and I gave your friend the same science book, but new? How would your learning be different from your friend's? Will you be able to read every page? (M)

5. Our identity can help define who we say we are in a community. People identify themselves based on gender, ethnicity, race, socioeconomic status, age, job, and so on. Who do you say you are? (P) Who gets to choose who you say you are? Explain. (P)
6. How would it make you feel if someone told you something not nice and not true (we call this negative stereotypes) about your identity? Is this fair or unfair? Explain. (M/P)

(M = moral, C = conventional, P = personal)

Question 3 asks students to problem solve and discuss a distribution of resources task. Developmental research by Rutland and Killen (2015) shows that students in 1st grade (6–7 years old) are at a transition point in how they attend to rectifying inequalities when it comes to allocating resources. They also point out that in-group concerns can compete with students' willingness to prioritize equity during the allocation of resources between unequal groups.

Following this moral discourse, there would be a series of activities designed to engage students in taking the perspective of students who participated in the Blowouts, as well as critically analyzing original images and texts from the movement. Examples of images can be found here: www.unitedwayla.org/en/news-resources/blog/historical-photos-from-the-1968-east-l-a-walkouts/. Rotating among different stations, students in small groups will examine images of students holding protest signs and walking out of school and practice making observations about the scene. This activity aligns with Grade 1 California state history and social science standards that dictate that students should: "Compare and contrast everyday life in different times and places around the world and recognize that some aspects of people, places, and things change over time while others stay the same." Finally, students will create posters and artwork in the style of the Chicano Blowouts to demonstrate the ideas they have learned.

3/4. Create and Implement a Plan of Action to Address the Problem

In lesson five of this unit, students will learn about how, as part of the protest, students presented a list of demands to the L.A. Board of Education. Students will critically analyze these demands using the RAFT writing strategy (role of the writer, audience, format, topic). Using a Theater of the Oppressed framework (Boal, 2002; Saxon, n. d.), students will reenact the walkout protests and the reading of the list of demands to the L.A. Board of Education.

The community action component of this unit was conceived in the summer of 2020 during a global pandemic (COVID-19) for a school community in Los Angeles that also faced economic hardship. During the pandemic, students were forced to stay home from school and engage in socially distanced learning online. However, many students did not have regular access to a computer or the Internet, much less a quiet place to focus and join online classes. Meanwhile, more privileged school districts in Los Angeles were able to provide their students with computers. In this action project, the teacher will help students connect the inequalities Mexican American students faced in 1968 to the inequalities their classmates are facing during the pandemic. Students will each draw a picture and write a letter to the Los Angeles Unified School District to show their concerns and demand for equity in education during socially distanced learning.

5. Analyze and Evaluate the Action

To help young children integrate the big ideas from the unit and the action project with their own identities as moral agents, the following reflection questions can be discussed in small groups:

1. What are some things you can do when you see unfairness?
2. Walking out of school was against the rules. Why do you think some people protested by walking out of school anyway?
3. Why do you think some people were scared to protest/walk out?
4. If none of your friends or teachers walked out of school, would you still protest/walk out? How come? How would you feel?

Following this general discussion, teachers could engage students in reflecting on their own actions:

1. How did writing a letter about your experiences during socially distanced learning make you feel?
2. How do you hope your audience feels when they read your letter?

As can be seen in the above lesson, young children can engage in action projects if the teacher establishes a context and activities that are age appropriate. Additional materials for working with younger students can be obtained from the website Black Lives Matter at School (www.blacklivesmatteratschool.com). This website provides a library of free curriculum resources aimed at helping educators bring antiracist pedagogy that centers on and lifts up Black voices into the classroom. In this library, Tarilyn Little has contributed a 5-day unit plan for grades 3 and older called "Children and Youth as Changemakers" (Little, 2020). The first lesson helps students understand what it means to stand up for a "cause" and identify a cause that they feel strongly about. After that, students learn about youth activism (past and present), creating positive change, and then identifying challenges in their own community. The fifth, culminating lesson asks students to take action: create signs and stage a hallway protest, write a letter to an official, or record a PSA. The lessons in "Children and Youth as Changemakers" would need to be modified to include domain-based moral discourse and reflection in order to promote students' moral growth as was illustrated above in the lesson created by Maria Ramos Rojas on the Chicano Blowouts.

Police Violence and Black Lives Matter (Middle School Civics)

Students in middle school are beginning to form an understanding of societies as rule-based systems. About half of students in the 8th grade, however, have not yet constructed an understanding of conventions as playing this societal role. For that reason, they are less likely to attend to the law and order considerations, and more likely to focus on the moral issues of fairness and harm that may be underplayed by their counterparts. As was illustrated in the conversation we shared in Chapter 8, this mixture of students often gives rise to rich transactive, morally engaged conversations that spur development and cross-domain coordination. Participation in the following set of activities is ideal for this grade level. The action project should be completed within heterogeneous working groups of five students and then shared as a whole-class activity.

1. Identify the Problem

Open a discussion with students on their own experiences with police and their knowledge of police treatment of people of color. This can be done at first in small groups and then opened to the entire class. In classrooms with predominantly White students, the reported experiences with police may be more positive than those reported in classrooms with a mixture of White students and students of color, or classrooms composed predominantly of students of color. Students from different backgrounds may also report different degrees of knowledge about police treatment of people of color, particularly the treatment of Black Americans. However, nearly all students in the United States should have awareness of publicized incidents of police shootings of unarmed Black men. Across these settings, the teacher should encourage honesty and openness to the varieties of personal experience. A constructive discussion will depend on the teacher and class having had experience engaging in transactive discussion and engaged reasoning as addressed throughout this book.

Drawing from the class discussion, the teacher can ask the students to frame what will emerge as a statement of the problem:

> Differential treatment by police of people of color and use of violence against Black men.

2. Analyze the Problem

The analysis would begin with prompts from the teacher to consider the moral and societal role of the police, and to guide the students into an exploration of the history and record of police conduct in their own community and the country in general. Among the issues to consider in an initial transactive discussion would be:

1. Is there a necessary role for police in an organized society? What is that role? (C/M)
2. Should policing be conducted in the same way regardless of the background of the people in the community? (M/C)
3. Should the way that police interact with citizens be the same regardless of the level of crime within the community? (M)
4. Are police justified in using lethal force? If so, under what conditions? (M)

(M = moral, C = conventional)

Following this initial domain-based discussion, the students would move into an investigatory phase to examine the history of police treatment of people of color, especially Black men, and learn about current movements responding to police violence against Black men. To aid in this analysis, the UVA "Educating for Democracy" program provides background materials in the form of handouts that cover the following (educatingfordemocracy.dev8.uvaits.virginia.edu/):

1. History of police violence originating in slave patrols assigned to capture runaway slaves, followed by Jim Crow laws in the south, incidents of lynching, and police violence toward protestors during the civil rights movement, legislation targeting the Black community such as the "War on Drugs," and recent acts of police violence toward Black men, such as the beating of Rodney King and the shooting by police of Black men recorded on video.
2. The origins of the Black Lives Matter movement following the murder of Trayvon Martin by a White man, who had stalked Martin and shot him in the belief that Martin, an unarmed Black teen, was a threat. The shooter, George Zimmerman, was acquitted of murder.
3. Information about the three women who founded the Black Lives Matter (BLM) movement. This handout provides an example of how citizens can take steps to address social injustice.
4. A handout detailing the criticism of BLM and the emergence of a counter movement, "All Lives Matter," that mistakenly

frames BLM as not caring about the lives of non-Black citizens. The handout also covers criticism from civil rights leaders who express concern that BLM exacerbates racial tension. The handout concludes with an expression of support for the notion that women, and not just men, care about these issues and can organize effectively to promote social justice.

In addition to making use of these UVA resources, students could examine the available data regarding policing in their own community as a function of the ethnic and racial backgrounds of individuals interacting with police. Many states post detailed records online within each locality of police actions such as traffic citations and arrests made as a function of the race and ethnicity of individuals. These statistics can be matched against the proportion of people in the community by race and ethnicity, allowing for a measure of discrepancy rates of police action by background. Middle school students in Chicago, Illinois, and Oakland, California, that we have worked with have used this tool to uncover disproportionate rates of discretionary traffic stops and misdemeanor arrests for Latino and Black men.

3/4. Create and Implement a Plan of Action to Address the Problem

There are many directions that students can take at this step. Among the first steps would be to explore the recommendations offered by community and political leaders for addressing policing in the United States. This could include examining the proposals put forward by Campaign Zero (www.joincampaignzero.org/) or President Obama's organization My Brother's Keeper (www.obama.org/mbka/). For students in the Oakland community who we work with, this step has added force because the Oakland mayor, Libby Schaaf (as of 2020), is on record as steering the Oakland Police Department toward alignment with those recommendations. Students could contact the Oakland Police Commission as well as the mayor's office to interview them about how they plan to reduce police violence. Oakland high school students enrolled in Heath Madom's, English 2 "Law and Society" course are provided a template for how to call a public official, and are taught how to write a script to effectively deliver their message. Students record a video of themselves making the call on a cell phone using the speaker option. In addition, students could create a website tracking the yearly trends in police activity for the city of Oakland and inform the mayor's office and police commissioner that they are monitoring these statistics. Finally, students could elect to join the peaceful protests against police violence such as those taking place in Oakland at the time we were writing this chapter, or help to organize a peaceful protest in conjunction with other local high school students.

5. Analyze and Evaluate the Action

Following completion of the action project, the teacher would engage the class in a transactive discussion relevant to their focal problem. This discussion would make use of their experiences and knowledge gained. The following illustrative example is drawn from the UVA materials developed for this unit. It centers on the controversial proposal to address police violence by defunding the police.

> After George Floyd and Breonna Taylor were killed by police officers in 2020, there were nationwide protests against police brutality and racial injustice toward Black Americans. These protests have called for policing in America to be reformed and reimagined in significant ways. One solution that has gained increased attention amidst these protests is to defund the police. The idea behind defunding the police is that money that is allocated toward police departments would be reinvested toward other public services and forms of public safety, such as education, housing, or health care. In many cities across America, police departments receive the largest amount of a city's budget compared to other services. Chicago, for instance, allocates 40% of its city's general funds toward policing. Protestors argue that increasing budgets for policing and police reform has not been effective and that communities could improve if money was distributed toward other forms of public safety. However, some critics worry that defunding the police is not the right solution to make communities safer and that supporters of the idea do not have a well-developed plan for how crime would be dealt with. Opponents claim that defunding would increase crime, extend wait times on 911 calls, and make police investigations longer to complete. According to a poll conducted in June 2020, 64% of Americans were opposed to defunding police departments.

The above information is followed by the quotes from politicians representing each side of the issue:

> A new way forward can't be put in place if we have a department that is having a crisis of credibility, if we have a department that's led by a chief who's suited for racism, if we have a department that hasn't solved homicide—half of the homicides in Minneapolis police department go unsolved. There have been cases where they've destroyed rape kits. And so you can't really reform a department that is rotten to the root. What you can do is rebuild. . . . If you had a company that wasn't producing, you wouldn't just pour more money into it so that it would produce. You would step back and say, let's look at what works, what doesn't work, and how do we move forward. —Ilhan Omar, U.S. Representative from Minnesota

Nobody is going to de-fund the police. We can restructure the police forces. Restructure, re-imagine policing. That is what we are going to do. The fact of the matter is that police have a role to play. What we've got to do is make sure that their role is one that meets the times, one that responds to these communities that they operate in. . . . This is a structure that has been developed that we have got to deconstruct. So I wouldn't say defund. Deconstruct our policing. —James Clyburn, U.S. Representative from South Carolina

Discussion Questions

1. Given what you have learned from your action project and what you have read, including the quotes above, which perspective on this topic do you align with more, and why?
2. Can you integrate the two perspectives or find a compromise between them?
    a. If not, why?
    b. If so, what would the solution look like?

Following this discussion, the students would be asked to reflect in their small groups on the impact of their project on the community and on themselves. The following are some key questions that can be used to lead this reflection:

1. What impact do you feel your activities have had on other people?
2. What impact do you think your activities have had on our local community and your goal of affecting police violence toward people of color?
3. How does that make you feel about yourself?
4. What changes do you see in yourself as a result of your participation in this activity?

Students would be instructed to write out the answers to these questions, but not necessarily turn them in. The group would complete a final report of the action project to be turned into the teacher. We will discuss the issue of grading at the end of this chapter.

INTEGRATING MORAL DEVELOPMENT WITHIN AN ACTION PROJECT

Another educational approach that aligns with the cycle of praxis is to allow students to self-select the social issue they want to address. This removes the action project from tight alignment with a mandated curriculum. For this reason, such student-selected projects can only be asked of students within traditional curricula as an additional assignment. Alternatively, some states afford schools broad latitude to meet state standards for aspects of the curriculum at particular grade levels. This is the case for California high school social studies. What we will turn to now is a discussion of the "Take Action Project" (TAP) that is a major component of 9th-grade social studies within the Oakland Public Schools. The TAP was designed using the principles of the cycle of praxis. In the following discussion, we will present a modified summary version of the TAP to incorporate attention to moral development. We do this with thanks to Jah-Yee Woo and Brenda Rivera of the Oakland Unified School District, who provided us with access to the TAP materials.

Take Action Project

**Illustrative Example:
The Relationship Between Air Pollution and Oakland Neighborhood**

---

1. Identify a Problem

The first component of TAP asks students in groups of five to brainstorm and select a social issue they wish to address. To aid in their brainstorming, the TAP materials provide them the following list of systems within society that they can refer to in pondering the issue they want to address.

> **Food** (creation and distribution of food)
> **Justice** (management of crime: law enforcement, court system, prison/jail, bail)
> **School** (primary, secondary, and higher education: curriculum, funding, career prep, support services)
> **City planning/development** (zoning, rent control, housing, design of roads, neighborhoods & buildings)
> **Corporate world** (freedom/restriction of corporate activities, monopolies, investors' rights)
> **Economic development** (financial support for small businesses: creation of local jobs & markets)
> **Health care** (preventative and responsive care: quality and cost of doctor's visits, hospitals, medicines)
> **Child care** (manner in which children are cared for: quality and cost of childcare, pre-K)
> **Eldercare/aging** (manner in which the elderly are cared for: quality and cost of various services)
> **Environmental management** (manner in which natural resources are used and taken care of)

> **Media** (manner in which information is disseminated to the public: TV, social media, books, magazines)
> **Transportation** (manner in which people get from place to place: cars, buses, trains, planes, bikes, etc.)
> **Governance** (manner in which the government itself functions: elections system [i.e., electoral college, ranked choice], taxation systems, voting rights, diplomacy)
> **Immigration** (manner in which people enter this country to live here: green cards, visas, DREAM Act)

To further inform the selection of a topic, students are encouraged to interview a community or family member to obtain their view of what issues are of concern from among the list of possible systems they might tackle through their action project. The example topic provided in the TAP materials for teachers is the relationship between levels of air pollution and neighborhood within the city of Oakland. Oakland is on the east side of the San Francisco Bay. The city neighborhoods range from very low-income homes close to the bay to luxury homes in the wooded hills on the eastern side of the city. The statement of the problem is as follows:

> Is there a relationship between neighborhood location and income, and the level of air pollution?

2. Analyze the Problem

As with the examples above, the teacher would work with the students to identify the societal and moral issues at play in the problem and create a set of questions for the students to discuss prior to delving into their research. Students in the 9th grade have typically constructed an understanding of societies as normative systems structured by societal conventions. They have also begun to emerge from the bottom of the U-shaped curve in moral reasoning typical of early adolescence and are becoming better able to coordinate multifaceted elements of moral problems. This makes engagement with social injustice a particularly relevant and motivating concern for these students.

Among the issues the students could engage through transactive moral discourse would be the following:

1. Is it the responsibility of citizens of Oakland who live in more affluent neighborhoods to be concerned about levels of air pollution and other forms of environmental pollution in poor neighborhoods? Why? After all, somebody has to live near the oil refineries and highways. (M/C)
2. We live with tradeoffs all of the time. You can't have a pollution-free world and still have industry. If we keep adding laws and

controls on pollution, then only the wealthy will be able to buy anything. Wouldn't that hurt the people who live in low-income neighborhoods? (Moral versus pragmatic)
3. What do you think about requiring industries that cause pollution to be distributed across the city instead of being concentrated near the bay? That way the negative effects of pollution would not be on one group of people. Would that be fair to people who have the means to buy into more affluent neighborhoods? (M/C)

(M = moral, C = conventional)

As was the case with the action projects connected with the curriculum, the students engaged with TAP would use library, Internet, and investigatory methods to research the problem. Within the TAP protocols, these would be considered secondary sources of information. In addition to such secondary sources, students are also required to contact at least two primary sources of information in their local community. The students who took on air pollution as their topic did Internet and library research. They also conducted a survey of 70 residents of Oakland about their experiences and concerns about air quality. These students also interviewed an individual who worked for a nonprofit group concerned with air quality and other environmental problems.

3/4. Create and Implement a Plan of Action

Following their exploratory research, these students set about creating an informational video around the relationship between air pollution and neighborhood wealth in the city of Oakland with plans to post it on YouTube. Here again we see the connection to the use of media as discussed in Chapter 10. They also set up an air pollution measurement device called AirBeam in various parts of the city, and posted the data on a website geared toward youth. Their stated goal was to stimulate young people to become aware of the issue and to take action for change.

5. Analyze and Evaluate the Action

As described above regarding curriculum-based action projects, these students reflected on the impact of their project. As part of TAP, this group of five students did a presentation about their project to their entire class and turned in a report for a grade by the teacher. We would add the following elements for this final phase of TAP: We would have the teacher set aside time prior to the class presentation for the small groups to engage in the reflection we describe above for the police violence action project. This would include revisiting the initial domain-based transactive discussion on the moral and societal issues associated with air quality and neighborhood wealth, as well as the following questions:

- What impact do you feel your activities have had on other people?
- What impact do you think your activities have had on our local community and your goal of affecting police violence toward people of color?
- How does that make you feel about yourself?
- What changes do you see in yourself as a result of your participation in this activity?

Indeed, an interesting way for each of the action groups to present their projects would be to lead the entire class in a 10-minute conversation about the questions that frame each group's domain discourse. In this case, the group of five students could lead the class in a discussion of where pollutive factories should be located. The entire class would be engaged in reflection on the moral elements of each project, and not simply be consumers of a presentation.

PIVOTING AND RESPONDING TO AN EMERGENT ISSUE

The tools and examples in this chapter so far all aim to help teachers prepare for and plan meaningful action projects in their classrooms. However, critical moral educators also must be flexible and able to pivot when emergent, relevant social issues arise in one's community. At the time of writing this book, several events interrupted and disrupted students' lives in North America and across the world, including: a global pandemic (COVID-19), the killing of George Floyd by a White police officer and massive subsequent protests against anti-Black racism and police violence, brutal wildfires in California and extreme weather across the country.

Students and their families will feel the impacts of these events physically, economically, and emotionally. The pandemic resulted in mass unemployment in many cities, as well as major restrictions in social interaction. After the killing of George Floyd, many Black students experienced fear and anxiety in public spaces, as well as rage, helplessness, and pain. In order to help students process their emotions and critically analyze the events around them, teachers might consider engaging them in the cycle of praxis: identifying the problem, analyzing it through moral discourse and research, creating a plan of action, and reflecting on the moral and societal impact of their actions on the community and themselves. Students might very well demand some sort of classroom response to an epic event, as their own minds and bodies are consumed by its effects.

We realize this means creating space and time in an already packed schedule of learning. Three days after George Floyd was killed by police, grade 7 teacher Sarah Moore tweeted: "I need to scrap all my lessons for the last 4 weeks of grade 7 and do a read aloud of Stamped by @DrIbram and @JasonReynolds83. I'll be starting Monday." On top of navigating online learning in the midst of a pandemic, and without the support of her co-teacher, she launched an antiracism book club (online) in which she facilitated discussions about *Stamped: Racism, Antiracism and You: A Remix*, which is a young adult version of Ibram Kendi's *Stamped from the Beginning: The Definitive History of Racist Ideas in America*. This responsiveness gave students a chance to ask questions about the protests they were seeing on the news and systemic racism, examine their own identities and actions, reflect on the moral and societal impact of these events, and brainstorm what they could do.

Emergent events can also provide opportunities to discuss societal inequalities. Inevitably, a seismic event will be felt differently by each school and potentially each classmate, depending on circumstances and unique identities. For example, in Toronto, Canada, people of color made up 83% of those hospitalized due to COVID-19 (as of July 2020), while only constituting half of the city's population (Cheung, 2020). The CDC echoed these disparities (Killerby et al., 2020). Students with housing instability or who lived in densely populated areas were more vulnerable to the virus as well. Teachers can draw students' attention to the ways in which certain groups of people will be disproportionately affected by social events, and brainstorm with students some ways to address these inequalities.

Finally, we do not mean to say that teachers need to wait for a seismic event to integrate community issues into their curriculum. In fact, we might encourage teachers to constantly seek out relevant issues in their community that are evolving in real time in order to continually pivot their students' attention toward tensions, policies, conflicts, struggles, and changing elements of society to which they can be active witnesses or agents of change. These events could also be highly local—a serious incident of bullying in a school community, the deportation of a classmate, or school district budget cuts.

ISSUES OF GRADING AND ASSESSMENT

A key concern of teachers is how to assess and grade student work. This becomes a potentially thorny issue when attempting to evaluate the impact of our efforts to stimulate moral growth. The examples of lessons we have provided in these final three chapters have all been integrated within the academic goals of teachers. Academic goals, such as conducting research or constructing a thesis statement, should be assessed and graded using the rubrics normally employed in academic subjects. For example, the essays generated as homework or in-class writing assignments in Chapter 9 would be assessed using relevant academic criteria. In a similar fashion, the Oakland teachers have generated rubrics for grading the academic elements of action projects. The main categories of the rubric used in Oakland are: Issue Analysis, Evidence, Organization, Language, and Group Work. Student performance within each category is assigned an evaluation in a 4-point scale from Incomplete Understanding to Highly Skilled. In none of these rubrics are students assessed in terms of the moral or political position taken in their essays, podcasts, or project reports.

At this point, it is reasonable to ask how teachers will know whether their efforts at stimulating moral development and student tendencies to engage in cross-domain coordination have been effective. We need to clarify the distinction between assigning grades to individual students and evaluating the overall effectiveness of our educational efforts. We argue that it is *enough* to witness collective classroom change in terms of critical moral and social reasoning, and that it is not necessary to translate research tools that assess transactive discourse or moral growth into student assessment measures. In fact, doing so may lead to an unintended quantification and ranking of students according to hypothetical moral scenarios. Instead, throughout the school year, as they engage their students in discourse, exploring texts, conducting research, and community action projects, teachers should attend to the following classroom and grade-level cohort indices of student growth:

- *Shifts in discourse:* In both small-group and whole-class discussions, there should be movement away from competitive argumentation toward responsive engagement in which students make use of the ideas offered by their peers and engage in serious efforts to find common ground. The level of sophistication of the discourse will vary by grade level, but teachers should look for evidence that students are making use of the ideas advanced by their peers and not simply reiterating their own favored stance.
- *Shifts in moral and societal cognition*: Chapter 3 of this book provides a broad overview of age-typical shifts in the moral, societal, and personal domains. Teachers can use these descriptions as general guidelines for what can be expected in terms of changes within students' arguments and reasoning in their own classroom. This is especially the case in grade levels that are points of transition. We should see emerging evidence, for example, of an understanding of societies as systems among 8th- and 9th-graders, or an understanding of fairness as equity for elementary students.
- *Cross-domain coordination*: Beginning in upper elementary and at the middle and high school levels, we would expect to see increased attention in student essays and assignments to competing personal, societal, and moral elements in multifaceted contexts, such as the labor practices used to produce inexpensive products that

students may purchase. We should see a reduction in the tendency to subordinate these complex issues to a single domain, such as morality, and an increase in the ability to bring competing elements of morality, convention, and personal preferences into balance. This capacity for cross-domain coordination is essential for a critical moral perspective on existing social structures and norms.

- *Novel ideas*: We should see the emergence of novel ideas that demonstrate developmental movement in a classroom community, signaling that the pedagogy has made space for wrestling with relevant moral and social conflicts and tensions. While not every grade 9 student may have a conception of a society as a system that functions to organize group life, by creating opportunities for group interaction and discourse, students will get exposed to these arguments and construct new meaning from their peers. This is in keeping with the ideology of constructivist, problem-posing education that argues against a one-way transmission of information from teachers to students.
- *Microgenetic shifts*: Teachers should keep a record of student work over the course of the year and look for evidence of movement in the elements outlined above. This could even be accomplished in end-of-year portfolio reviews in conjunction with students themselves. Small changes, referred to as microgenetic shifts, in student reasoning will provide teachers data points for assessing their pedagogy from one year to the next.
- *Increased student engagement*: Finally, evidence from research (Nucci et al., 2015) indicates that this approach to teaching has a positive impact on student engagement and improved performance on the academic content. Teachers should see evidence of broad student participation in classroom discourse, a reduction in the need for the teacher to engage in behavioral management, and an increase in the completion of assignments.

CHAPTER 12

Closing Thoughts

In this book we have made the case for integrating moral education with critical pedagogy. We have shown how these two powerful tools for empowering students to move toward a more just and caring society share common assumptions about the constructivist nature of learning and knowledge formation. We have drawn from decades of careful research identifying the universal core of moral development and have demonstrated how to link those elements of moral judgment with a critical stance toward societal norms and institutions. Throughout the book we have grounded our attention to research and theory with actual classroom practices. That includes attention to the development of students' social and emotional capacities through a nonpunitive approach to classroom management and conflict. In sum, we have provided an integrative theoretical framework and a road map for achieving moral education for social justice within the school setting.

As we were writing this book in 2020, the United States was holding a presidential election. During the campaign the sitting president issued a directive against using taxpayer dollars to support "divisive, un-American propaganda training sessions." This directive explicitly flagged trainings about critical race theory and White privilege. In doing so, this misguided directive effectively placed us as the authors of this book among the researchers and educators presumed to be engaging in the promotion of "un-American propaganda." We see things very differently. The research on moral development has clearly demonstrated that the child's understandings of fairness and human welfare emerge through processes of construction and reflection that are antithetical to direct instruction or indoctrination. These understandings and capacity for moral judgment sit in dialogue with the child's conceptions of convention and their personal wants and goals. Our entire approach to moral education is consistent with the promotion of fairness and moral autonomy. We do not advocate for moral education that simply promotes the teacher's value system. Instead, we rely on student discourse around contentious topics that seeks to find common ground through responsive engagement. Such discourse is the opposite of indoctrination and in keeping with the goals and traditions of a democratic society (Erickson & Thompson, 2019).

Where we would attract the ire of the former president and his allies is in our attention to the needs of students whose social class, ethnicity, race, gender, or disability leaves them shortchanged by the educational system and the larger society. Addressing the historical, social, and systemic roots of these inequalities is at the heart of critical pedagogy and an imperative of moral education worthy of the name (Erickson & Thompson, 2019). In this book we have addressed how domain-based moral education functions within the cycle of praxis. Instead of undoing American culture, the cycle of praxis connects students directly with the challenges facing society and promotes civic engagement and democracy. We have illustrated how teachers can match the design of their lessons and activities with the moral developmental levels of their students to allow for effective pedagogy across ages.

ADDRESSING STUDENT EMOTIONS AND POTENTIAL RESISTANCE

The process of critical inquiry and domain-based moral discourse may unearth deep-seated emotions and feelings. The educational process we have described will affect more than the capacity to reason about fairness, or to understand the abstract features of social systems. As students from marginalized groups confront the reality of their own position in relation to historical and current social inequalities, they may experience rage or depression. We noted in the previous chapter that such emotions can emerge in response to actual events, such as the killing of George Floyd, but they can also be unearthed as students become aware of the historical basis of systematic factors contributing to their own, or their family's, oppression. In this book we have emphasized the importance of the social–emotional climate of the school and classroom. We have positioned critical inquiry and moral discourse within this emotional framework because moral dialogue is more than cool rational reflection. Elements of outrage, care, and reason are all at work as students grapple with solutions to longstanding forms of inequality. In Chapter 8, in our discussion on responsive engagement, we offer words of wisdom from critical educators about valuing stories of lived experiences with oppression in the classroom. Part of fostering narrative moral agency is making sense of lived experiences in new ways. The engagement in praxis guided by moral discourse places the students in a proactive rather than reactive position, and a focus on community action projects may afford a channel for the emotional outrage or pain students may experience.

Our own experience with students participating with the lessons and forms of praxis presented in this book is that the students find them engaging, and more relevant than traditional instruction. However, we openly acknowledge the possibility that for some students, especially White males in middle school and high school, the honest appraisal of the ways in which current society affords them privilege may be met with resistance. This would be especially the case for students who view themselves as fair-minded and not personally engaging in acts of oppression. Student resistance may take the form of silence, withdrawal, immobilizing guilt, feeling overly hopeless or overly hopeful, rejection, anger, sarcasm, and argumentation (Sensoy & DiAngelo, 2017). Each of these forms of resistance would potentially undermine efforts to engage students in constructive dialogue at the heart of our educational approach. These student reactions are understandable because the broad social narrative about American society is that it is democratic, fair, and inclusive. Among the statements students may offer in defense of their resistance to critical analysis are the following (Sensoy & DiAngelo, 2017, p. 3):

"I accept people for who they are."

"I see people as individuals."

"It's focusing on difference that divides us."

"My parents taught me that all people are equal."

"I was always taught to treat everyone the same."

"I've been discriminated against so I don't have any privilege."

"Our generation is more open-minded."

"I have friends from all races and we are all fine with each other."

"I don't think race and gender make any difference—as long as you work hard."

"It's White males who are the minority now."

"Women are just as sexist as men."

Similarly, Adams and Bell (2016) write about social identity development theories and models as being a helpful tool in social justice classrooms to help students normalize their emotional reactions to content and expand their view of who they can be. They write that social identity development models, such as specific ethnic or racial identity models, usually outline a series of phases individuals move through:

> 1) accepting and internalizing the dominant ideology of the subordinated group, 2) questioning, rejecting, and resisting the dominant ideology and oppressive systems and thus the way their social group is characterized, 3) exploring, redefining, and developing a new sense of social identity that is not rooted in the norms and values of superiority and inferiority, and 4) integrating and internalizing the new identity along with a commitment to social justice. (2016, p. 36)

These authors are quick to point out, however, that stage models of identity development have been critiqued for being overly linear and simplistic. Additionally, categorizing social groups as being on opposite sides of privilege (e.g., advantaged vs. disadvantaged) does not provide enough nuance to capture an individual's intersecting identities, and how shifting social contexts interact with one's identity.

However, they suggest that exposing students to social identity development models—for a specific social identity—might be a powerful way to engage students in a process of metacognitive growth. If they recognize their own thinking in the model, it may help normalize their feelings and envision an identity that has reconciled contradictions or painful emotions. They write, "Social identity development theories also offer participants a framework for examining current ways of thinking and feeling, and to see the possibility of moving to a position that feels more authentic and liberating. . . . For people who may be struggling at the earlier phases, the latter phases offer positive images of what continued growth can look like. This can be especially important for participants who feel mired in difficult emotions such as guilt, shame, and rage" (2016, p. 37). If using these models, they argue, educators should be sure to recognize that "stages" are metaphors for types of meaning-making with regard to identity and justice, and not meant to label students as "low" or "high," or restrict your perception of what students are capable of.

The educational approach offered in this book anticipates and addresses forms of resistance by emphasizing the role of respectful engagement in the process of information gathering and dialogue in which the goal is not to win an argument, but to search for common ground. This removes the need to defend a prior position in the face of counter evidence, and allows students to unburden themselves of viewpoints or arguments as tied to their moral identity. As with the case of the emotional responses of students from marginalized groups, the overall affective climate of the school and classroom that emphasizes mutual respect and *care* for all students affords the emotional safety needed to confront a personal position of privilege with a positive sense of growth rather than resistance. Engagement in praxis places all students in positions of solidarity and problem solving rather than defensiveness or blaming, and engagement in critical media production places students in an agentic role to create counter-narratives about their communities and identities.

bell hooks offered reflections on grappling with teaching students who are coming to terms with their own privilege in her book *Teaching to Transgress: Education as the Practice of Freedom* (1994). She wrote that she expects students to experience pain and discomfort as they forfeit familiar worldviews, and she respects that pain, even if it means they do not love her classes. She wrote, "We have to learn how to appreciate difficulty, too, as a stage in intellectual development. Or accept that that cozy, good feeling may at times block the possibility of giving students space to feel that there is integrity to be found in grappling with difficult material, whether that material comes from confessional narratives, books or discussions" (p. 154). So, even as we discuss the need for an environment of care, emotional safety, and trust, this does not mean seeking immediate resolutions to all emotional disruptions, but embracing the capacity of your classroom community to hold discomfort together.

WALKING THE WALK: STEPS FOR EDUCATORS

The blueprint outlined in this book cannot guide teachers to successful, justice-oriented classrooms unless they are simultaneously engaged in a process of critical self-reflection. We encourage students to have dialogic mindsets and engage in heteroglossia, and so must we. The words of bell hooks about university professors in this regard apply to all educators: "If professors are wounded, damaged individuals, people who are not self-actualized, then they will seek asylum in the academy rather than seek to make the academy a place of challenge, dialectical interchange, and growth" (1994, p. 165). Seeking self-actualization is, therefore, a social justice education project. We draw on the work of Yolanda Sealey-Ruiz and others to offer ideas for how teachers can actively cultivate practices and perspectives that are justice oriented and support education as a liberatory and critical endeavor for all students.

Racial Literacy

Sealey-Ruiz (2011) suggests that teachers need to cultivate racial literacy in order to be effective social justice educators. This means teachers must acknowledge the enormous role that race plays in systemic educational injustice. This literacy is sustained and developed through self-reflection, learning about systems of inequality, and then explicitly teaching their students about these systems (2011, p. 118). Teacher education, she argues, should provide space to confront and discuss concerns and fears about embracing antiracist pedagogy. She suggests five principles that teachers and teacher education programs can embrace "as they move their students toward deep self-reflection, an equity mindset, and development of racial literacy" (p. 118): (1) Read critical texts that deal with race, racism, and discrimination so you are equipped with vocabulary to combat racial stereotypes in schools, (2) Examine long-held assumptions about race, Black children, and children of color, (3) Hold teachers/teacher candidates accountable for practicing racial literacy in classrooms, (4) Dissect personal experiences with race as a group, and (5) Take action against racist policies (p. 118). Maisha Winn echoes these sentiments as she described teacher education that holds teachers accountable for identifying institutional racism—especially in the realm of discipline. "Teachers must unlearn racist ideas that manifest in punishing their Black and Latinx students more than their White and Asian peers" (2018, p. 145).

The idea of fostering a literacy for *reading* injustice and inequality in educational environments applies to our students with disabilities, multilingual students, LGBTQ students, undocumented students, and nonbinary students. Sealey-Ruiz's five principles can guide us toward becoming literate in the types of oppression that all our students face.

Emotional Literacy

In addition to fostering transformative social–emotional learning with students, Jagers and colleagues (2019) argue that educators should apply "adult SEL," and strive to cultivate social–emotional competencies within themselves. This, they claim, will prepare educators to commit to institutional cultural change. Jagers et al. (2019) argue:

> When we reflect on our existing views, assumptions, and perspectives, we employ components of two SE competencies: self-awareness and social awareness. Reexamining our perspectives on the intersections between our sense of self and how society may view us and those around us is fundamental to creating educational equity, for two reasons.
> 1. It allows us to consider the world from the viewpoint of someone different from us: Do the students in my classroom have similar opportunities and experiences that I did when I was growing up? If not, why?
> 2. Reexamining perspectives can lead to action. We see the world differently, which prompts us to change. My students have had different opportunities and experiences than me—how can I address and empathize with their needs? (p. 4)

The Greater Good Science Center also identifies self-awareness and self-management as critical skills for teachers. Among the skills they list that can build self-awareness are labeling and recognizing one's emotions, identifying emotional triggers, cultivating a growth mindset, and understanding the relationship between one's thoughts, emotions, and behaviors. Emotional literacy can lead to more positive relationships with students and more equitable classrooms in terms of discipline and expectations (Greater Good Science Center, n.d.).

Similarly, in writing about healing-centered engagement as a strategy for going beyond "trauma-informed" education, Ginwright (2018) urges educators to take emotional risks with their students in order to build empathy. He wrote: "To create this empathy, I encourage adult staff to share their story first, and take an emotional risk by being more vulnerable, honest and open to young people. This process creates an empathy exchange between the adult and the young people which is the foundation for healing centered engagement (Payne, 2013)." In sum, we as educators must be constantly putting in effort to awaken our own critical consciousness in relation to our students and our society. Among other things, this includes cultivating racial and emotional literacy within ourselves.

CONCLUSION

In closing, we invite you as teachers, prospective teachers, teacher educators, and researchers to join us in implementing and improving on the practices and underlying research presented in this book. Collectively we can move education toward the goal of developing young people, who are moral, caring, and committed to a genuinely inclusive democratic society. This book is the start of a working agenda that will continue to evolve as research and reflection on practical classroom experience raise new questions and offer even more effective practices. We invite you to visit our website, www.moraledk12.org, which provides additional resources, and to remain in contact with us.

References

Adams, M. E., & Bell, L. A. E. (2016). *Teaching for diversity and social justice* (3rd ed.). Routledge/Taylor & Francis Group.

Agrawal, N. (2019, September 10). California expands on "willful defiance" suspensions in schools. *Los Angeles Times*, https://www.latimes.com

Aknin, L. B., Hamlin, J. K., & Dunn, E. W. (2012). Giving leads to happiness in young children. *PLoS one*, 7(6), e39211.

Armbrester, S. (2017, December). I am a cheerleader, and here's why I take a knee. NPR's *All Things Considered*. www.npr.org/2017/12/01/567845804/i-am-a-cheerleader-heres-why-i-take-a-knee

Arthur, J., Kristjánsson, K., Harrison, T., Sanderse, W., & Wright, D. (2016). *Teaching character and virtue in schools*. Routledge.

Bakhtin, M. M. (1981). The dialogic imagination: Four essays. (Michael Holquist, ed.; Caryl Emerson and Michael Holquist, trans.). University of Texas Press, 1981.

Beachum, L. (2020). Student will be barred from graduation unless he cuts his dreadlocks, school says. *The Washington Post*. www.washingtonpost.com/education/2020/01/23/texas-dreadlocks-suspension/

Berkowitz, M. W., & Gibbs, J. C. (1983). Measuring the developmental features of moral discussion. *Merrill-Palmer Quarterly (1982–)*, 399–410.

Bhandary, A. (2019). *Freedom to care: Liberalism, dependency care, and culture*. Routledge.

Bigler, R. S., & Liben, L. S. (2006). A developmental intergroup theory of social stereotypes and prejudice. *Advances in Child Development and Behavior*, 34, 39–89.

Blair, J., Mitchell, D., & Blair, K. (2005). *The psychopath: Emotion and the brain*. Blackwell Publishing.

Blum, L. (2013). Political identity and moral education: A response to Jonathan Haidt's The Righteous Mind. *Journal of Moral Education*, 42(3), 298–315.

Blum, L. (2015). Race and class categories and subcategories in educational thought and research. *Theory and Research in Education*, 13(1), 87–104.

Blumenfeld, P. C., Pintrich, P. R., & Hamilton, V. L. (1987). Teacher talk and students' reasoning about morals, conventions, and achievement. *Child Development*, 58(5), 1389–1401.

Boal, A. (2002). *Games for actors and non-actors*. Psychology Press.

Bochenek, M., & Brown, A. W. (2001). *Hatred in the hallways: Violence and discrimination against lesbian, gay, bisexual, and transgender students in U.S. schools*. Human Rights Watch.

Brown, C. S., & Anderson, R. E. (2019). It's never too young to talk about race and gender. *Human Development, 69*, 1–3.

Brummett, J. (2003, April 13). United Christian states of America (Column). *Las Vegas Review-Journal*, A15.

Chen-Gaddini, M., Liu, J., & Nucci, L. (2020). "It's my own business!": Parental control over personal issues in the context of everyday adolescent–parent conflicts and internalizing disorders among urban Chinese adolescents. *Developmental Psychology, 56(9)*, 1775–1786.

Cheung, J. (2020, July). *Black people and other people of colour make up 83% of Covid-19 cases in Toronto*. CBC News. www.cbc.ca/news/canada/toronto/toronto-covid-19-data-1.5669091

Costello, M., & Dillard, C. (2019). *Hate at school report*. Southern Poverty Law Center.

Curwood, J. S., & Gibbons, D. (2009). "Just like I have felt": Multimodal counter-narratives in youth-produced digital media. *International Journal of Learning and Media, 1(4)*, 59–77.

Dahl, A. (2016). Infants' unprovoked acts of force toward others. *Developmental Science, 19(6)*, 1049–1057.

Dahl, A., & Tran, A. Q. (2016). Vocal tones influence young children's responses to prohibitions. *Journal of Experimental Child Psychology, 152*, 71–91.

Damon, W. (1977). *The social world of the child*. Jossey-Bass.

Darnell, C., Gulliford, L., Kristjánsson, K., & Paris, P. (2019). Phronesis and the knowledge-action gap in moral psychology and moral education: A new synthesis? *Human Development, 62(3)*, 1–29.

Davidson, M. (1974). *Nine true dolphin stories*. Scholastic.

Dean, T. (2008, May 27). Students object to graduation dress code. *Oak Park Wednesday Journal*. www.oakpark.com/News/Articles/5-27-2008/Students-object-to-graduation-dress-code/

Dolan, M. C., & Fullam, R. S. (2010). Moral/conventional transgression distinction and psychopathy in conduct disordered adolescent offenders. *Personality and Individual Differences, 49(8)*, 995–1000.

Doyle, A. (1998). "Cops": Television policing as policing reality. *Entertaining crime: Television reality programs* (pp. 95–116). Routledge.

Duncan-Andrade, J. M. R., & Morrell, E. (2008). *The art of critical pedagogy: Possibilities for moving from theory to practice in urban schools* (Vol. 285). Peter Lang.

Durkheim, E. (1973/1925). *Moral education: A study in the theory and the application of moral education*. Free Press.

Dweck, C. (2015). Carol Dweck revisits the "growth mindset." *Education Week, 35(5)*, 20–24.

Eccles, J. S., Wigfield, A., & Schiefele, U. (1998). Motivation to succeed. In W. Damon (Ed.), *Handbook of child psychology* (5th ed., Vol. 3, pp. 1017–1095). Wiley.

Eisenberg, N. (2014). *Altruistic emotion, cognition, and behavior (PLE: Emotion)*. Psychology Press.

Eisenberg, N., Cumberland, A., Guthrie, I. K., Murphy, B. C., & Shepard, S. A. (2005). Age changes in prosocial responding and moral reasoning in adolescence and early adulthood. *Journal of Research on Adolescence, 15(3)*, 235–260.

References

Ellsworth, E. (1989). Why doesn't this feel empowering? Working through the oppressive myths of critical pedagogy. *Harvard Educational Review*, 59(3), 297–324.

Erickson, J. D., & Thompson, W. C. (2019). Preschool as a wellspring for democracy: Endorsing Traits of reasonableness in early childhood education. *Democracy and Education*, 27(1), 1.

Fancher, M. (2018, August 3). Elementary school kids don't belong in handcuffs. *ACLU Blog*. www.aclu.org/blog/juvenile-justice/school-prison-pipeline/elementary-school-kids-dont-belong-handcuffs

Freire, P. (1973). *Education for critical consciousness* (Vol. 1). Bloomsbury Publishing.

Freire, P. (2005). *Pedagogy of the oppressed* (30th anniv. ed.). Continuum. (Original work published 1970)

Furrer, C., & Skinner, E. (2003). Sense of relatedness as a factor in children's academic engagement and performance. *Journal of Educational Psychology*, 95(1), 148–162.

Gaffney, C. (2019). When schools cause trauma. *Teaching Tolerance*, Issue 62. www.tolerance.org/magazine/summer-2019/when-schools-cause-trauma?fbclid=IwAR3lP1zdlVYOTVjdIbHgegAZffBvDjbzrJwRWh0xnSpMfLIJW9q2HGpFwSM

Gelman, S. (2003). *The essential child: Origins of essentialism in everyday thought*. Oxford University Press.

Ginwright, S. (2018). The future of healing: Shifting from trauma informed care to healing centered engagement. Occasional Paper, 25. https://ginwright.medium.com/the-future-of-healing-shifting-from-trauma-informed-care-to-healing-centered-engagement-634f557ce69c

Greater Good Science Centre. (n.d.). SEL for adults: Self-awareness and self-management. https://ggie.berkeley.edu/my-well-being/sel-for-adults-self-awareness-and-self-management/

Greenberg, M. T., Weissberg, R. P., O'Brien, M. U., Zins, J. E., Fredericks, L., Resnik, H., & Elias, M. J. (2003). Enhancing school-based prevention and youth development through coordinated social, emotional, and academic learning. *American Psychologist*, 58(6–7), 466–474.

Gregory, A., Clawson, K., Davis, A., & Gerewitz, J. (2016). The promise of restorative practices to transform teacher-student relationships and achieve equity in school discipline. *Journal of Educational and Psychological Consultation*, 26(4), 325–353.

Gregory, A., & Weinstein, R. S. (2008). The discipline gap and African Americans: Defiance or cooperation in the high school classroom. *Journal of School Psychology*, 46(4), 455–475.

Griffin, B. W. (2002). Academic disidentification, race, and high school dropouts. *High School Journal*, 85(4), 71–81.

Gutiérrez, K. D., Asato, J., Santos, M., & Gotanda, N. (2002). Backlash pedagogy: Language and culture and the politics of reform. *Review of Education, Pedagogy & Cultural Studies*, 24(4), 335–351.

Gutiérrez, K. D., Larson, J., & Kreuter, B. (1995). Cultural tensions in the scripted classroom: The value of the subjugated perspective. *Urban Education*, 29(4), 410–442.

Gutiérrez, K. D., & Rogoff, B. (2003). Cultural ways of learning: Individual traits or repertoires of practice. *Educational Researcher*, 32(5), 19–25.

Habermas, J., Lenhardt, C., & Nicholsen, S. W. (1991). *Moral consciousness and communicative action*. MIT Press.

Haidt, J. (2012). *The righteous mind: Why good people are divided by politics and religion*. Vintage.

Hamlin, J. K., & Van de Vondervoort, J. W. (2018). Infants' and young children's preferences for prosocial over antisocial others. *Human Development*, 61(4–5), 214–231.

Hart, S. C., DiPerna, J. C., Lei, P. W., & Cheng, W. (2020). Nothing lost, something gained? Impact of a universal social-emotional learning program on future state test performance. *Educational Researcher*, 49(1), 5–19.

Hartshorne, H., & May, M. A. (1928). *Studies in deceit*. Macmillan.

Hasebe, Y., Nucci, L., & Nucci, M. (2004). Parental control of the personal domain and adolescent symptoms of psychopathology: A cross-national study in the United States and Japan. *Child Development*, 75(3), 815–828.

Helwig, C. C., Zelazo, P. D., & Wilson, M. (2001). Children's judgments of psychological harm in normal and noncanonical situations. *Child Development*, 72(1), 66–81.

Hidalgo, M., Ehrensaft, D., Tishelman, A., Clark, L., Garofalo, R., Rosenthal, S., Spack, N., & Olson, J. (2013). The gender affirmative model: What we know and what we aim to learn. *Human Development*, 56(5), 285–290.

hooks, b. (2014). *Teaching to transgress*. Routledge.

Horn, S. S. (2003). Adolescents' reasoning about exclusion from social groups. *Developmental Psychology*, 39(1), 71.

Horner, R., & Goodman, S. (2009). Using rewards within school-wide PBIS. https://www.pbis.org/resource/using-rewards-within-school-wide-pbis

Hull, G. A., & Katz, M. L. (2006). Crafting an agentive self: Case studies of digital storytelling. *Research in the Teaching of English*, 41(1), 43.

Hytten, K., & Bettez, S. C. (2011). Understanding education for social justice. *Educational Foundations*, 25(1–2), 7–24.

Ilten-Gee, R. (2020). From pen to podcast: Critical reasoning transformations in narratives of personal conflict. *Media Education Research Journal*, 9(2), 10.

Ilten-Gee, R., & Nucci, L. (2018). From peer discourse to critical moral perspectives: Teaching for engaged reasoning. *Precollege Philosophy and Public Practice 1*, 58–74.

Immordino-Yang, M. H. (2016). Emotion, sociality, and the brain's default mode network: Insights for educational practice and policy. *Policy Insights from the Behavioral and Brain Sciences*, 3(2), 211–219.

Jackson, R. (2016). If they gunned me down and criming while White: An examination of Twitter campaigns through the lens of citizens' media. *Cultural Studies ↔ Critical Methodologies*, 16(3), 313–319.

Jacobs, J., & Levin, D. (2018, August 21). Black girl sent home from school over hair extensions. *New York Times*. www.nytimes.com/2018/08/21/us/black-student-extensions-louisiana.html?smid=em-share

Jacobson, D. (2012). Moral dumbfounding and moral stupefaction. *Oxford studies in normative ethics* (Vol. 2). Oxford University Press.

Jagers, R. J., Rivas-Drake, D., & Williams, B. (2019). Transformative social and emotional learning (SEL): Toward SEL in service of educational equity and excellence. *Educational Psychologist, 54*(3), 162–184.

Jain, S., Bassey, H., Brown, M. A., & Kalra, P. (2014). Restorative justice in Oakland schools. Implementation and impacts: An effective strategy to reduce racially disproportionate discipline, suspensions, and improve academic outcomes. www.ousd.org/cms/lib/CA01001176/Centricity/Domain/134/OUSD-RJ%20Report%20revised%20Final.pdf

Jambon, M., & Smetana, J. G. (2014). Moral complexity in middle childhood: Children's evaluations of necessary harm. *Developmental Psychology, 50*(1), 22–33.

Kellner, D., & Share, J. (2007). Critical media literacy, democracy, and the reconstruction of education. In D. Macedo & S. R. Steinberg (Eds.), *Media literacy: A reader* (pp. 3–23). Peter Lang.

Kelly, D. M., & Arnold, C. (2015). Cyberbullying and Internet Safety. In B. Guzzetti & M. Lesley (Eds.), *Handbook of research on the societal impact of digital media* (pp. 529–559). IGI Global.

Kelly, D. M., & Brooks, M. (2009). How young is too young? Exploring beginning teachers' assumptions about young children and teaching for social justice. *Equity & Excellence in Education, 42*(2), 202–216.

Killen, M. (2019). Developing inclusive youth: How to reduce social exclusion and foster equality and equity in childhood. *American Educator, 6*(2019), 7.

Killen, M., Lee-Kim, J., McGlothlin, H., Stangor, C., & Helwig, C. C. (2002). How children and adolescents evaluate gender and racial exclusion. *Monographs of the society for research in child development, 67*(4), i–129.

Killen, M., Mulvey, K. L., & A. Hitti. (2013). Social exclusion in childhood: A developmental intergroup perspective. *Child Development 84*(3): 772–790.

Killen, M., Pisacane, K., Lee-Kim, J., & Ardila-Rey, A. (2001). Fairness or stereotypes? Young children's priorities when evaluating group exclusion and inclusion. *Developmental psychology, 37*(5), 587.

Killen, M., & Smetana, J. G. (1999). Social interactions in preschool classrooms and the development of young children's conceptions of the personal. *Child Development, 70*(2), 486–501.

Killerby, M., Link-Gelles, R., Haight, S., Schrodt, C., England, L., Gomes, D. . . . & CDC Covid-19 Response Clinical Team. (2020). Characteristics associated with hospitalization among patients with COVID-19—Metropolitan Atlanta, Georgia, March–April 2020. *Morbidity and Mortality Weekly Report, 69*(25), 790–794. https://dx.doi.org/10.15585/mmwr.mm6925e1

Kilman, C. (2013, Summer). The gender spectrum. *Teaching Tolerance, 44*. www.tolerance.org/magazine/summer-2013/the-gender-spectrum

Kress, G. R. (2003). *Literacy in the new media age*. Psychology Press.

Kumashiro, K. K. (2000). Toward a theory of anti-oppressive education. *Review of Educational Research, 70*(1), 25–53.

Kuyel, N., & Cesur, S. (2013, June 6). *The connection between religious rules and the moral judgments of less religious and more religious Turkish Muslims*. Paper presented at the annual meeting of the Jean Piaget Society, Philadelphia, PA.

Kuyel, N., Sorkabi, N., Nucci, L., & Yildiz, M. (2019, November 8). Sunni Muslims' reasoning about God, justice and human welfare. Paper presented at the annual meeting of the Association for Moral Education, Seattle, WA.

Laden, A. S. (2012). *Reasoning: A social picture*. Oxford University Press.

Lapsley, D. (2016). Moral self-identity and the social-cognitive theory of virtue. In J. Annas, D. Narvaez, & N. E. Snow (Eds.), *Developing the virtues: Integrating perspectives*. Oxford University Press.

Laupa, M., & Turiel, E. (1993). Children's concepts of authority and social contexts. *Journal of Educational Psychology, 85*(1), 191–197.

Lee, C., & Soep, E. (2018). Beyond coding: Using critical computational literacy to transform tech. *Texas Education Review, 6*(1), 10–16.

Lefebvre, J. P., & Krettenauer, T. (2020). Is the true self truly moral? Identity intuitions across domains of sociomoral reasoning and age. *Journal of Experimental Child Psychology, 192*, 104769.

Leslie, A. M., Mallon, R., & DiCorcia, J. A. (2006). Transgressors, victims, and cry babies: Is basic moral judgment spared in autism? *Social Neuroscience, 1*(3–4), 270–283.

Li, G., Wu, A. D., Marshall, S. K., Watson, R. J., Adjei, J. K., Park, M., & Saewyc, E. M. (2019). Investigating site-level longitudinal effects of population health interventions: Gay-straight alliances and school safety. *SSM-Population Health, 7*, 100350.

Lipman, M. (2003). *Thinking in education*. Cambridge University Press.

Little, T. (2020). Teaching about youth activism 5-day plan: Unit plan: Children and youth as changemakers. Black Lives Matter at School. www.blacklivesmatterat school.com/curriculum.html

Liu, J. (2018). Chinese adolescents' conceptions of teacher authority and their relations to rule violations in school. *Ethics in Progress, 9*(1), 99–117.

Losen, D. J., & Martinez, T. E. (2013). Out of school and off track: The overuse of suspensions in American middle and high schools. Eric document: ED541735. https://files.eric.ed.gov/fulltext/ED541735.pdf

Mahiri, J. (2011). *Digital tools in urban schools: Mediating a remix of learning*. University of Michigan Press.

Mahiri, J., & Sims, J. (2016). Engineering equity: A critical pedagogical approach to language and curriculum change for African American males in STEM. In Z. Bacaci-Wilhite (Ed.), *Human rights in language and STEM education* (pp. 53–70). Brill Sense.

Mayo, J. B., Jr. (2015). Youth work in gay straight alliances: curriculum, pedagogy, and activist development. *Child & Youth Services, 36*(1), 79–93.

McGrath, R. E. (2016, July). *Essential virtues*. Presented at the Workshop on Approaches to the Development of Character, National Academy of Sciences, Washington, DC.

McIntosh, P. (1988). White privilege: Unpacking the invisible knapsack. In M. B. Zinn, P. Hondagneu-Sotelo, & M. A. Messner (Eds.), *Gender through the prism of difference* (pp. 235–238). Oxford University Press.

Meagley, D. (2016, October 12). I'm just drawn this way: Teen finds gender identity through art. YR Media. www.npr.org/sections/health-shots/2016/10/12 /497468025/im-just-drawn-this-way-teen-finds-gender-identity-through-art

Midgette, A. (2018). Children's strategies for self-correcting their social and moral transgressions and perceived personal shortcomings: Implications for moral agency. *Journal of Moral Education, 47*(2), 231–247.

Midgette, A. (2020). Chinese and South Korean families' conceptualizations of a fair household labor distribution. *Journal of Marriage and Family, 82*(4), 1358–1377.

Midgette, A., Noh, J. Y., Lee, I. J., & Nucci, L. (2016). The development of Korean children's and adolescents' concepts of social convention. *Journal of Cross-Cultural Psychology, 47*(7), 918–928.

Midgette, A. J., Ilten-Gee, R., Powers, D. W., Murata, A., & Nucci, L. (2018). Using Lesson Study in teacher professional development for domain-based moral education. *Journal of Moral Education, 47*(4), 498–518.

Mills, K. (2011). "I'm making it different to the book": Transmediation in young children's multimodal and digital texts. *Australasian Journal of Early Childhood, 36*(3), 56–65.

Mirra, N., Morrell, E., & Filipiak, D. (2018). From digital consumption to digital invention: Toward a new critical theory and practice of multiliteracies. *Theory into Practice, 57*(1), 12–19.

Monk-Turner, E., Martinez, H., Holbrook, J., & Harvey, N. (2007). Are reality TV crime shows continuing to perpetuate crime myths? *Internet Journal of Criminology*, 1–15.

Narvaez, D. (2008). Human flourishing and moral development: Cognitive and neurobiological perspectives of virtue development. In L. Nucci & D. Narvaez (Eds.), *Handbook of moral and character education* (pp. 310–327). Routledge.

National Public Radio. (2019, April 26). Talking race with young children. *Life kit.* www.npr.org/2019/04/24/716700866/talking-race-with-young-children

New York Times Editorial Board. (2016, April 18). Transgender bathroom hysteria cont'd. www.nytimes.com/2016/04/18/opinion/transgender-bathroom-hysteria-contd.html

Noddings, N. (2002). *Educating moral people: A caring alternative to character education.* Teachers College Press.

Nucci, L. (2001). *Education in the moral domain.* Cambridge University Press.

Nucci, L. (2009). *Nice is not enough: Facilitating moral development.* Merrill.

Nucci, L. (2014). The personal and the moral. In M. Killen & J. Smetana (Eds.). *Handbook of moral development* (2nd ed., pp. 538–558). Routledge.

Nucci, L., Creane, M., & Powers, D. W. (2015). Integrating moral and social development within middle school social studies: A social cognitive domain approach. *Journal of Moral Education, 44,* 479–496. doi.org/10.1080/03057240.2015.1087391

Nucci, L., Turiel, E., & Roded, A. D. (2017). Continuities and discontinuities in the development of moral judgments. *Human Development, 60*(6), 279–341.

Nucci, L., & Weber, E. K. (1995). Social interactions in the home and the development of young children's conceptions of the personal. *Child Development, 66*(5), 1438–1452.

Nucci, L. P., & Nucci, M. S. (1982a). Children's responses to moral and social conventional transgressions in free-play settings. *Child Development, 53,* 1337–1342.

Nucci, L. P., & Nucci, M. S. (1982b). Children's social interactions in the context of moral and conventional transgressions. *Child Development*, 53(2), 403–412.

Overton, W. F., & Lerner, R. M. (2014). Fundamental concepts and methods in developmental science: A relational perspective. *Research in Human Development*, 11(1), 63–73.

Paris, D., & Alim, H. S. (2014). What are we seeking to sustain through culturally sustaining pedagogy? A loving critique forward. *Harvard Educational Review*, 84(1), 85–100.

Pasupathi, M., & Wainryb, C. (2010). Developing moral agency through narrative. *Human Development*, 53(2), 55–80.

Rawls, J. (2001). *Justice as fairness: A restatement*. Harvard University Press.

Recchia, H. E., Wainryb, C., Bourne, S., & Pasupathi, M. (2015). Children's and adolescents' accounts of helping and hurting others: Lessons about the development of moral agency. *Child Development*, 86(3), 864–876.

Rizzo, M. T., Elenbaas, L., Cooley, S., & Killen, M. (2016). Children's recognition of fairness and others' welfare in a resource allocation task: Age related changes. *Developmental Psychology*, 52(8), 1307.

Rogers, L. O., & Way, N. (2018). Reimagining social and emotional development: Accommodation and resistance to dominant ideologies in the identities and friendships of boys of color. *Human Development*, 61(6), 311–331.

Russell, S. & Horn, S. S. (2017). *Sexual orientation, gender identity and schooling: The nexus of research, practice, and policy*. Oxford University Press.

Rutland, A., & Killen, M. (2015). A developmental science approach to reducing prejudice and social exclusion: Intergroup processes, social-cognitive development, and moral reasoning. *Social Issues and Policy Review*, 9(1), 121–154.

Ryan, R. M., & Deci, E. L. (2017). *Self-determination theory: Basic psychological needs in motivation, development, and wellness*. Guilford Publications.

Saxon, L. (n.d.) Toolkit of the revolution: Theatre of the Oppressed. beautifultrouble.org/theory/theater-of-the-oppressed/

Sealey-Ruiz, Y. (2011). Dismantling the school-to-prison pipeline through racial literacy development in teacher education. *Journal of Curriculum and Pedagogy*, 8(2), 116–120.

Sensoy, O., & DiAngelo, R. (2017). *Is everyone really equal? An introduction to key concepts in social justice education*. Teachers College Press.

Sesame Street. (n.d.) Coping with incarceration. sesamestreetincommunities.org/topics/incarceration/

Shields, C. M. (2007). *Bakhtin primer* (Vol. 14). Peter Lang.

Shor, I. (1992). *Empowering education: Critical teaching for social change*. University of Chicago Press.

Shweder, R., Mahapatra, M., & Miller, J. (1987). Culture and moral development. In J. Kagan & S. Lamb (Eds.), *The emergence of morality in young children*. University of Chicago Press.

Sionti, M., Ai, H., Penstein Rosé, C. P., & Resnick, L. (2011). A framework for analyzing development of argumentation through classroom discussions. In N. Pinkwart & B. McClaren (Eds.), *Educational technologies for teaching argumentation skills* (pp. 28–55). Bentham Science.

Smetana, J. G. (2011). Adolescents' social reasoning and relationships with parents: Conflicts and coordinations within and across domains. In E. Amsel & J. G. Smetana (Eds.), *Interdisciplinary perspectives on knowledge and development: The Jean Piaget Symposium series. Adolescent vulnerabilities and opportunities: Developmental and constructivist perspectives* (pp. 139–158). Cambridge University Press.

Smetana, J. G., Ahmad, I., & Wray-Lake, L. (2015). Iraqi, Syrian, and Palestinian refugee adolescents' beliefs about parental authority legitimacy and its correlates. *Child Development*, 86(6), 2017–2033.

Smetana, J. G., Ball, C. L., Jambon, M., & Yoo, H. N. (2018). Are young children's preferences and evaluations of moral and conventional transgressors associated with domain distinctions in judgments? *Journal of Experimental Child Psychology*, 173, 284–303.

Smetana, J. G., & Bitz, B. (1996). Adolescents' conceptions of teachers' authority and their relations to rule violations in school. *Child Development*, 67(3), 1153–1172.

Soep, E. (2014). *Participatory politics* (p. 96). MIT Press.

Soep, E., & Chavez, V. (2010). *Drop that knowledge: Youth radio stories*. University of California Press.

Solé, E. (2018). A 14-year-old was suspended for his "distracting" haircut—but his mom says there's a bigger problem. Yahoo. www.yahoo.com/lifestyle/school-district-reimburses-other-sons-haircut-deemed-distracting-194525884.html

Spears Brown, C., & Bigler, R. S. (2004). Children's perceptions of gender discrimination. *Developmental Psychology*, 40(5), 714.

Srinivasan, M., Kaplan, E., & Dahl, A. (2019). Reasoning about the scope of religious norms: Evidence from Hindu and Muslim children in India. *Child Development*, 90(6), e783–e802.

Stack, M. (2015). "Vomitorium of venom": Framing culpable youth, bewildered adults, and the death of Amanda Todd. In D. S. Coombs & S. Collister (Eds.), *Debates for the digital age: The good, the bad, and the ugly of our online world* (pp. 249–271). ABC-CLIO/Greenwood.

Stack, M., & Kelly, D. M. (2006). Popular media, education, and resistance. *Canadian Journal of Education/Revue canadienne de l'éducation*, 29(1), 5–26.

Stanley, T. J. (2003). White supremacy and the rhetoric of educational indoctrination—A Canadian case study. In by J. A. Mangan *(Ed.), Making imperial mentalities: Socialisation and British imperialism*. Taylor & Francis Group.

Stavy, R. (Ed.). (2012). *U-shaped behavioral growth*. Elsevier.

Thornberg, R. (2010). A study of children's conceptions of school rules by investigating their judgements of transgressions in the absence of rules. *Educational Psychology*, 30(5), 583–603.

Thrift, E., & Sugarman, J. (2019). What is social justice? Implications for psychology. *Journal of Theoretical and Philosophical Psychology*, 39(1), 1–17.

Turiel, E. (1983). *The development of social knowledge: Morality and convention*. Cambridge University Press.

Turiel, E. (2002). *The culture of morality: Social development, context, and conflict*. Cambridge University Press.

Turiel, E. (2010). Snap judgment? Not so fast: Thought, reasoning, and choice as psychological realities. *Human Development*, 53(3), 105–109.

Turiel, E. (2015). The development of morality: Reasoning, emotions, and resistance. In W. Overton & P. Molenaar (Eds.), *Theory and method*. Volume 1 of the *Handbook of child psychology and developmental science* (pp. 554–583). Wiley.

Turner, V. D., & Berkowitz, M. W. (2005). Scaffolding morality: Positioning a sociocultural construct. *New Ideas in Psychology*, 23, 174–184.

United Way. (2018, February). The Walkout—How a student movement in 1968 changed schools forever. www.unitedwayla.org/en/news-resources/blog/1968Walkouts/

U.S. Department of Education Office for Civil Rights. (2014, March). Civil rights data collection: Data snapshot: School discipline. https://ocrdata.ed.gov/assets/downloads/CRDC-School-Discipline-Snapshot.pdf

Vakil, S. (2018). Ethics, identity, and political vision: Toward a justice-centered approach to equity in computer science education. *Harvard Educational Review*, 88(1), 26–52.

Vigdor, N. (2019, August 3). Georgia elementary school is accused of racial insensitivity over hairstyle guidelines display. *New York Times*. www.nytimes.com/2019/08/03/us/hairstyles-black-students-appropriate-inappropriate.html

Wainryb, C. (1991). Understanding differences in moral judgments: The role of informational assumptions. *Child Development*, 62(4), 840–851.

Wainryb, C. (2011). "And so they ordered me to kill a person": Conceptualizing the impacts of child soldiering on the development of moral agency. *Human Development*, 54(5), 273–300.

Wald, J., & Losen, D. J. (2003). Defining and redirecting a school-to-prison pipeline. *New Directions for Youth Development*, 2003(99), 9–15.

Waletzko, A. (2017, December 6). Why the Bechdel test fails feminism. Huffington Post. www.huffpost.com/entry/why-the-bechdel-test-fails-feminism_b_7139510

Walsh, G. (2017, Oct. 1) Character education and social justice. Curriculum for equity. https://curriculumforequity.wordpress.com/2017/10/01/character-education-and-social-justice/

Watson, M. (2018). *Learning to trust: Attachment theory and classroom management*. Oxford University Press.

Westheimer, J., & Kahne, J. (2004). What kind of citizen? The politics of educating for democracy. *American Educational Research Journal*, 41(2), 237–269.

Wilson, A. A., Chavez, K., & Anders, P. L. (2012). "From the Koran and *Family Guy*": Expressions of identity in English learners' digital podcasts. *Journal of Adolescent & Adult Literacy*, 55(5), 374–384.

Winn, M. T. (2018). *Justice on both sides: Transforming education through restorative justice*. Harvard University Press.

Young, I. M. (2011). *Justice and the Politics of Difference*. Princeton University Press.

Youniss, J., McLellan, J. A., & Mazer, B. (2001). Voluntary service, peer group orientation, and civic engagement. *Journal of Adolescent Research*, 16(5), 456–468.

Zehr, H. (2015). *The little book of restorative justice* (Rev. and updated). Simon and Schuster.

Index

Action project
  examples of, 179–187
  extending curriculum-based moral lessons, 178–187
  integrating moral development within, 187–191
Adams, M. E., 108, 197
Adjei, J. K., 86
Administrators, as proactive agents of social justice, 80–81
Adolescents, 12, 34–35, 66. *See also* Children
  African American, 34
  development of concepts of morality in, 45–56
  in middle school, 32–33
  and nonmoral rules, 12–13
  and privacy, 18
  school conventions and, 76–77
Adults
  Muslim, 13
  view on conventions, 11
African Americans, 34. *See also* Blacks
  as violent offenders, 166
Agrawal, N., 88
Ahmad, I., 18, 35
Ai, H., 126
Aknin, L. B., 64
Alim, H. S., 26
Anders, P. L., 169
Anderson R. E., 29, 115
Arbitrary conventions, 10
Ardila-Rey, A., 46
Aristotle, 59
Armbrester, S., 174–175
Arnold, C., 165
Arnold, DeAndre, 78–79

Arthur, J., 3, 27, 59
The Art of Critical Pedagogy (Duncan-Andrade and Morrell), 112
Assessment, of student work, 192–194
Autonomy, 83–84

Bakhtin, M. M., 121, 128, 169
Ball, C. L., 11
"Banking" model, 3, 118, 122
Barbers Hill High School, Mont Belvieu, 78–79
Bassey, H., 100
Beachum, L., 79
Bell, L. A. E., 108, 197
Belonging, 84–86
Berkowitz, M. W., 112, 126
Bettez, S. C., 2, 106
Bias-related harassment, 85
Bigler, R. S., 73, 89
"Bimbo the Big Bully" (story), 139–140
Bitz, B., 73, 74
Black Girls Code, 173
Black Lives Matter movement, 179
  police violence and, 183–187
Blacks. *See also* African Americans
  and injustice, 1
  students, 87
Blair, J., 64
Blair, K., 64
Bloch, Becca, 78
Blumenfeld, P. C., 73
Boal, A., 181
Bochenek, M., 86
Boston Tea Party, 128–129
Bourne, S., 60
Brees, D., 145
Brooks, M., 29, 106, 114, 115

Brown, A. W., 86
Brown, C. S., 29, 115
Brown, M. A., 100, 167–168
Brown students, 87

Calhoun, J. C., 125
Canonical texts, 156
Cesur, S., 12, 13
Chaos *vs.* conversation, 76
Character, 4
  components of, 4, 61–65
  defined, 58
  as developmental system, 58–66
  formation, 63–64
  good, 59
  linking to identity, 66
  model of, 59
  performance, 62
  and self-system, 60–61, 63
  traditional views, limits of, 59–61
  as virtues, 59–60
Character development, curriculum goals, 121
Character education, 3, 58
Chavez, K., 169
Chavez, V., 112, 169, 171
Cheng, W., 83, 87
Chen-Gaddini, M., 18, 35
Cheung, J., 192
Chicano Blowouts of 1968, 179–183
Children. *See also* Adolescents
  in early elementary, 30–31
  engagement in conflict resolution, 91
  interaction with mother, 22–23
  in middle elementary, 31–32
  and morality, 11, 12, 19–21, 45–56
  moral judgment, 47
  and nonmoral rules, 12–13
  and privacy, 18
  response to moral transgressions, 20
  response to social convention transgressions, 20–21
  and school rules, 72–77
  understandings of convention progress, 35–45
  view on conventions, 11
Christians, 12
  and nonmoral issues, 13

"Citizenship" award, 95
Civil Rights Project, 87
Clark, L., 31, 81
Classroom, 71–72
  dialogue and discourse, 112–114
  management. *See* Classroom management
  media production in, 163
  moral climate, elements of. *See* Moral classroom climate, elements of
  social conventions, 73–77
  strategies, 112–114
  third space in, 76
Classroom management, 89–90
  goals, 89
  and moral development, 90–93
  and social development, 94–98
Clawson, K., 98, 100
Code-switching, 72
Cognitive assumptions, 108
Commitment, steadfast, 62
Common-Ground Integration, operational transacts, 130
Competence, 86–87
Competitive extension, operational transacts, 129
Complex multidomain issues, 155–162
Confucianism, 40
Consciousness, 33
Constructivism, 107–109
Controlling praise, 95
Conventional domain, curriculum goals, 119–120
Conventions
  and adolescents, 76–77
  affirmation, as authority-based rules for social order, 38–39
  classroom, 73–77
  as constituent elements of society, 40–45
  developmental dynamics and, 34–35
  developmental factors and, 74–76
  development of concepts, 35–45
  issues, identification of, 124
  lesson plan for, 145–151
  morality and, 9–11
  negation, as empirical regularity, 37–38

Index   215

negation, as part of a rule system, 39–40
negation, as societal standards, 44–45
as reflecting observed social regularities, 36–37
religious, 14
Conversation, chaos *vs.*, 76
Cooley, S., 49
Cops (television show), 166
Counter consideration, operational transacts, 130
Counterscript, 76
COVID-19, 192
Creane, M., 3, 117, 123, 127, 128, 133, 170, 194
Critical consciousness, 101, 106, 110, 114–116, 120–121
Critical digital consumption, 165–167
Critical digital distribution, 170–173
Critical digital pedagogy, 163–176
 critical digital consumption, 165–167
 critical digital distribution, 170–173
 critical digital production, 167–170
 defined, 164–165
 examples of, 175–176
 invention, 172–173
Critical digital production, 167–170
Critical moral perspective, 109, 120–121
Critical pedagogy, 105–106
 alignment in classroom strategies, 112–114
 and constructivism, 107–109
 digital. *See* Critical digital pedagogy
 and informational assumptions, 111–112
 overview of, 106–107
 and reasoning transformations, 109–111
Critical transitivity, 110
Cross-domain coordinations, 24
Curriculum, 117–137
 goals, 119–121
 identifying and categorizing issues by domain, 123–124
 overlapping/multifaceted issues, 125
 principles for constructing lessons, 122–123
 usage of, 117–118
Curriculum for equity blog, 3
Curwood, J. S., 171
Cycle of praxis, 4
 integrating moral education within, 177–194
 and moral development, 177–178

Dahl, A., 11, 12, 19, 21, 28
Damon, W., 47, 48
Darnell, C., 60
Davidson, M., 139
Davis, A., 98, 100
Daydreaming, 76
Dean, T., 78
Debate *vs.* deliberation, 112
Deci, E. L., 31, 84, 94, 95
Decisions
 multidimensional uncoordinated, 52–55
 one-dimensional, 51–52
Deliberation, debate *vs.*, 112
Desocialization, 110
Developing Inclusive Youth, 85
Development
 and cross-domain interactions, 56–57
 dynamics between personal and conventional domains, 34–35
 harm, concept of, 49–56
 in high school, 33–34
 overview, 29–30
 personal domain, age-related changes in, 30–32
 of social convention concepts, 35–45
 welfare, concept of, 49–56
Developmental discipline, 31, 89–90, 98–99
Developmental factors, and social conventions, 74–76
Dewey, J., 80
Dialogue, 128
 classroom, 112–114
 and operational transacts, 126, 129–131
 and representational transacts, 126, 130

DiAngelo, R., 197
DiCorcia, J. A., 19
DiPerna, J. C., 83, 87
Discipline, 71
Discourse protocol, 135–137
Discourse skills, 65
Discrimination, 85
Distributive justice, development of, 47–49
Dogg, S., 155–159
Dolan, M. C., 64
Domain-based moral education, 105–116
Domain coordination, 24–25
  and pedagogy, 26–27
  and social justice, 25–26
Do the Right Thing (film), 143
Doyle, A., 166
Duncan-Andrade, J. M. R., 112, 113, 156, 163, 177
Dunn, E. W., 64
Durkheim, E., 71, 78
Dweck, C., 87

Early elementary, children in, 30–31
  convention as reflecting observed social regularities, 36–37
  intuitive morality, 47
Eccles, J. S., 77
"Educating for Democracy" project, 125, 179
Ehrensaft, D., 31, 81
Eisenberg, N., 47
Elaboration game, 135
Elementary school, social exclusion in, 85
Elenbaas, L., 49
Elias, M. J., 117
Ellsworth, E., 114, 132
Emotional literacy, 200–201
Emotions, 65, 196–199
Engaged reasoning, 127
England, L., 192
Equality
  morality of, 48–49
  strict, morality as, 48
Equity, morality of, 48–49
Erickson, J. D., 2, 195, 196
Expiatory punishments, 96–97

Factual assumptions, curriculum goals, 120
Fairness, 17, 46, 88–89, 115
  development of, 47–49
Fancher, M., 1
Feedback, 94, 95
Filipiak, D., 163, 165, 166, 167, 170, 172
Floyd, G., 166, 191, 196
Fredericks, L., 117
Freire, P., 3, 101, 106–108, 110, 111, 113, 122, 138, 165
Fullam, R. S., 64
Fundamental attribution error, 3
Furrer, C., 83

Gaffney, C., 85
Garofalo, R., 31, 81
Gelman, S., 30
Gender, and legal rights, 25–26
Gender-affirming stance, 81
Gender-based norms, 24
Gerewitz, J., 98, 100
Gibbons, D., 171
Gibbs, J. C., 112, 126
Ginwright, S., 177, 178, 200
Goals, curriculum, 119–121
  character development, 121
  conventional domain, 119–120
  coordination across domains, 120
  critical moral perspective/critical consciousness, 120–121
  factual assumptions, 120
  moral domain, 119
  personal domain, 120
  praxis, 121
Gomes, D., 192
Good character, 59
Good discussion, rules for, 133–135
Goodman, S., 94
Grading, of student work, 192–194
Gramsci, A., 164
Greenberg, M. T., 117
Gregory, A., 78, 88, 98, 100
Griffin, B. W., 78
Growth mindset, 87
Gulliford, L., 60
Gutiérrez, K. D., 72, 76

Habermas, J., 112
Haidt, J., 12, 16
Haight, S., 192
Hamilton, V. L., 73
Hamlin, J. K., 11, 19, 64
Harassment, bias-related, 85
Harm, 97
  development of concept, 49–56
Harrison, T., 3, 27, 59
Hart, S. C., 83, 87
Hartshorne, H., 59
Harvey, N., 166
Hasebe, Y., 35
Head coverings, 12, 13, 14, 16
Helping, 53–54, 55
Helwig, C. C., 46, 61, 111
Heteroglossia, 128
Hidalgo, M., 31, 81
High school
  affirmation of convention as mediated by social system, 40–45
  development in, 33–34
  moral development in, 141–143
  multidimensional uncoordinated decisions, 52–54
Hindus, 12
Hispanics, 166
Hitti, A., 111
Holbrook, J., 166
hooks, b., 110, 132, 198, 199
Horn, S. S., 44, 86
Horner, R., 94
Huckleberry Finn (Twain), 155–159
Humanization, 100, 101
Hytten, K., 2, 106

Identity, linking character system to, 66
Ilten-Gee, R., 113, 118, 121, 131, 163, 168, 169
Immoral education, 80
Immordino-Yang, M. H., 76
Informational assumptions, 27–28, 111–112, 125–126
Injustice, 1
Interactions, 21–24

Jackson, R., 168
Jacobs, J., 35
Jagers, R. J., 4, 5, 82, 117, 200
Jain, S., 100
Jambon, M., 11, 46
Jews, 12
  and nonmoral issues, 13
John Brown's raid, 141–143

Kaepernick, C., 144–145
Kahne, J., 3, 164, 178
Kalra, P., 100
Kaplan, E., 12, 28
Kellner, D., 164, 165
Kelly, D. M., 29, 106, 114, 115, 164, 165, 166
Killen, M., 46, 49, 61, 74, 85, 111, 181
Killerby, M., 192
Kilman, C., 149
King, M. L., Jr., 143
Kozol, J., 113
Kress, G. R., 167
Krettenauer, T., 66
Kreuter, B., 76
Kristjánsson, K., 3, 27, 59, 60
Kumashiro, K. K., 71
Kuyel, N., 12, 13

Laden, A. S., 65, 99, 112, 118, 127, 128, 131, 171
Lapsley, D., 66
Larson, J., 76
Latinos, 1–2
Laupa, M., 73
Lee, C., 175, 176
Lee, I. J., 10, 36, 40, 41, 42
Lee-Kim, J., 46, 61, 111
Lefebvre, J. P., 66
Legal rights, gender and, 25–26
Lei, P. W., 83, 87
Lenhardt, C., 112
Lerner, R. M., 4
Leslie, A. M., 19
Lesson planning
  for moral development and social justice, 138–162
  principles of, 122–123
Levin, D., 35

LGBTQ+, 26, 44, 86
Li, G., 86
Liben, L. S., 73
Life Kit (podcast), 115
Link-Gelles, R., 192
Lipman, M., 127
Little, T., 182
Liu, J., 18, 35, 74
Losen, D. J., 1, 87, 98
Love Don't Live Here No More (Dogg), 156–159

Mahapatra, M., 27
Mahiri, J., 163, 165, 169, 173
Malcolm X, 143
Mallon, R., 19
Marshall, S. K., 86
Martinez, H., 166
Martinez, T. E., 87
May, M. A., 59
Mayo, J. B., Jr., 86
Mazer, B., 178
McGlothlin, H., 46, 61, 111
McGrath, R. E., 59
McIntosh, P., 26, 65
McLellan, J. A., 178
Meagley, D., 148, 149
Meaning-making process, 108
Media education, 164–165. *See also* Critical digital pedagogy
Media production, 163
Mediasmarts.ca, 166
Men, and legal rights, 25–26
Middle elementary, children in, 31–32
  morality as strict equality, 48
  negation of convention as empirical regularity, 37–38
Middle school, adolescents in, 32–33
  moral development in, 141–143
  multidimensional uncoordinated decisions, 52–54
Midgette, A., 10, 36, 40, 41, 42, 60, 118, 131
Miller, J., 27
Mills, K., 168
Mirra, N., 163, 165, 166, 167, 170, 172

Misbehavior, response to, 96–98
Mitchell, D., 64
Monk-Turner, E., 166
Moore, S., 192
Moral agency, 60, 108
Moral classroom climate, elements of
  autonomy, 83–84
  belonging, 84–86
  competence, 86–87
  fairness, 88–89
  respect, 87–88
Moral cognition, 62–64
Moral complexity, 24–27
Moral development, 1. *See also* Development
  lesson plans for, 138–162
  in middle school and high school, 141–143
  in primary grades, 139–141
  through social problem solving, 90–93
Moral domain, curriculum goals, 119
Moral education, 1, 3–4
  approaches to, 4–5, 19
  critical, 114–116
  and critical pedagogy. *See* Critical pedagogy
  domain-based, 105–116
  framework for, 2, 3
  purpose of, 109
Moral issue, 15–16
Morality, 64
  children and, 11, 12, 19–21, 45–56
  defined, 9
  intuitive, 47
  issues, identification of, 124
  and moral cognition, 62–64
  and religious rules, 11–17
  rules and, 72–73
  and social convention, 9–11
  as strict equality, 48
Moral judgment, informational assumptions on, 27–28
Moral reasoning, 45–46
Moral transgressions
  adult responses to, 21
  children's responses to, 20–21

Moral wellness, 61, 82
  components of, 61–62
Morrell, E., 112, 113, 156, 163, 165, 166, 167, 170, 172, 177
Mother–child interaction, 22–23
Multidomain issues, 155–162
Mulvey, K. L., 111
Murata, A., 118, 131
Muslims, 12, 13
Mutual respect, 88

Naïve transitivity, 110
Narrative moral agency, 99–100
Narvaez, D., 58, 60, 63
National Public Radio, 115
Nazis, 62
Needs, 97
Nice Is Not Enough (Nucci), 4
Nicholsen, S. W., 112
Nine True Dolphin Stories (Davidson), 139
Noddings, N., 45, 83
Noh, J. Y., 10, 36, 40, 41, 42
Nonmoral (conventional) issues, 12–13, 16–17
Nonviolent protest, 144–145
Nucci, L., 3, 4, 9, 10, 12, 13, 17, 18, 20, 21, 22, 29, 30, 35, 36, 37, 38, 39, 40, 41, 42, 46, 49, 51, 60, 63, 83, 109, 111, 112, 113, 117, 118, 121, 123, 127, 128, 131, 133, 164, 170, 179, 194
Nucci, M. S., 20, 21, 35, 37, 38, 39

Oak Park and River Forest High School, Illinois, 78
Obligations, 99
O'Brien, M. U., 117
Olson, J., 31, 81
Operational transacts, 126, 129–131
Optimization, 159–162
Out of School and Off-Track (report), 87, 88
Overlapping/multifaceted issues, curriculum, 125
Overton, W. F., 4

Paggett, E., 79
Pang, O., 115–116
Paris, D., 26
Paris, P., 60
Park, M., 86
Pasupathi, M., 60, 99, 170, 175
PBIS (positive behavioral instructional support), 94–96
Pedagogy
  critical. *See* Critical pedagogy
  domain coordination and, 26–27
Pedagogy of the Oppressed (Freire), 106
Penstein Rosé, C. P., 126
Performance character, 62
Personal domain
  age-related changes in, 30–32
  curriculum goals, 120
  developmental dynamics and, 34–35
  lesson plan for, 152–155
  of privacy, 17–19, 33
  social interactions and, 21–24
Philosophy for Children movement, 127–128
Phronesis, 60
Piaget, J., 107
Pintrich, P. R., 73
Pisacane, K., 46
Podcasts, production of, 169–170
Positive behavioral instructional support (PBIS), 94–96
Positive feedback, 94
Powers, D. W., 3, 117, 118, 123, 127, 128, 131, 133, 170, 194
Praise, 95–96
Praxis, 107, 121, 170
  cycle of. *See* Cycle of praxis
Primary grades, moral development in, 139–141
Privacy, personal domain of, 17–19, 33
"Problem-posing," form of education, 107
"Protectionist approach," to media education, 164
Punishments, expiatory, 96–97

Questioning phase, podcasts
   production, 169

Racial disparities, 1–2
Racial literacy, 199–200
Rawls, J., 65
Reasoning
   defined, 127
   domain, 166–167, 169–170,
      171–172, 173–174
   engaged, 127
   transformations, 109–111
Reasoning critique, operational
   transacts, 130
Rebuttal game, 135
Recchia, H. E., 60
Refinement, operational transacts,
   129
Regressions, 36
Religion, morality and, 11–17
Religious conventions, 14
Representational transacts, 126, 130
Resnick, L., 126
Resnik, H., 117
Respect, 87–88
Responsive engagement, 112,
   118, 121
Restorative conferences, 100
Restorative justice (RJ), 87, 89, 98–101
   characteristics of, 98–99
"Revealed truth" religions, 13
Rivas-Drake, D., 4, 5, 82, 117, 200
Rizzo, M. T., 49
Roded, A. D., 11, 46, 49, 51, 60, 63,
   109
Rogers, L. O., 34, 78
Rogoff, B., 72
Rosenthal, S., 31, 81
Russell, S., 86
Rutland, A., 181
Ryan, R. M., 31, 84, 94, 95

Sabbath, 13
Saewyc, E. M., 86
Sanderse, W., 3, 27, 59
Savage Inequalities (Kozol), 113
Saxon, L., 181
Schiefele, U., 77

Schools, 71–72
   elementary, social exclusion in, 85
   high. *See* High school
   legitimate authority, 73–74
   middle. *See* Middle school
   as primary social institution, 71
   rules. *See* Schools rules
   and self-awareness promotion, 82
Schools rules
   children and, 72–77
   and social justice, 77–81
School-to-prison pipeline, 1
Schrodt, C., 192
Science (journal), 11
Script, 76
Sealey-Ruiz, Y., 199, 200
SEL. *See* Social and emotional learning
   (SEL)
Self-control, 84
Self-determination, 84
Self-regulation, 84
Self-system, character and, 60–61, 63
Sensoy, O., 197
Sesame Street (television show), 116
Share, J., 164, 165
Shields, C. M., 128
Shor, I., 110, 113, 115
Shweder, R., 27
Simple affirmation, representational
   transacts, 130
Sims, J., 173
Sionti, M., 126
Skinner, E., 83
Smetana, J. G., 11, 18, 19, 25, 34, 35,
   46, 73, 74, 76, 88
Social and emotional learning (SEL), 4,
   83, 139
   supplements, 141
   transformative, 4, 82, 117
Social cognitive domain theory, 108,
   109
Social conventional transgressions
   adult responses to, 21
   children's responses to, 20–21
   classroom, 75
Social conventions. *See* Conventions
Social development, classroom
   management and, 94–98

Index

Social-emotional capacities
  other-regarding, 64
  self-regarding, 64–65
Social exclusion, 85–86
Social experiential origins, of children's morality, 19–21
Social foundations theory, 12
Social interactions, and personal domain, 21–24
Social justice, 2
  domain coordination and, 25–26
  lesson plans for, 138–162
  school rules and, 77–81
Social justice education, 2–3, 108
  critical pedagogy. *See* Critical pedagogy
Social norms, 9, 10–11
Social order, affirmation of convention as authority-based rules for, 38–39
Social system, affirmation of convention as mediated by, 40–45
Societal standards, negation of convention as, 44–45
Soep, E., 112, 169, 170, 171, 175, 176
Solé, E., 79
Sorkabi, N., 12
Spack, N., 31, 81
Spears Brown, C., 73, 89
Srinivasan, M., 12, 28
Stack, M., 164, 165, 166
Stangor, C., 46, 61, 111
Stanley, T. J., 58
Stavy, R., 36
Steadfast commitment, 62
Stealing
  indirect, 52, 53, 54
  as moral issue, 15–16
Student circle keepers (SCKs), 99, 100
Students
  as allies, 79–80
  Black, 87
  Brown, 87
  emotions, 196–199
  engagement, 126–137
  LGBTQ+, 86
  misconduct, ethical response to, 97–98
  praise to, 95
  preparation, to engage in productive discussion, 132–133
  responsive engagement, 127–131
  and rules for good discussion, 133–135
  social-emotional and moral growth in. *See* Moral classroom climate, elements of
  space to "agree to disagree," 131–132
  work, grading and assessment, 192–194
Students with disabilities, 1, 2
Sugarman, J., 3
Systemic school-based injustice, 1

Take Action Project (TAP), 188–191
Teachers
  common questions asked by, 135–137
  as proactive agents of social justice, 80–81
  and self-awareness promotion, 82
Teaching Children About Social Issues: Kidpower (Pang), 115–116
Third space, in classrooms, 76
Thompson, W. C., 2, 195, 196
Thornberg, R., 72
Thrift, E., 3
Tishelman, A., 31, 81
Tran, A. Q., 11, 21
Transactive discourse, 112
Transactive statements, 126
Transformations, reasoning, 109–111
Transformative SEL, 4, 82, 117
Transgressions
  moral, 20, 21
  social convention. *See* Social conventional transgressions
Turiel, E., 10, 11, 25, 26, 35, 37, 45, 46, 49, 51, 60, 63, 65, 73, 109, 156
Turner, V. D., 126
Twain, M., 155–159
Twitter, 167–168
"Two Boys One Chair" (video), 92

University of Virginia
  "Educating for Democracy"
    curriculum, 125, 179
Unlearning truths, 110
Unobserved entities, 28
Unprovoked hitting, 10

Vakil, S., 164, 173
Van de Vondervoort, J. W., 11, 19
Vigdor, N., 35
Violence, 143
  police, and Black Lives Matter
    movement, 183–187
Virtues, character as, 59–60
Voting rules, 125

Wainryb, C., 60, 64, 99, 111, 170, 175
Wald, J., 1, 98
Waletzko, A., 166
Walsh, G., 3, 5
Watson, M., 31, 74, 80, 83, 84, 89, 95, 96, 97, 141
Watson, R. J., 86
Way, N., 34, 78
Weber, E. K., 22
Weinstein, R. S., 78, 88
Weissberg, R. P., 117

Welfare, development of concept, 49–56
Westheimer, J., 3, 164, 178
"White Privilege: Unpacking the Invisible Knapsack" (McIntosh), 26
Wigfield, A., 77
Willful defiance, 87–88
Williams, B., 4, 5, 82, 117, 200
Wilson, A. A., 169
Wilson, M., 46
Winn, M. T., 87, 98, 99, 100–101, 199
Women and girls
  and legal rights, 25–26
Wray-Lake, L., 18, 35
Wright, D., 3, 27, 59
Wu, A. D., 86

Yildiz, 12
Yoo, H. N., 11
Young, M., 78
Youniss, J., 178
YR Media, 163, 171

Zehr, H., 98
Zelazo, P. D., 46
Zins, J. E., 117

About the Authors

Larry Nucci is an adjunct professor in the Graduate School of Education at UC Berkeley and professor emeritus of educational psychology at the University of Illinois at Chicago. Nucci has published extensively on children's moral and social development and education. His eight other books include *Nice Is Not Enough: Facilitating Moral Development* and *Education in the Moral Domain.* In 2017, his work in moral education was recognized by the Association for Moral Education with the Kuhmerker Career Award for Outstanding Contributions to Research and Practice in Moral Education. He also received the Sanford N. McDonnell Award for Lifetime Achievement in Character Education (given by the Character Education Partnership, 2020). He is a pioneer in the educational application of what is referred to as domain theory, in which distinctions are drawn between morality and the conventions of society. An aspect of his work on social development has focused on children's judgments about issues considered personal matters of privacy and discretion. This research has been carried out in a number of cross-cultural contexts including Asia and Latin America. He served as editor in chief of the journal *Human Development* from 2007 through 2019 and is a member of the editorial boards of *Cognitive Development, Parenting Science and Practice,* and the *Journal for Research in Character Education.*

Robyn Ilten-Gee is an assistant professor in education at Simon Fraser University in British Columbia, Canada. She started her career as a middle school English language arts teacher in San Francisco, California. She also worked at YR Media (formerly Youth Radio) in Oakland, California, as a youth media producer and education reporter. She received her PhD from the Graduate School of Education at the University of California, Berkeley. Her research examines the overlap between critical pedagogy and moral development, as well as opportunities for critical moral reasoning in media education, specifically podcasting. She has published research in several academic journals, including *Media Education Research Journal, Journal of Moral Education,* and *Ethnography and Education.*